Readings in Medieval Rhetoric

Readings in Medieval Rhetoric

Edited by

Joseph M. Miller
Michael H. Prosser
Thomas W. Benson

INDIANA UNIVERSITY PRESS
Bloomington and London

PUBLISHED IN CANADA BY FITZHENRY & WHITESIDE LIMITED,
DON MILLS, ONTARIO
LIBRARY OF CONGRESS CATALOG CARD NUMBER: 73-77857
ISBN: 0-253-34878-1 CL.   0-253-34879-X PA.
MANUFACTURED IN THE UNITED STATES OF AMERICA

To Harry Caplan and James J. Murphy
Two Pioneering Scholars in Medieval Rhetoric

CONTENTS

PREFACE

Like grammar, rhetoric enters the Middle Ages in association with the artes liberales. As part of the "authoritative traditional stock," it was conserved by the schools. Thenceforth its destiny is no longer a living growth. It exhibits symptoms of degeneration, atrophy, distortion. ERNST R. CURTIUS, *European Literature and the Latin Middle Ages.*

The consignment of rhetoric to the function of adorning and dilating took from it something of its former vitality in the intellectual processes of composition. SISTER JOAN MARIE LECHNER, O.S.U., *Renaissance Concepts of the Commonplaces.*

Examining Professor Curtius' evaluation of the status of rhetoric during the early Middle Ages and Sister Joan Marie's comment on its position in the later Middle Ages, most historians of culture and education would agree in the apparent conclusion that traditional rhetoric had little impact during the years between the death of Augustine and Poggio Bracciolini's rediscovery of Quintilian. Certainly scholars, even the most renowned, produced little or nothing new or original to add to the corpus of material called rhetoric; rather they concentrated on preserving unchanged the principles of the past, and on demonstrating the permanent values of those principles to a civilization operating from a quite different set of presuppositions.

To the extent that such a conservative approach is a demonstration of torpor, atrophy, distortion, it is true that rhetoric was comatose; however, it is dangerously inaccurate to presume that such retrenchment meant the death, even temporarily, of the art itself. Actually, a close study of typical pedagogical works from every century reveals that the rhetorical theories of Cicero, Quin-

tilian (and, by implication, Aristotle), and lesser-known authorities of the past had significant impact on generation after generation of learned men after Augustine, from Boethius and Bede to
the Dominican preachers of the thirteenth and fourteenth centuries. If Cassiodorus, Alcuin, Rabanus Maurus, Alberic of Monte
Cassino, Alan of the Isles and Brunetto Latini confined their con-
tributions to paraphrases and explanations of the *Ad Herennium,*
Cicero's *De inventione* and Augustine's *De doctrina christiana*
with few exceptions, yet even such limited and repetitious treatment discloses a strong awareness of the role classical theories of
rhetoric ought to play in every branch of learning during the
Middle Ages.

Perhaps the simplest way to explain this influence is to note that
it lay primarily in the area of practical application. During the
millennium in question, oratory came to have ever less influence
on political and social behavior; only in such restricted fields as
missionary preaching in pagan lands did oratory retain even a
vestige of its traditional grandeur (and there the persuasiveness
of the orator depended more frequently on the sharpness of the
sword than on the aptness of the word). Nonetheless, it remains
a fact that the use of rhetorical techniques did develop greatly
during these centuries. Admittedly, this development did not show
itself in an improvement in the quality of oral discourse; rather
it became apparent in the opening up of new areas for the application of the ancient principles.

Boethius considered himself a philosopher and logician, not a
rhetorician. His brief treatises on commonplaces and on rhetorical
argument grew out of his study of logic; they dealt only tangen-
tially with the art of persuasion. The result, however, was the development of a rhetorical facet in the study of philosophy. Rabanus Maurus was more interested in formulating a program for
the training and education of young clerics than in teaching them
how to preach. His treatment of rhetoric was an unabashed pla-
giarism of parts of Augustine's *De doctrina christiana;* yet he
added to the ecclesiastical discipline a clear rhetorical dimension.
Alberic of Monte Cassino expounded an epistolary art completely
unrelated to oral discourse. Yet his presentation of the old princi-

ples in a new context was not a perversion; rather it was the discovery of a new frontier, the addition of new territory to old, the
broadening of an already far-ranging horizon. Seldom, if ever, did
these men or others like them add new principles or theories to
the existing body of knowledge; almost invariably they brought
the existing *corpus* to bear on new and growing areas of practical
need.

Among the multitude of factors contributing to this development of rhetorical thought during the Middle Ages, three in particular deserve close attention; they stand out in the selections in
this volume. The first was the strong hostility which marked the
attitudes of Christian scholars toward an art which they viewed as
reminiscent of all the immorality of pagan Rome. The contempt
which Jerome had expressed for all forms of classical literary elegance, even while he was himself practising such elegance, found
a frequent echo during the Middle Ages in ominous warnings
against caring more for style and delivery than for substance. Because of this hostility, nearly every Christian scholar of these centuries, especially those who preceded the establishment of the
great universities in the thirteenth century, relied almost exclusively on Augustine's *De doctrina christiana* and the classical
works it had baptized into respectability. Cicero's youthful *De
inventione*, his *De oratore* (in fragmented forms), and the pseudo-
Ciceronian *Rhetorica ad Herennium* became the bases for all rhetorical theory, if for no other reason than that the principles they
enunciated seemed broad enough to transcend pagan oratorical
goals and to offer some valuable suggestions to the Christian
writer and preacher.

Secondly, the rapid spread of monasticism after the fifth century played a major role in shaping the attitudes men held toward
rhetoric. Very soon after Benedict of Nursia (*c*.480–547) introduced his concept of spirituality to the western world, schools began to exist as extensions of monasteries, and as the great abbeys
and priories took control of the life of their communities, the
values of the monks began to permeate the culture of the time.
This state of affairs continued until the universities began replac-
ing the cathedral and monastery schools; thus the teachers who

shaped the minds of those young people fortunate enough to receive an education were themselves imbued with the sense of
values and the order of priorities inherent in a cenobitic–contem-
plative life. Not only were these theological–ecclesiastical values;
more important, they gave much greater emphasis to personal and
individual spiritual needs than to social responsibility. The monk
was more interested in attaining personal holiness than he was in
converting others, more concerned that he himself should come to
a deeper understanding of the implications of Scripture than that
he communicate such understanding to others through preaching.
As a result, his students came to view logic, the science of reasoning accurately to valid conclusions, as more important than dialectic, the science of exchanging conclusions with others, and both
logic and dialectic as far more necessary than rhetoric, the art of
winning others to an acceptance of one's own position. In this
view of the trivium, one studied in order to find God, the goal of
every individual's earthly pilgrimage. Even the traditional medieval definition of rhetoric as "the art of speaking well in secular
matters," tacitly accepted this attitude, since as Wibaldus of
Covey indicated and as every monk knew, the only matters worth
discussion were spiritual, theological, or ecclesiastical—never
secular.

Thirdly, there recurs throughout the Middle Ages an ever increasing tendency to view rhetoric as a tool of administrative procedure rather than as a means of persuasion, somewhat in the
manner of administrative journalism in certain modern authoritar-
ian states. This new vision of the role of rhetoric seems to flow
automatically from the monastic influence already noted; if one
has no business attempting to influence the behavior of others
through persuasion, then the alternative seems to be to influence
that behavior through the passage and administration of laws.
This principle meant that those who were responsible for laws
were more inclined to communicate with one another than they
were to seek approval from those whom they governed. For them,
rhetoric provided rules for the composition of formal letters and
official documents. Even during the Merovingian and Carolingian
periods, model letters and *formulae* were staples in royal and

ecclesiastical chanceries; the collected letters of Pliny, Cicero, Seneca, and other venerated correspondents of the past were universally studied as patterns of style. It is not surprising, then, that this emphasis finally led in the eleventh century to an attempt to subordinate all rhetoric to the art of epistolary composition and to the production of an *ars dictaminis* as an independent rhetorical form.

Of course these were not the only significant trends in medieval rhetoric. The student of the various documents treated in this volume, some as incisive as Alcuin's *Dialogue* and others as unimaginative as Isidore's catalogue of definitions and examples, will quickly become aware of others; they range from Bede's emphasis on figures and tropes in Scripture, through Rufinus of Antioch's labored discussion of verse metres suitable to the orator, to John of Salisbury's urgent (if somewhat subversive) demand for a return to practical dialectic and rhetoric. An effort to represent as many of these divergent trends as possible was one consideration governing the selection of material for this volume.

A second consideration was our desire to include selections from all periods of the Middle Ages. Scholars seem to agree that the Middle Ages lasted just about one thousand years, though they do not always agree on which thousand. Some view the Christianization of the Roman Empire under Constantine (c.350) as the beginning, and the advent of vernacular literature as the end of medieval growth; others consider Augustine to have been the last voice of Classicism, and Aeneas Silvius Piccolomini, the great poet and intellectual who became Pope Pius II (1458–1464), the patron saint of the Renaissance. Certainly, however, there is real agreement in the underlying belief that the classical period ended when the later Fathers of the Church managed to establish the new non-artistic norms of spirituality and ecclesiasticism as measuring sticks for intellectual activity, and that the Renaissance began when the growing influence of the universities and the first rejection of clerical authority (as a courtier in the imperial court, Piccolomini had written an attack on Papal authority) opened the way for a Da Vinci, a Columbus, a Peter Ramus to challenge the stereotypes of the past. We have, for convenience, adopted the dates 430 (the death of Augustine) and 1416 (the rediscovery of Quintilian) to enclose the period.

By developing the volume chronologically, and by selecting treatises from nearly every century, we have tried to present a feeling of the diversity of interests as well as of the continuity of approach which marked the rhetoric of the Middle Ages. If we seem to have included too much material on preaching which seems out of touch with rhetoric, we note that preaching was the only form of oral discourse which persisted throughout every century; only in this practical use of public address, and in its adherence to or deviation from standards of rhetorical excellence can we understand the implications of the new emphases on certain aspects of theories preserved (and often distorted) from the past.

Despite the appearance in recent years of several significant works about medieval rhetoric, including Richard McKeon's near-classic, "Rhetoric in the Middle Ages" (*Speculum* 17, 1942; since reprinted in Schwarz and Rycenga's *The Province of Rhetoric*), most of the original sources have not until now been translated into English, or, if translated, have remained either unpublished or available only in obscure or out-of-print volumes. Recognizing this imbalance (recently alleviated by the welcome appearance of *Three Medieval Rhetorical Arts*, James J. Murphy, ed.), the editors of this collection have endeavored to bring together as many of these previously unavailable works as possible, even though that policy sometimes meant the omission of a major work already easily accessible in English in order to make room for some little-known treatise of minor historical or pedagogical value. For such major treatises as Alcuin's *Dialogue*, Geoffrey of Vinsauf's *New Poetic*, and Harry Caplan's translation of the Pseudo-Aquinas *De arte praedicandi* (to mention only three), we have included a brief commentary essay together with references indicating the source in which the reader can locate the translation of the entire work.

In general we have included complete works or complete sections of long works rather than brief excerpts. Not all will agree with our choices; this, however, must be the fate of any editor or editorial committee relying on personal judgment, and it becomes more likely when no previous editor has made the necessary errors.

As we have already indicated, we included few previously published translations; the only exceptions to this rule were in those cases where the translation is not easily accessible (again, a matter of editorial judgment). Where unpublished or unavailable translations were made accessible to us, we used them; in their absence we made or commissioned translations with a view to avoiding excessive literalness, seeking readable English rather than slavish fidelity to frequently barbaric Latin. Most of the original Latin texts appear either in Halm's *Rhetores Latini Minores* (hereafter identified as *RLM*) or in Migne's *Patrologia Latina* (hereafter identified as *PL*). Where more definitive recensions of texts were available, we endeavored to consult them.

James J. Murphy of the University of California at Davis made our task of selection and editing much easier. By conferring with us personally, by corresponding with us, by making available to us the galley proofs for his *Medieval Rhetoric: A Select Bibliography,* and by inspiring us through his own published work, he broadened our horizons considerably. Edwin S. Ramage of the Department of Classics at Indiana University and J. Jeffrey Auer of the Department of Speech there provided useful and welcome advice, as did Mrs. Barbara Halporn and Anthony Shipps of the Indiana University Library. Through the Board of Research and Advanced Studies at Indiana University we received a grant which assisted us as the project developed. Our colleagues and students at St. Meinrad School of Theology, Indiana University, and the Pennsylvania State University provided us with ideas and criticisms as the volume was being completed. To all of them we extend our thanks. We alone, of course, are responsible for the plan of the book and the translations made and selected for it.

Joseph M. Miller
Michael H. Prosser
Thomas W. Benson

Readings in Medieval Rhetoric

1. MARTIANUS MINNEUS FELIX CAPELLA

De nuptiis Philologiae et Mercurii, V: "The Book of Rhetoric" (EXCERPT)[1]

Translated by Joseph M. Miller

It seems incredible that a work so sneered at as *De nuptiis Philologiae et Mercurii* could have any importance to the modern reader. After noting that this monumental work of Martianus Capella (*fl.*410–429) remained the authoritative treatment of the liberal arts for the duration of the Middle Ages, Ernst Curtius comments, "It is a huge work, filling over five hundred pages of print; for the modern reader's taste it is indigestible."[2] Likewise, Percival Cole notes that Martianus is one of those "men of whom we should care to know little if the intrinsic merit of their work were the only thing concerned, but of whom we cannot know enough because of the influence they have exerted upon the subsequent course of human affairs. . . . [Martianus] was the author of . . . the most successful textbook ever written."[3]

Martianus Capella flourished during the early fifth century; most scholars agree on a period prior to the fall of Carthage in 439.[4] Thus he becomes the final product, the ultimate representative of the Second Sophistic. His style is typical of that genre: he has culled whatever he needs from earlier sources and has superimposed on that material a

---

1. Martiani Minnei Felicis Capellae *Liber de arte rhetorica* (*De nuptiis, liber V*) in *Rhetores Latini Minores*, ed. Carl Halm (Leipzig: Teubner, 1863; Dubuque: Wm. C. Brown Reprint Library, n.d.), 449–492. This excerpt is from pp.449–451.

2. Ernst R. Curtius, *Europaische Literatur und lateinisches Mittelalter* (Bern: A. Francke AG, 1948), p.46.

3. Percival Cole, *Later Roman Education in Ausonius, Capella and the Theodosian Code* (New York: Columbia University, 1909), p.16.

4. F. Eyssenstadt, ed., *Martianus Capella* (Leipzig: Teubner, 1866), p.viii; also Cole, *Later Roman Education*, p.16.

1

fantastic allegory composed of pedantic humor, obscure metaphor, and ponderous verbosity. In the first two books of *De nuptiis* he describes the marriage of the God Mercury to the nymph Philologia; in the remaining seven he describes the seven liberal arts, personified as seven beautiful maidens dedicated to the bride's service. Thus the full title of the work is *De nuptiis Philologiae et Mercurii et de septem artibus liberalibus libri novem* (*Nine Books concerning the Marriage of the Nymph Philology to Mercury and concerning the Seven Liberal Arts*).[5]

In Book V, *Rhetorica*, Martianus draws his information from the *Liber de figuris sententiarum et elocutionis* (*A Book about the Figures of Thought and of Speaking*) by Aquila Romanus, a minor fourth-century rhetorician and grammarian. To discuss this material, he describes the imposing Dame Rhetoric, who talks about herself, describing her purpose and method.

---

1. And now the braying trumpet splits the air
And cracks the heavens with its alien sound;
    The gods fall back aghast, the godlings huddle
Trembling, not aware of why; their hearts quail
With fear, lest Phlegra's crime be theirs.[6]
Then Amnes and the fauns of Pan, Pales,
The Ephialtes and the woodland Nymphs,[7]
All watch their masters rise without delay.
All stunned they watch, and, one by one adoring,
Marvel at the peace which fills their hearts.
Then comes Silvanus from the sacred grove,
The first to move, and, overcome with awe,
His hand unweaponed bravely stretches out,
Seeking Apollo's bow, the club of Herakles;
For Proteus' three-pronged lance he cries aloud,
Not daring to demand the shaft of Mars;
Resigned to battle, he searches for the scythe
of Saturn on the battlefield; his life
Despairing now, awaits Jove's thundering blow.

5. For a fuller background to the *De nuptiis*, see Cole, *Later Roman Education*, pp.16–28.
6. Phlegra's crime = hubris (arrogance before the gods).
7. The erudition of these references to minor deities furnishes an excellent example of the erudition criticized by Curtius and Cole.

2. But while all the multitudes of the gods of the earth were so disturbed, there entered a magnificent woman of noble bearing, beautiful of face, impressive of stature and completely poised, wearing on her head a helmet, upon which rested a royal crown. The weapons she carried in her hands, with which she was equally adept at defending herself and at wounding her foes, shone with blinding flashes of brilliance. The garment beneath her weaponry was like a mantle of state which hung in folds about her shoulders, falling around her in the Roman mode; the beauty of the individual folds seen as distinct from one another seemed to emphasize the full beauty of the whole. Her breast was covered with precious stones of the most exquisite splendor. When these ornaments struck against her armor as she walked, the effect was like the booming crash of a bolt of lightning, so that you might say the thunderclaps rattled; no wonder it was easy to believe that she was the very image of Jupiter, able herself to hurl his thunderbolts. For she had the power, so to speak, of a queen over all things, able to lead men where she would and to hold them back when she would, to bring them to tears or to rouse them to frenzy, and to bring about a change in attitudes and convictions in governments as well as in armies at war, wheresoever she was able to stand before an assemblage of people. Report held that she had subdued the senate house and the public podium as well as the courts of law among the descendants of Romulus, that she had mastered for her own purposes the council chamber and the public meetings and the theatres of Athens, and that she had shaken all of Greece to the very heart when she spoke. Ah, how beautiful was her face, how striking the melody of her voice, how glorious her language! To hear her performance was a reward even among those already named [the sisters Grammar and Dialectic], so witty was her invention, so rich and lush her style, so spacious her storehouse of memory and recall; the order of arrangement she followed was quite perfect, the tone of voice in which she spoke was completely appropriate, the movements with which she gestured were unvaryingly graceful, her insight was always thorough. She was subdued when speaking of minor matters, fluent when speaking of ordinary things, overpowering when dealing with

subjects of moment; she rendered her listeners docile when there was doubt; by persuasion she won them to agreement, by her attacks she roused them to anger, by her praise she appealed to their pride. Moreover, when she raised her voice in accusation against someone in the public eye everything seemed to be in turmoil, in chaos, to be consumed with rage.

3. And so a great crowd of illustrious men followed this woman with her golden voice as she scattered the jewels of her crown and her kingdoms. Among them, the two who stood nearest her were especially striking because of their unusual apparel and because of their homelands; one wore a Greek mantle and the other a Roman toga.[8] The sound of their voices was different, for one said that he had studied Greek in Athens and also that he had both been exposed to the exercises of the gymnasia and been a consistent participant in the quarrelsome disputes of the academy; both were young men, escaping from the embrace of poverty; while the father of one was a knight of the Quirinal, the labor of an artisan raised up the other; so outstanding were they in the brilliance of their speech that after the end of their burdens and their unfortunate deaths, they ascended to the stars because of their power and dominated history by the immortality of their names. Of the one, whom the people of Athens and a whole entourage of Greek admirers followed, there was a report common that he was more vehement and formidable in his thunderings than the roar of a pounding ocean: there was even a verse which said of him that he was

> *deinos aner; tacha ken kai anaition aitooto* (a powerful man; he accused even when there were no grounds for the accusation).
> Homer, *Iliad* ll.654.

The other, however, wore the consular purple and built his strength on a victory over a destroyed conspiracy; he soon reached the highest chamber. There he offered his thanks to Jupiter for watching over him, and began to exclaim joyously, "How happy

---

8. As is apparent from what follows, the reference is to Demosthenes and Cicero.

are we, how fortunate the republic, how glorious the fame of my consulship!" (Cicero, *In Catil.* II.5.10). After these two came outstanding orators in two groups; you could see Aeschines, Isocrates and Lysias bearing before them the the emblems and banners of their eloquence. Then come in togaed ranks the Sosantii, the Gracchi, Regulus, Pliny, and Fronto. But before any of them, and even leading the woman herself who commanded all, there marched an old man carrying an impressive marshal's staff in the manner of a Roman lictor; on the top of the staff was a raven[9] with a golden beak portrayed in flight to provide an omen of good for the woman who followed. But the man carrying the staff, Tisias by name, seemed both older and nobler than the others; holding the raven aloft, he reminded all his youthful companions, even including the lady herself, that they were his sons and she his daughter. Moved by this argument, a great many people considered her to be one of the noblest daughters of the gods, either related to Apollo (if Greek) or belonging to the Valerian family Corvinus (if she was of Roman birth). To this riddle was added the fact that she appeared both fearless and as clearly trusted by Pallas Athena as she was beloved by Mercury himself, so that her spirit displayed evidence of a real bond of intimacy with both.

9. Obviously Martianus intends a pun when he uses the word *corax* to identify the emblem carried by Tisias, a pupil of Corax.

2. (PSEUDO) AURELIUS AUGUSTINE

On Rhetoric: Additional Material[1]

Translated by Joseph M. Miller

Although this treatise bears the name of Augustine at its head, it is almost certainly not his work; scholars usually identify it as Pseudo-Augustine.

In his *Retractationum duo libri,* I.6, Augustine tells how he composed a series of treatises on five of the liberal arts during his sojourn in Milan before his baptism. He concludes the interlude: "Of the five works so undertaken, the *Dialectic,* the *Rhetoric,* the *Geometry,* the *Arithmetic,* the *Philosophy,* only the prefaces remain; and even these I have somehow managed to lose, though I suppose that someone must have a copy."[2] Although the present work easily fills the description, there seems to be no other reason to consider it the second of these incomplete treatises.

There seem to be two significant reasons for doubting the Augustinian authenticity of the tract. First, "there is no primary manuscript copy of this work extant,"[3] an apparent indication that the work may have been the fruit of the labors of some enthusiastic admirer of the Second Sophistic, who attributed his work to Augustine in order to increase its acceptance. This probability gains likelihood in view of the fact that the oldest printed texts of the work, under the title *Supplementary Material about Rhetoric by Aurelius Augustine,* invariably appear as a conclusion to the *Three Books of Rhetoric* by Chirius Fortunatianus,[4] excerpts of which form the next reading in this volume. Perhaps the true author of this *De rhetorica* hoped to establish, through the use of Augustine's name, a better ethos for a subject fast sinking into disrepute; perhaps he intended only to recognize the fact that the most respected

1. Aurelii Augustini *de rhetorica quae supersunt,* in *RLM,* pp.136–151.
2. *Retractationes* I.6; *PL* 32.591.
3. Comment by the editor, *PL* 32.1439 fn.
4. *RLM,* praef., p.x.

educator of Christian tradition was a rhetorician and might be expected to approve the work. At any rate, the medieval veneration accorded Augustine's name assured the preservation of the work.

The second fact which throws doubt on Augustine's authorship of the tract is the totally un-Augustinian use of Greek, "which the author relies upon far beyond what is needed, contrary to the habit of Augustine,"[5] who disliked Greek. In addition to these two pieces of internal evidence, we should also note that the treatise is quite unimaginative, a mere rehash of second-rate pedanticism, more like the work of an Aquila Romanus than the brilliant analysis of *De doctrina christiana*, the one authentic Augustinian rhetorical work. In short, it is obvious that Augustine did not compose *De rhetorica quae supersunt*.

---

1. The duty of the orator is to understand immediately, as soon as a civil question is brought up, whether general or specific, if it is simple or if it involves several issues, if it is to be treated on its own merits or as it relates to something else. After he has ascertained this, he must find out the appropriate divisions of the subject, so that he can properly arrange his observations about either the moral or the intrinsic issues. From this point he must proceed to evaluate what he has found pertinent, so that he can reject those points which seem vulnerable to attack; then what he deems worthy of retaining he must put in proper order. Even though there may be many quite relevant facts at his disposal, if each does not have its own place in the speech assigned to it according to its importance and length, those facts will probably hamper the case, or at best not further it very much. Immediately after this organization of material, the orator will have to prepare the exact text of his presentation of the issues; this involves two steps: the structure in which the ideas are put together, and the careful choice of words. He must then commit all this to memory; most of the Greeks insist that this is among the most necessary of the orator's duties, as also does the great teacher M. Tullius [Cicero], who writes in words something like this, I believe, in his first book about the orator: "I come now to memory, the storehouse for

5. *PL* 32.1439 fn.

everything; if we do not use it to keep all we have thought of and put in order, then everything, no matter how familiar to the orator, will, as we know, perish."[6] The next step after memory must be impressive delivery; Demosthenes considers this as either the first or the only concern among the duties of the orator. It consists of two elements: the movement of the body and the control of the voice. This brief summary seems sufficient to touch on the obligations of the orator; it remains to us now to determine what his chief purpose is.

2. In all things the chief purpose is, as I see it, that to which all else is directed, that for the sake of which everything else is done. The name which the Greeks give it is *telos;*[7] philosophers make it the subject of almost all their disputations: thus they ask, "What is the chief purpose of living well, virtue or pleasure?" and other questions like this. Every commentator views the chief purpose of the orator's work in a different way: some think that the whole reason the orator has for what he does is bound up in his speaking well; to others the purpose seems to lie in speaking correctly; to still others it seems to lie in persuading. But even those who think that the chief purpose of the orator's task is to speak well or to speak correctly do not deny that the final goal of these purposes is persuasion; they merely say that it is the goal of the orator to speak well, and that it is the goal of speaking well to persuade. Thus all seem to agree that the ultimate purpose of the orator's labor is to persuade. Yet this could lead one to fall into a trap (for an orator does not succeed every time in persuading; yet he does not lose the name or talent of an orator when he fails to persuade); therefore to avoid such a trap, Hermagoras added and left in writing the statement that it is the goal of the orator to persuade insofar as circumstances and conditions allow.

3. From that same word, persuade, there also arise certain other misconceptions, begun by Plato and discussed at great length in the Gorgias, and impudently rediscovered in more recent times by

6. *De oratore* I.18. There is a slight divergence from the original.
7. Because the author's use of Greek is inconsistent, and because this problem is compounded by editorial errors, the Greek appears here without correction. All Greek characters have been transliterated.

certain clever craftsmen, opponents of Hermagoras. They absolutely deny that persuasion is the proper goal of the orator's work
exclusively, holding rather that he holds that goal in common with
nearly everyone; that it is the mathematician's task to persuade
regarding those matters which fall in his area of competence, the
doctor's to persuade regarding what comes into his purview, and
that laborers, merchants, and artisans, as well as any other persons,
ought to be able to offer an effective argument about whatever it
might be that they do. Thus it is not exclusively the chief purpose
of any one person in a community to persuade, for the act of persuading is the common responsibility of many and cannot be the
chief goal of the orator alone. To this error Hermagoras offers a
very clear answer. He says that it is the function of the orator to
persuade insofar as circumstances and conditions allow, but only
regarding civil questions; questions pertaining to doctors, philosophers, and so forth, fall outside the scope of civil concern, which
the Greeks call *politikēn*.

4. Of course there are civil questions whose study can fall
within the common interest of all those who think; these the
Greeks call *koinēn ennoian*. Let us, then, try to explain a little
more clearly what this kind of issue is, what makes a civil question. A civil question is any question of the kind that people would
be embarrassed not to understand, of the kind that a person pretends to know all about even though he is actually quite ignorant
about it, of the kind that everyone is willing to comment on when
it comes up for discussion. What I am trying to point out is this: if
someone were to ask you the weight of something, you would not
blush because you didn't know how many pounds it was; if someone ask you a measurement, you would not blush because you
didn't know how many feet long it was; and there are many other
such questions, too many to enumerate here. Now when questions
like this come up for discussion, even though there is real dis-
agreement, there is still not a civil question. But when we are trying to decide whether something is just or unjust, honorable or dishonorable, praiseworthy or contemptible, deserving of reward or
punishment, expedient or inexpedient, and so forth, there is no one
who would not be ashamed to admit that he didn't know even

though he had no training in any art or science. This is why everyone is convinced (or at least has no doubt that he can convince
others) that he understands the difference between justice and injustice, honor and dishonor, and between all the other opposing
concepts we have noted here. Thus when disputes arise in any of
these areas, they are called civil questions; they are not the exclusive preserve of a select few, but are the common concern of all.
As a result, since these things are evident even to the untrained,
the questions which come within the category of *koinēi ennoiai*
are called civil. They are the ones in which the orator must take
an interest so that he can assume a position of leadership.

5. There are basically two general kinds of civil questions. One
of these the Greeks call the thesis, the other the hypothesis. We
have been able to give to the former no other name than that
Greek one; the same is true of the latter also, although we may
seem to have been able to find a Latin term. But what we call the
controversia can really be understood to embrace both the thesis
and the hypothesis, for both deal with a question; in each, therefore, there is a *controversia*. Besides the meaning of the word hypothesis seems to be explained by the structure of the word, *hypo
tēn thesin,* which indicates that it comes under the thesis in the
manner of a species under a genus.

The thesis is a subject which lends itself to logical discussion
without reference to a specific person; the hypothesis or *controversia* (to use the term loosely) is a subject which lends itself to
such discussion only in reference to a specific person. Perhaps the
best way to explain this is with an illustration. A thesis is a question like this: "Should people go sailing?" or "Should people study
philosophy?" An hypothesis is a question of this type: "Should a
reward be bestowed on Duillius?" There are not lacking, however,
those who challenge Hermagoras in this; not least of these is Apol-
lodorus, who denies that there is any difference between the thesis
and the hypothesis, holding that the distinction of persons is of no
importance. Hermagoras, they say, seems to have made a very
careful distinction between these kinds of question; however the
question in any hypothesis is in reality no less unlimited or unre-

stricted than that in a thesis. For, they say, when we ask the question, "Should Orestes not be punished?", it is not the person but the fact that is at issue, and it is the same as if we asked, "Should a matricide not be punished?" If they are right in this, then there is no difference between the hypothesis and the thesis.

6. In response to this, here is our comment: first of all, it is the identity of the persons involved which makes the difference in questions. It often happens in these hypotheses (or *controversiae*) that certain acts are held to be deserving of punishment or no punishment, of praise or blame, not so much from the caliber of the action as from the position of the one who acted. Thus the two types of question differ at least in this, that in the thesis there occurs the evaluation of an act, while in the hypothesis there is a dispute about it; to the extent, therefore, that there is a difference between an examination of an act and a quarrel about it, to that extent there is a difference between thesis and hypothesis. Again, in a thesis the question centers on what would be best for everyone to do, while in an hypothesis it deals with one or two or a few, a certain specified kind of person. There is this difference also, that in a thesis we ask as though we are ignorant and unsure of what is best to do, while in the hypothesis we ask as if knowing and wishing to defend a position. Then too, the thesis is always about the future, the hypothesis very rarely so; the latter deals almost exclusively with the past or with what is already being done. No one can be accused of an act unless he has already done it or at least is said to have done it; nor can any one seek a reward if he has not already earned it or at least claimed to have earned it. This also applies to those who are accused of attempted tyranny or treason or poisoning or parricide or whatever other crime you might want to name. They are charged with planning to commit a crime, and this is their crime. For example, one may be charged with a plan to commit treason; we do not try to find out if he committed an act still in the future, but whether he laid a plan to commit treason sometime in the past. So the would-be tyrant is asked if he planned to commit tyranny, and the same with the planner of parricide and of poisoning. So in an hypothesis, the investigation al-

ways centers around the past or the present, but in a thesis only
around the future. And if we are right in all this, then the difference between the two is established.

7. Now since we have said enough about the difference between
general and special questions and have distinguished the thesis
from the hypothesis in the manner of distinguishing the reality
from the abstraction, it seems that the next step must be to identify what makes the hypothesis, or *controversia.* So, it is the circumstances of the act, what Hermagoras calls the *peristasin;* without this there can be absolutely no *controversia* at all. What this
peristasis is can be explained more easily by breaking it down into
its components than by defining it. Actually, there are seven parts
of the context or peristasis; Hermagoras calls them *moria perista-
seōs,* and Theodorus the *stocheia tou pragmatos* or "components,"
because cases to be argued are the immediate result of their being
put together in just the same way that nouns and verbs are seen to
result from the putting together of their letters. But whether they
are more correctly called *stocheia* or *moria* is immaterial to us; we
are more interested in what they are. And here is what they are:
who? what? when? where? why? how? by what means (which the
Greeks call *aphormas*)? When all of them, or at least most of
them, come together logically, the result is a subject to be argued.
It is only right to examine each of them, therefore.

8. "Who?" has reference to the identity of the speaker. This can
be established in two ways, by name or by position. By name, the
speaker might be Camillus, C. Marius, L. Sulla; by position he
could be a rich man or a poor, a magistrate or an emperor. Either
he is identified specifically by name or generally by a description
of his personal qualities; his name is simply what he is called, but
his personal qualities can include his fortune, his age, his rank, his
education, and an infinite range of other things. "What?" has reference to the thing spoken about: whether it was done or said or
planned by someone, whether it is being done or said or planned,
or whether it is going to be done or said or planned; also whether
it is good or bad, honorable or dishonorable, just or unjust, necessary or unnecessary, important or insignificant, customary or unusual. "When?" has reference to the time of the occurrence, such

as whether it happened during the day or at night, on a sacred day or an ordinary one. It also concerns itself with such accidental circumstances of time as may give it a special character, as a time of war or a time of peace, during a time of revolution or during a period of harmony, during independence or under oppression, and anything else that might come into such a category. "Where?" has the purpose of identifying the place where the act occurred, whether inside the city or outside, in a sacred place or a profane one, at sea or on land. "Why?" inquires as to the cause of the act or the word or the plan, which I consider an item of the first importance in building the whole case. "How?" has reference to the actual performance of the act as it was done or as it is being done or as it is supposed to be done; asking is it overt or secret, an act of open violence or of clandestine treachery, or whatever else of this nature might enter into the investigation. The *aphormai*, which we have called the tools, have the purpose of identifying the instruments by which something is supposed to have been done, such as a rope, a sword, poison, a letter, a messenger, commands, a servant, a conspirator, an assassin. The logical assembling of all these elements makes, as I have indicated earlier, a civil question.

9. "Rational" questions are those which Hermagoras calls logical. It seems more correct to call them this than to call them "verbal," since the experts who call them "logical" do so not in reference to words, but in reference to reasoning, and *logos* sometimes means "word" and sometimes "idea." These rational or logical questions are of four kinds, asking definite information: did anything happen? what happened? what are the particular qualities of what happened? and, should the event be brought up for a judgment? When we ask if anything happened, this is the kind of question that Hermagoras calls *stochasmos* and we call conjecture; Theodoros calls it *peri tēs ousias,* which means "about the substance." Nothing can be examined as a fact if it does not have substance; nothing can be planned which does not have the potential of substance. Some call this kind of question *an sit,* from the fact that what we are asking is, "Is anything there?" Another rational question is that which Hermagoras calls "the end"; The-

odoros calls it *peri tēs idiotētos,* which means "about the uniqueness," some others use the term *quid sit,* and some even call it
peri tou autou kai thaterou, "about this and that." For the third
rational question, all authorities agree on the same name,
"quality."

10. The fourth issue is, as we have noted above, whether to
bring the question up for a decision at all; there is much controversy about this one. There are many who deny that it can be an
issue if the matter is already called up for judgment. Against
these, however, stands the opinion of Hermagoras that it is a real
issue, that it is very important, that it is a proper subject for argument in court, and even that it ought to be treated along with the
other questions of status from the very start of the case if the entire structure is to be perfectly clear. I can think of nothing more
important to the persons on whose behalf a judgment is sought
than a refusal to pass judgment; indeed, I believe that the very
refusal is in itself a kind of judgment. For if any matter can be so
treated that a person who does not want his case judged has the
power to refuse to submit it, then there never was a real question.
Still the fact is that there are always some who want to impede
justice; the very fact that one asks for judgment and the other refuses to submit makes the question the kind of *controversia* which
Hermagoras calls *metalēpsin.* A few contemporary authors call it
reprehensio, and others *translatio,* both groups following sound
reasoning. Those who say *reprehensio* stress the fact that as soon
as the case is called for decision some attack it (*reprehenditur*)
and others defend it (*retrahitur*) as it were. Those who call it
translatio note that the accused does not deny that he did the
action; instead he challenges the present consideration of it by
asking that it be transferred to another kind of decision, either one
already concluded or one still to come.

11. There are four other questions, called by their developers
the *nomikas,* which we call the legal issues. These include *scrip-
tum et voluntas,* which many call *rhēton kai dianoian; antinomia,*
which we call the conflict between contradictory laws; ambiguity,
which the Greeks call *amphibolian;* and inference, which they call

syllogismon. These I shall treat in greater detail later on, explaining each as to meaning and identifying for each its divisions.

But first it seems to me that we ought to see what bones and members fit together to make each question a perfect whole. First there is some kind of statement, which the Greeks call the *phasin.* This is broken down into two parts, one being the *ketaphasis,* the other the *apophasis.* We can identify the *cataphasis* (it would not be enough just to call it the assertion) as the phrase in which the accusation actually appears; in other words, it is the word which names the crime: "You struck him, you betrayed him, you killed him." What some call the *apophasis,* we call the rejection of the charge which the accuser makes: "I did not strike him, I did not kill him, I did not betray him." From these two elements, assertion and response, charge and denial, the question emerges. Thus: the charge is, "You killed," and the denial is, "I did not kill"; the question is then, "Did he kill?" But if we move beyond the first investigation, the charge becomes, "You killed unjustly," and the denial is, "I killed, but not unjustly"; then the question is, "Did he have the right to kill?" So it is with every legal status: The charge is always, "The law did not permit you to do this," and the answer is, "The law did permit me to do it"; then the question is always, "Does the law permit a person to do this thing?"

12. Some (and we among them until now) have called this issue "the question," and others have identified it as "the *status* of the question." It is obvious that this is because it really is both the preliminary statement and the whole point of the argument. It is the latter in this sense: when two people who have not yet come together in battle stand apart from one another, as it were, and say, "This was done," on the one hand, and, "It was not done," on the other, they are not yet engaged in fighting, but only in determining the ground for the fight that is to come. But when they draw nearer to one another, coming face to face with each other, and hurl the charge and the denial back and forth, the question clearly arises between them whether or not it was done. On this everything else hinges; all that was said previously is ignored; in this case, the "question" can also be called the "*status.*" Theodoros

calls this the *kephalion,* using the image of the chief part of the human body, because it can serve either of two purposes, both of which could be called, as it were, "the head of the entire *controversia.*"

13. The next step is at least equally important, if not even more so; it is the demonstration of what the case is, what the grounds for the case are, and what the point actually at issue is. Identifying the case Hermagoras calls the *aition,* the grounds for the case he calls the *synechon,* and the point at issue the *krinomenon.* The case is whatever has happened before *controversia* can be said to have begun. What I mean is this: "The son is disinherited by his father" is not a statement of a case, because there is no reason given for the disinheriting, there is nothing that happened earlier. But when we add a cause, the controversy is immediately laid out: "A son has sworn that he will never marry, and so his father has disinherited him." The fact that he has sworn is the *aition;* that is, it is the cause for which he is disinherited. The *synechon,* or grounds for the case, is what appears as the explanation given in answer to the *aition;* here is an example: "A commander has killed a soldier who had sworn that he intended to desert; the comander is now charged with murder." Here the *aition* or cause of the case is the fact that the commander killed the soldier; after all, he would not be on trial if he had not killed the man. But the *synechon,* or grounds for the case, is that which drove him to kill, the oath which the soldier had sworn that he intended to desert. It is this that Hermagoras calls the *synechon,* or the grounds for the case; he also calls it the *aition aitiou,* or the cause of the cause. For just as the fact that he killed the soldier is the cause of his being accused, so the cause of the killing is that the soldier had sworn that he was going to desert.

14. Now, since we know what the cause is and what the grounds for the cause are, we must find out also exactly what the point at issue is, which is *to krinomenon.* It is really nothing more than the probing of *to synechon,* that is of the grounds for the case. To illustrate, let me continue with the same *controversia,* so that my point will be clearer. The *aition* is the fact that this commander killed this soldier; the *synechon* is what the accused man swears

happened, that is the reason he gives for killing the man, which is that he swore that he was going to desert; the *krinomenon* is the investigation of this latter point which the accused man has brought up in his own defense. For example it would be necessary to inquire whether the commander might have killed the soldier for another reason and made this up as a pretext. Such would be the case if it seems that the killing took place not because the soldier had sworn that oath, but for some other reason, such as jealousy or rivalry. In this case, the entire contention would be treated as follows: "Even if he had sworn so, this would hardly stand up as a just cause for killing him." And the whole investigation of the entire *synechon* as it is presented in answer to the *aition* is called the *krinomenon*. Now it can sometimes happen that the *aition*, the *synechon*, and the *krinomenon* do not all appear at once in a single *controversia;* more usually they appear one after the other as the case unrolls. Thus the *controversia* may be "Ulysses is charged with a crime against the state because he has killed the suitors." Here the *aition* is that he killed them; the *synechon*, or *aition aitiou*, is that he killed those who were pillaging his goods and plotting against the chastity of his wife; the *krinomenon* is whether this, even though it may have really happened, is indeed the reason for the killing or only a pretext in place of some other reason, and also whether he ought to have killed even the very vilest of criminals if they have not yet been formally sentenced. Then Ulysses offers a *synechon* for this *krinomenon:* that he killed them on the command of Minerva. But this *synechon* demands a *krinomenon*, whether perhaps he killed, but not because of Minerva's command at all, and also whether in such a matter he ought perhaps not to have obeyed Minerva. So it is exclusively the right of the accuser to formulate the *aition;* it is that of the defendant to formulate the *synechon;* and it is the right of either party to present a *krinomenon*.

15. The next point that I think needs to be made is to explain what *controversiae asystatae* are and how many kinds there are. As a matter of fact, they ought not be called *controversiae* at all, but irrational mouthings or *aloga*. Now there are four kinds of *asystatae*. The first is that in which something is missing from the

context (and the importance of the context has already been noted above); for example if the act itself or the actor or the place cannot be identified, or if any of the other elements are unclear from which the context ought to be established. This kind of *asystaton* cannot be the subject of study in school, however, simply because there is no theme to be handled at all if the context is incomplete. Nevertheless the fact is that it sometimes turns out that even though one of these elements is lacking, yet because of the carelessness of the speaker such an irresponsible case comes before the judge. There is a second kind of *asystaton,* which the Greeks call *kat' isotēta.* Unfortunately we cannot give it a Latin name; nevertheless we must try to understand it. When the very same things can be said on both sides and there is not the slightest shade of difference to be discerned, then this kind of *plegma* befouls the status; the two parties are equally guilty. Take for example two young men who have beautiful wives; at night they encounter one another in the darkness and accuse each other of adultery. Now whatever the first young man can say, the second has an equal right to say exactly the same way. If the first says, "It looks very much as though you wanted to commit adultery, since you are a young man," the other can say, "It looks very much as though you had the same intention, since you too are young." If the first says, "It looks as though you wanted to, because I have a beautiful wife," the other responds, "That is equally true of you, because my wife is pretty too." "The fact that you are my neighbor gives you the opportunity." "You are my neighbor too and have the same opportunity." "Why were you going toward my house in the middle of the night?" "Well, weren't you coming to my house in the same way?" There is absolutely no way to distinguish between the two; so if either of them accuses the other he automatically incriminates himself, and if he defends himself, he also removes all suspicion from the very neighbor he wants to accuse.

16. The third kind of *asystaton,* which the Greeks call *kath' heteromerian,* is that in which the accused can offer no defense. In this kind of case there is found either no complexion of circumstance which can be established for certain at all or almost none which can even be demonstrated probably. Thus my mentor Dem-

ocrates[8] was wont to say that those questions in which a long search
is necessary to shed any new light do not have a status. He was,
however, too unyielding; I would allow any defense to be suggested, no matter how barely probable it is. But if the case as presented is clearly full of holes, then it is proper to throw it out on
the basis of *heteromeria*. Also, there sometimes come up certain
questions, especially regarding the truth, which give a definite
advantage to the accuser and none to the defendant; these we do
not call *controversiae* but commonplaces, because they center
around not proof of the crime but a dramatic presentation which
makes the act seem more shocking.

Fourth, there is a kind of *asystaton* so very sneaky that it sometimes takes in even quite learned men. It bears a resemblance to
material which can be proved and which holds up under scrutiny.
This is the kind in which the judge is unable to find a reason for
rendering a decision. The Greeks call this *aporon*. Let us make
use of an example here: one man demands that another pay interest on some money, charging that it was a loan; the other admits that he received the money, but he maintains that it was
entrusted to him as a deposit. He says that he will return the
money without interest. While they are waiting for a decision, a
new law is passed which cancels all debts. The first man then
says he wants his deposit back, but the second refuses, saying now
that it was a loan after all. I do not see on what grounds the judge
can reach a decision, since the petitioner first says he loaned the
money, then says that he deposited it; likewise the other says first
that he received a deposit, then that he received a loan. Neither
holds to his original claim, but each takes the position originally
held by the other.

17. It seems now that it would be quite proper for us to spend
a little time studying the forms of the *controversiae* and how they
differ from one another, so that we may better understand how we
should treat each one. There are, then, four kinds of structure, or
forms, in *controversiae:* they are *endoxos,* when we speak to those

8. The identity of this Democrates is unclear. Perhaps the author used the
phrase "my mentor" to identify his own tutor rather than Augustine's.

who hold us in good opinion; *amphidoxos,* when we speak to those whose opinions are mixed; *paradoxos,* when we speak to those whose opinion is hostile. There are some people who do not speak Greek very well who would say that *paradoxa* can refer to those things we respect very highly; thus, the word is popularly applied to the victors in Olympic games and other sacred contests more because of habit than of logic. But it is my opinion that *paradoxon* comes from *para tēn doxan,* which means "against good opinion." Moreover, even though we prefer to demand that they justify giving such an inaccurate meaning to that word, yet for now, since many things are given new names either by experts or by philosophers, we ought to accept the meaning which is dictated not by habit or custom or popular usage, but by the demands of the situation. The fourth form of *controversia,* which is called *adoxos* in Greek, is our expression not of opposition, as is commonly believed, but of indifference; by it we label the theme low and worthless. But these will all be clear in the following examples.

18. *Endoxos* is an argument of the kind in which both the person speaking and the topic are honorable, as in this example: "After his victory in the Punic War, Scipio asks that his reward be a laurel crown bestowed at the games." Now the person of Scipio is certainly honorable, and what he asks is not contemptible. *Amphidoxos* is an argument in which the foulness of the subject vitiates the nobility of the speaker, as in the case of the same Scipio in the same circumstances asking, under the pretense of asking a reward, the death of Tiberius Asellus. Certainly the person of the petitioner is honorable, but what he asks is loathsome. The exact opposite would also be an example of this: if a disinherited son acts nobly and asks that, as his reward, he be allowed to return to his father's house. Now the person asking is in disgrace, disinherited, but what he asks for is praiseworthy, to be allowed to return to his father's house. *Paradoxon,* as I defined it above, is the kind of argument in which both are dishonorable, the petitioner and his theme; for example, "a man accused of adultery acts nobly and asks as his reward the death of his accuser." The petitioner is dishonorable, being accused of adultery, even though the nobility of his later act helps to diminish the magnitude of his shame, and

what he asks is contrary to honor. *Adoxon* is a kind of *controversia* without any strong opinion on either side, low and petty. "A poor man," for example, "sells some clothing; another poor man comes up and makes a claim against the first, saying that the clothing belonged to him and the first man took them away in a theft; the seller maintains that he took them from a man caught in adultery; then they continue hurling accusations back and forth, the one of adultery, the other of theft." In this case both of the two men are of low degree, and the matter which they seem to make the point at issue, the claiming and counterclaiming about the clothing, is petty; so, even though the crime of adultery is not petty, yet since there are so many mean and shallow elements *en tē peristasei*, these detract from the dignity of the whole *controversia*. When there is agreement on everything else, then we must recognize the difference between these forms of the *controversia* from the very beginning, so that we can find an approach to the question, a technique for presenting it in keeping with the status of the theme. For the same kind of beginning is not suitable for all four themes, *endoxos, amphidoxos, paradoxos,* and *adoxos;* rather each deserves its own kind.

19. First of all, Hermagoras denies that any preliminary statement at all is necessary in the kind of matter which is *endoxos*. For, he says, if we are accustomed to begin by saying a few words to win good will, then there is nothing to be gained by doing so when the question itself already has the esteem of the audience, as in the first example of Scipio; those to whom we are going to speak are already favorably inclined, so there is no reason to do what has already been done. But it seems otherwise to me, and with all due respect to such a man, I must say so; authority is not always to be followed blindly, especially if it must give way before logic. I think there is nothing in the kind of material comprising *endoxos* which excludes an introductory statement. I see nothing wrong with speaking pleasantly so as to make a good-natured judge even better-natured; or if we see that others have been offended by our opponent, then we should try to increase that antipathy by our own presentation. Besides, we see that even bards and minstrels and other entertainers of that kind always say

a little something first, and they are not getting ready to deliver an oration. Since a speech before an action is badly defective and lacking in integrity if it dispenses with the introduction and plunges directly into the heart of the matter, then we ought to use an introduction even in those questions where the good will of the audience is assured. However it should be somewhat shorter and more to the point, confident and marked with dignity, without display; thus the subject will not antagonize anyone. This was the method of M. Tullius [Cicero] when he spoke against the election of Metellus; he seemed to rise above himself as he attacked that tribune: "What right at all does he have even to stand forth for election? I feel as though I am chasing him like a fugitive at this point, since I cannot manage to confront him like an adversary."[9] Surely he would never have begun to speak so eloquently at the very outset unless his own dignity as speaker was notable and his subject not to be held in contempt. Likewise, in another place, he spoke about the reading of auguries; he said, "I notice, Fathers of the Senate, that all of you have turned your faces and your eyes to me,"[10] and so forth. All of this is of such a nature that the speaker seems to have confidence both in his own dignity and in the dignity of the subject about which he intends to speak; he is certain that both are most deserving of honor. In the case of some *exordia*, says G. Gracchus, the nobler the subject is, the more elevated the delivery. Certainly no one, not even an army could hold back M. Erucius when he spoke, or any one of those men who fought at Cannae.

20. In the kind of material which demands *amphidoxos*, a certain mildness is needed at the beginning of the presentation, so that we may both [de-emphasize] the foulness which is so much a part of the case [by covering it up][11] and stress the dignity of the person or the act by enhancing it. In this way we will mingle the two elements so that the nobility of the one part will over-

9. *Fragm.* I (Halm's identification).

10. *Oratio in Catilinam Quarta* I.1.

11. The bracketed words represent a phrase whose insertion is suggested both by Halm and by the editor of the text in *PL* 32.

shadow the vileness of the other, using not so much the kind of eloquent display which characterizes the kind of case mentioned above as a sort of confident reserve. If it is the theme which lacks respectability, then we will, as best we can, call the judge's attention to the merit of the person; if the person is of questionable honor, then we will take refuge in the nobility of the act, moving as it were from the dangerous ground to a safer location. When we do this, we must admit it briefly and in passing so that we may seem rather to dismiss the accusation that we are afraid than to be afraid. We will also work to this end, so that when we have tied the two elements together, the dignity of the theme and that of the person, we may seem to have done so more in honest confidence than in trembling doubt. But to make this kind of introduction more clear, I turn to the example furnished by M. Tullius when he spoke in behalf of M. Scaurus. This was a real case of *amphidoxos* in the material, since he wished to stress the personal prestige of M. Scaurus and at the same time to cover up his foul crime of accepting bribes. The orator therefore immediately tied the two things together at the very beginning so that he could bury the vileness of the crime under the honor of the person; yet he did this not in an effusive or overblown way, but in such a way, indeed, as to express a certain trace of fear: "M. Scaurus truly hopes, oh judges, that [you will hear his case] without any prior hatred of any one, without taking offense, without irritation,"[12] and so forth.

21. In *paradoxos*, which is a situation involving hostility, where the dignity of both person and subject labor under a cloud, it is wise to use a longer introduction. Thus for the purpose of allaying suspicions, we should pay homage to the deeds [of the judges]; we should speak modestly both as to our content and as to our phrasing, so as to charm them by flattery; and we should offer a complaint about the unjust accusations of crime and the false charges leveled against us by those who hate us. The whole body should be kept under control so that it projects an aura of mod-

12. *Fragm.* I (Halm).

esty, the face should be cast down, the eyes fixed on the ground. And none of this should be done bitterly, but as far as possible in a gentle tone of voice.

In *adoxos*, which is a speech about something quite petty, the introductory remarks ought to be very conversational; do not argue in high-flown sentiments or with outrageously flowery phrases, use no weighty brief; but be relaxed and unaffected. The point of everything said in these preliminary comments ought to be this: we want to take what is of merely personal interest and present it to a wider audience; we want to prove that the matter under consideration is of importance to all. To this purpose we maintain that the very fact that it seems small indicates how frequently and to how many people it can happen. Further, we point out that the case should be studied not on the basis of the importance of the issue or the people involved, but in terms of justice and injustice, truth and falsehood; in these questions the smallest matters are just as significant as the greatest. Demosthenes frequently used such introductions in speaking to those freedmen who were considered unlearned; they were used even more frequently by Lysias and by our own ancients. Certainly M. Tullius did not use any other approach when he spoke on behalf of Archias.

3. C. CHIRIUS FORTUNATIANUS

Artis rhetoricae libri tres, I (EXCERPT)[1]

Translated by Joseph M. Miller

C. Chirius Fortunatianus was a Roman rhetorician who flourished around 450 A.D. Although his *Three Books on the Art of Rhetoric* is not itself an important work in the development of rhetorical theory, it is of historical interest for two reasons: first because of the unusual question-and-answer format in which Fortunatianus expounds traditional post-Classical rhetorical theory and, second, because of its great popularity as a textbook in the schools of the later Middle Ages.[2]

The importance of the work appears in two facts concerning the work. First, as Halm points out,[3] the treatise always preceded the Pseudo-Augustinian *Rhetoric* in one volume, indicating that Fortunatianus somehow shared in the reflected glory of the most venerated Christian scholar; second, Cassiodorus, the much more renowned contemporary of Fortunatianus, pays tribute to him by quoting him by name as a highly respected authority in the field of rhetoric.

---

1. Whoever wants to hasten down rhetoric's highway
Toward the handling of laws and cases first must master
This study of the art, that he may escape the traps of the maze.

What is rhetoric? The knowledge of how to speak well.
What is an orator? A good man skilled at speaking.
What is the function of the orator? To speak well on civil questions.

---

1. C. Chirii Fortunatiani *Artis rhetoricae libri tres*, in *RLM*, pp.81–84.
2. *Nouvelle Biographie Generale*, ed. M. le Docteur Hoefer (Paris: Firmin Didot Frères, 1851), vol. 18, p.232.
3. *RLM*, p.136.

To what end? In order to persuade, insofar as the state of affairs and the attitude of the audience permits, in civil questions.

What are civil questions? Those which can be understood by ordinary intelligence; those which everyone can grasp, as an investigation whether something is just or good.

How many kinds of civil questions are there? Three. What are they? Demonstrative, deliberative, judicial. What are these called by some? Kinds of speaking.

What is the demonstrative kind? That in which we point out that there is something which gives cause either for praise or condemnation. What do the Greeks call this? *Epideiktikon* or *enkomistikon*. What is the deliberative kind? A speech in which an effort is made to persuade or to dissuade. What do the Greeks call this? *Symbouleutikon*. What is the judicial kind? That in which there occurs either an accusation or a defense. What do the Greeks call this? *Dikanikon*.

How many steps are there to the orator's task? Five: analysis, organization, composition, memory, delivery. What are they called by the Greeks? *Erga tou rhētoros*.

2. When a subject for argument has been suggested, what is the first thing we must look for? Whether it holds up as an issue. How can we determine this? By examining the charge and the response.

What is the charge? The statement that the first person makes when he raises the question. What do the Greeks call this? *Katabasis*. What is the response? The answer that the second person makes to the charge. And what do the Greeks call this? *Apophasis*.

Where does the *katabasis* get its force? From the *aetion*. What is the *aetion*? The cause of the litigation, the point concerning which judgment is sought.

Where does the *apophasis* get its force? From the *synekon*. And what is the *synekon*? The statement which contains the essence of the entire defense.

From the *aetion* and the *synekon* what results? The *krinomenon*. What is the *krinomenon*? The point concerning which judgment must be given.

What issues have no right to be considered at all? A charge against which there is no defense, and a charge which is leveled dishonestly or unfairly. What are such cases called by the Greeks? *Asystata*.

2.[4] How many kinds of *asystata* are there? According to Hermagoras, there are four; they are *ellipousa* and *isazousa* and *monomerēs* and *aporos*.

What is *ellipusa?*[5] It is the lack of some element in the circumstances which affect the question; if someone disinherits his son, for example, and gives no explanation for the disinheriting. On the other hand, if we offer a reason, such as, "He is lustful," or "He lacks friends," or something of that kind, then the issue will stand as valid. Is *ellipusa* ever called by other names? Sometimes it is called *kat' ellipes* or *kata morion* or *kat' aperistaton*.

What is *isazusa?* A case in which each of the two parties can say exactly the same thing, so that nothing is applicable exclusively to one or the other. Thus: "Two young men who are neighbors both have beautiful wives; they come upon one another during the night, whereupon each accuses the other of adultery." In this case, whatever one party says, the other can also say. Do people call *isazusa* by other names? Yes, *isomerē* or *kat' isotēta* or *priona*.

What is *monomeres?* A case in which all the evidence seems to support one side only, so that nothing can be said on behalf of the other; *monomeres* is much like a commonplace. Give an example. "A procurer knows the place where some youths are planning to meet; during the night he digs a pit and covers it over; the youths die in this trap; he is arrested and accused of planning to cause their deaths." There is no defense for the procurer against this charge. What else is *monomeres* called? *Heteromerēs* or *kath' heteromerian*.

What is *aporos?* A case in which the judge cannot find any basis for a decision. For example: "Three men set out on a journey together, but only two return; each accuses the other of murder. In such a case, the judge cannot determine what really happened,

4. This inconsistency of numbering two consecutive sections with the same number occurs in *RLM*, p.82. No explanation appears, but the numbering continues from this point.

5. The variations in the Greek spellings result from the fact that the translator has transliterated the Greek directly to English, but has accepted the spelling of Fortunatianus in those places where he transliterated to Latin.

since each maintains that the other killed the missing man; thus there is no way to obtain proof so long as that circumstance is not cleared up.

3. Are these the only species of *asystatae?* There are also some others which we find mentioned by various commentators on the arts. What are they? *Antistrephousa, achromos, adunatos, apithanos, aprepes, anaisynchtos, par' istorian, alogos.*

What is *antistrephusa?* When the two litigants change positions in the case, so that neither is upholding the contention with which he began, but each is now taking the position his opponent inaugurated. Give an example. "A man demanded that his friend pay back some money with interest, on the claim that it had originally been a loan; the other offered to pay it back without interest, maintaining that it had been a deposit. While they were waiting for a decision, a new law was passed, cancelling all debts; now the first man wants his money back as a deposit, but the other insists that he owes nothing because it was a loan."

What is *achromos?* A case in which there are no details to color the fact; for example, "Ten soldiers amputate their fingers in time of war; they are charged with treason against the state."[6] How does *monomeres* differ from *achromos?* In the fact that *monomeres* is the absence of all defense, while *achromos* is the absence of shading details only.

What is *adynatos?* A case where something is brought into the charge which is completely impossible by the very nature of things, like accusing an infant of adultery because he sleeps with someone else's wife.

What is *apithanos?* The discovery of a circumstance in the case which most probably did not occur in the way described. For example, if the speaker says that the eyes of a blind man were restored to him or that the inhabitants of a besieged city sent messengers out to someone; it is however, possible that it ought to be accepted. Why is this so? Because, even though it is most unlikely. that a blind man should recover the use of his eyes, yet we can

6. Those were guilty of treason who rendered themselves unfit for military service.

believe that it is possible for this to happen through an act of God; also, it is possible that the inhabitants of a city under siege might have sent out messengers by taking advantage of the time when those besieging were asleep, or by finding a part of the city where they had been careless about maintaining the siege. What do we call arguments of this kind? *Cacosystatae.* What are *cacosystatae?* Arguments which are not solidly established. How many kinds of *cacosystatae* are there? Three: those called *cacosystatae* because they are not solidly established; others called *asystatae* because they have no foundation for acceptance at all; and still others which cannot even be called arguments because they are contrary to reason in the way they are fashioned, that is they are *aloga.*

4. What is *aprepes?* A case in which something incongruous is brought out about a person, such as: "This courageous man demanded a reward; it is true that he acted bravely, but then he demanded the marriage of his daughter as his reward."

What is *anaesynchtos?* It is a case in which the party bringing the charge is found to be completely without honor. For example, "A lecherous father disinherits his son for being decent" would illustrate this, if the father does indeed disinherit the son for that reason; moreover, even if he proves that he did not disinherit his son, the charge of plotting to do so would still hold up, even though the act were never actually carried out. Therefore we must understand that there are some *controversia* which can be argued on the grounds of intention, even though the plan is not implemented.

How does *monomeres* differ from *aeschyntos?* In the fact that *monomeres* is a case in which the defendant has nothing to present, while *aeschyntos* is one in which the accuser has nothing.

What is *par' historian?* A case in which something comes out during the testimony which seems directly opposed to what really happened. For example, "Q. Hortensius is indicated on a charge of demanding tribute from innocent citizens while he served as consul." This would be *par' historian* if we discover that the consul who did this was not Hortensius but Tullius. Is this kind of error discovered only in regard to the person named in the charge? Not at all. It can apply to any of the circumstances: to the act it-

self, to the time, to the place, to the cause, to the manner, to the
means used, and to anything else that might be inserted in the
story contrary to what we know to be true.

What is *alogos?* An argument which is composed without regard to logic. Although it is true that all *asystatae* can be called
alogos, yet the term applies specifically to those in which no logic
at all appears.

5. When we know that a case will hold up in court, what is the
first thing we must look for? An approach to the case. What does
approach mean? The proper way to put the entire case together.
What is the difference between the approach (*ductus*) and the
method (*modus*)? Approach involves the structure of the entire
oration, while method deals with only one part of the oration.

How many approaches are there? There are five: simple, subtle,
contrived, oblique, and mixed.

What is the simple approach? When we do exactly as we have
proposed in our opening statement.

What is the subtle approach? When we say one thing in our
statement of purpose, but have in mind the intention of doing
something different.

What is the contrived approach? The approach we use when
shame keeps us from speaking out openly.

What is the oblique approach? When danger keeps us from acting openly.

What is the mixed approach? When the approach is not any one
of these.

Where should we look for the approach? In the plan. How? If
the plan is straightforward, the approach should be simple; but if
the plan is not straightforward, then the approach will not be simple, but either subtle, if the intention is to say one thing at the outset and then to do something different, or contrived, if shame
keeps us from saying openly what we intend, or oblique if fear of
danger keeps us from taking direct action, or mixed, if there is not
any single approach.

6. Where do we look to determine our plan? At the time involved. How? If we are dealing with something from the past,
then our plan should be straightforward; but if the time in ques-

tion is the present or the future, the plan will not be straightforward.

On what basis do we evaluate the time in question? According
to the cause of the trial. See, for example, how the approach is discovered in each of these cases. "The corpse of a recently murdered
man is found next to him, therefore he is charged with murder."
The cause of the trial is that the corpse has been found; it follows
then that the plan is straightforward and the approach simple.

How is the subtle approach found? "He has no friends, so he
should be disinherited." The cause of the litigation is that he has
no friends, which is a situation presently in existence; it does not
call for a straightforward plan, nor, as a consequence, does it call
for the simple approach. What approach will be appropriate,
then? The subtle, because it proposes to do one thing but actually
intends to do something quite different. In this case, it pretends to
oppose the conclusion, "he should be disinherited," but actually
deals with the reason for the disinheriting; it seeks to persuade the
judge that he does have friends.

How is the contrived approach found? "It is lawful to kill adul-
terers. A foul wretch defiles his own daughter-in-law. His son finds
the adulterer with his face masked and does not kill him. The
father asks the son who the adulterer was that he spared; the son
does not answer and the father disinherits him." The cause of the
case is that the son refuses to speak, which is a situation of the
present; there is no call, therefore, for a straightforward plan, nor,
consequently, for a simple approach. What is the approach, then?
It is contrived, because it is shame which keeps the son from saying outright to his father, "You were the adulterer."

How is the oblique approach found? "A tyrant relinquished his
power under a treaty of amnesty: now he wishes to seek a magistracy and is being opposed." The cause of the opposition is that he
is seeking a magistracy, which is a present act dealing with a future situation; therefore there is no call for a straightforward plan,
nor, consequently, for a simple approach. What is called for then?
The oblique approach, since the opponent is prevented by fear
from making any mention of the tyranny.

How is the mixed approach found? "The wretch who defiled his daughter-in-law lived in a castle: he called his son to him and asked whether he believed the rumor; the son said that he did not believe it. The father then let him depart from the territory under a treaty of amnesty; the son put aside his wife. The father asks the cause of the repudiation; the son does not answer and is disinherited." The cause of the trial is that the son does not explain the cause of the divorce; this is a situation of the present which does not call for a straightforward plan, nor, consequently, for a simple approach. What does it call for? Mixed, that is both contrived and oblique approaches: contrived because shame keeps the son from saying to his father, "You were the adulterer on whose account I divorced my wife," and oblique because fear keeps him from making any mention of the tyranny.

4. EMPORIUS THE ORATOR

Concerning Ethopoeia[1]

Translated by Joseph M. Miller

Although Emporius the Orator flourished toward the end of the Second Sophistic, a contemporary of Fortunatianus, Martianus Capella, and Pseudo-Augustine, his contribution to rhetoric deserves attention only because it represents a typically pedestrian treatment of the predominant elements of rhetoric as seen by the less-gifted rhetoricians of the time. Little is known of him beyond the period of his activity; his surviving works include the present discussion of ethopoeia as well as a manual of commonplaces (*Praeceptum loci communis*), a manual concerning the use of demonstrative material (*Praeceptum demonstrativae materiae*), and a manual concerning the use of deliberative material (*Praeceptum deliberativae materiae*). The four items occupy a total of about thirteen pages in *RLM*.

Although impersonation is not the whole substance of the orator's duty, still it is a major part of the material and is necessary in the preparation of all the material. Attitudes are, after all, essential to all orations, and major attention must be given to the art of reproducing them. Some there are who call this use of material *ethopoeia*, because it brings out the character or the emotional state of the speaker. Besides it furnishes an opportunity for discipline in choosing an appropriate style. For since there are three approaches [to style], the expansive, the subdued, and the middle, which the Greeks call the Asian, the Attic, and the Rhodian characters, we must consider how to render the form of the feelings, thoughts, and words appropriate to the content in these styles. Otherwise one may begin or continue his speech as though angry, another timorously, another cheerfully, another sadly, another in

1. Emporii Oratoris *De ethopoeia*, in *RLM*, pp.561–563.

the manner of an old man, another as a youth, another as a man, another as a woman. It is important in speaking to know whether [the speaker] is a god or a man, playful or morose, cowardly or brave, learned or uneducated. So let the speech of a happy man be brisk, that of a boastful man pompous, that of an abrupt man short and to the point, that of a prostitute enticing and sensuous, that of a matron serious, that of old men thoughtful, that of a boy uninhibited, that of a lowly man supplicating, that of a man who is sure of himself long and covering everything, that of a hypocrite ingratiating, that of a mother anxious, that of a country fellow unpolished, that of an orator brilliant. Moreover we should express in every phrase the life-style of him whose words are being created. And this kind of impersonation, as we have already noted, is called *ethopoeia*.

Pathopoeia is also valuable, being an extension of ethos. Through it we also imitate those attitudes which are not natural, but are cultivated. Those writers err seriously who distinguish between this material and *ethopoeia* on the grounds that whatever makes people happy is ethical, while anything that brings out sadness is pathetic. Some accident of mood often undermines one's natural approach to life, and nature often undergoes a definite strain when he who is speaking deviates from his customary style of speaking. Thus Hercules, whose speech was always strong, begins to weep for his crime of patricide; or Homer tells how Achilles, always fearsome, sobs when he finds himself surrounded by a river; or the ever cruel Mezentius begs either Turnus to allow him sanctuary or Aeneas to grant him burial. Thus ethos turns out to be personal character, pathos to be the cause of that character. So when a passing mood is predominant, then the process of imitation is called *pathopoeia*, although the native character is not completely eliminated still. Mazentius did not appeal to Turnus in such a way, nor did Mars groan over his wound in this way so as to gain the sympathy of Venus. So the inborn characteristic is usually the most important, though we seek also with great effort to master that which is a later addition if its force truly dominates the substance; but if it is ineffectual, then the attitude which comes later should be worked in only lightly. There is a third kind of *ethopoeia*, which is introduced only on account of the thing to be done;[2] such would be, "Go forth my son and summon the Zephyrs" (*Aeneid* 4.23), and "Oh citizens, we have seen Diomede" (*ibid.* 11.243); this approach is called the attorney's (*pragmaticus*). It is brought in once in a great while so that a certain attitude will not appear at all or will appear very vaguely, as in the case above where Venulus is eager to praise his own work but instead refers to Diomede. There is also a fourth kind of impersonation, which is frequently adopted by great orators in especially serious or tragic cases; it involves giving words to the dumb and creating a person who does not really exist, as when M. Tullius [Cicero] attributes words to the province of Sicily or represents the republic as speaking; this is called *prosopopoeia*.

Having examined the kind of material to be used, therefore, and having adjusted our thought patterns according to the type of speaking to be done, it is necessary to find a way to begin. The opening phrase can be drawn either from the persons involved or from the matter itself or from the time or from the place. First of all, if it is drawn from the persons involved, it may refer to our own person, or to the person to whom we are addressing ourselves, or to the person about whom we are speaking. It can refer to ourselves, as in the speech which Vergil attributes to Juno, "I have begun; shall I now give up?" (*ibid.* 1.37), or in the speech of Turnus, "I have certainly deserved it, nor will I attempt to minimize . . ." (*ibid.* 12.931). It may also refer to the person to whom we are addressing ourselves, as in the same author's, "To you, Aeolus . . ." (*ibid.* 1.65) and the apostrophe, "Oh you, of such great fame . . ." (*ibid.* 11.124). Reference to the person about whom we are speaking would include, "Juno's terrible anger . . ." (*ibid.* 5.781), and "Should she be handed over to exiles?" (*ibid.* 7.359). An introductory phrase based on an event would be, "These solemn rites we celebrate, this festive banquet . . ." (*ibid.* 8.185) and "The greatest event . . ." (*ibid.* 11.14). One based on the time is "While at war with Argolis . . ." (*ibid.* 8.374), and

---

2. As will be clear from what follows, Emporius means by this creating an imaginary agent for a desired action.

"Have you at last come?" (*ibid*. 6.687). One based on place is, "There is here no fixed abode . . ." (*ibid*. 6.673).

Now these elements are not always present all together in every topic; each must be studied carefully so that, after all things have been dealt with, that which is most appropriate may be chosen. However, it sometimes happens that one piece of material involves two or even three elements from the list. This occurs once in a while, as it does in the words of the Trojan who refers to the person addressed, "Oh, queen appointed to found this new city . . ." (*ibid*. 1.522), and to the person speaking, "We wretched Trojans beg of you . . ." (*ibid*. 1.524), and to an event, "We have not come to decimate the Libyans with the sword . . ." (1.527).

Thus, having examined the opening words, and having brought them in suitably, the speaker must organize his material according to the order of time. For it is only natural that we first set forth what has already been done, then what is now being done, and finally what will be done in the future. In following this division, there is need for discretion, so that everything will not come across through narration or as a story. As a result we must choose only what pertains to a theme, what is relevant to the issue. For this reason we must here consider carefully that not every element applies equally in all material, but that some topics are richer, others poorer; in almost every case, however, the topic lacks some of the elements. Take as an example the speech attributed by Vergil to Juno when she saw Aeneas in Italy. There is the person of whom she speaks, "Oh accursed offspring . . ." (*ibid*. 7.293); then there is a reference to the past, "Did they perish on the plain of Sigeum?" (*ibid*. 7.294), and another, "What help lay in the wastes of Charybdis?" (*ibid*. 7.302). A reference to the present is, "They drive the Trojans from the beach they seek . . ." (*ibid*. 1.172). One to the future is, "Granted that it will not be in my power to keep him from the Latin throne . . ." (*ibid*. 7.313), and the other things that follow.

5. RUFINUS OF ANTIOCH

Verses of the Famous Scholar, Rufinus, on Word Arrangement and Metres in Oratory[1]

Translated by Ian Thomson

Rufinus of Antioch was a fifth-century Latin author, a contemporary of Emporius. Although the title of this work in *RLM* identifies him as a famous scholar, little is actually known of him beyond the fact that he is not to be confused with the fourth-century Rufinus of Aquilaeia, an ecclesiastical author, or with the Rufinus mentioned by Libanius of Antioch as a fourth-century teacher of eloquence.

These verses comprise part of a longer work, *Rufinii comentarii de metris comicorum et de numeris oratorum,* "A Commentary by Rufinus on the Metres used by the Comic Poets and the Rhythms used by the Orators."[2] In one eighth-century codex, the *Commentarii* is linked with five works of Priscian (two on arangement and three on grammar) and a hymn by Remus Favinus. This translation reveals the close bond these early scholars discerned between rhetorical theory and poetics, as well as the strong Ciceronian influence which still dominated works on style.

Professor Ian Thomson of the Department of Classics at Indiana University prepared this translation especially for *Readings in Medieval Rhetoric.*

Poets, the children of the muses, seek rhythm and metre. The orator seeks rhythm, lest through aimless wandering he prove ignorant of his praiseworthy craft. This is his prime virtue. The

---

1. *Versus Rufini V.C. Litteratoris de Compositione et de Metris Oratorum,* RLM, 575–584.
2. The Latin text of the entire *Commentarii* appears on pages 547–578 of *Scriptores artis metricae,* the sixth volume of *Grammatici Latini,* 8 vols., ed. Heinrich Keil (Hildesheim:Georg Olins, 1961).

dactyl is the weapon of the Latin and Greek orators. It was Cicero's weapon, as were the iambus, the heavy spondee, the paean with its excellent rhythm, and their equivalents in time, even with a syllable added.[3] Avoid many of the same feet in succession; the result is verse. The best orator follows the poets in method; his is a kindred art. Although he rejects metre, he, too, tries by means of rhythm to bridle words that would otherwise stray.

Again as follows: The learned Aristotle praises two kinds of paean. The one beginning with a long syllable as exemplified in *aspicere* (‒◡◡) will enhance the opening of a sentence. Its opposite is the final paean.[4] Cicero praises the one which has its penultimate syllable long. *Esse* (‒◡) is a trochee, and in *videantur* (◡◡‒◡) we have the third variety of what antiquity, in its devotion to the muses,[5] calls a paean. This rhythm, the third syllable of which is long, is better for the members.[6]

Verses of the famous scholar, Rufinus, on rhythm and metrical feet in oratory.

The dochmiac makes a nice rhetorical ornament. Its first part will be a bacchius (◡‒‒), and an iambus (◡‒) will end it. To describe the same things in different terms, an iambus will come first, then a cretic (‒◡‒) completes it: first a short syllable, then two longs, a short, and a final long. The example you will get will be *respublica* in the genitive, the case in which Cicero likes to put it.[7]

---

3. The substitution of a dactyl (‒◡◡) for a spondee (‒‒), or a tribrach (◡◡◡) for an iambus (◡‒), or a paean (see n.4) for a cretic (‒◡‒) would add one syllable to the measure, but the time taken to pronounce it would not be altered, since a long syllable counted as the equivalent of two shorts.

4. There were four varieties of paean, easily distinguished by the relative position of the long syllable: ‒◡◡◡ (first), ◡‒◡◡ (second), ◡◡‒◡ (third), ◡◡◡‒ (fourth or final).

5. The paean was originally a hymn in honor of Apollo, patron god of the arts, and the term came to be applied also to the prevailing metrical foot in such hymns.

6. For the technical meaning of "members," see n.17.

7. The Latin reads, *Exemplumque artis dabitur res publica vobis,/ Quam Cicero casu genitivo ponere gaudet.* The circumlocution Rufinus uses is necessary, since *rei publicae* (◡‒‒◡‒), the dochmiac to be exemplified, cannot fit into his hexameters. Here, as occasionally elsewhere, I have departed from a strictly literal rendering in order to make the meaning clear.

This well-ordered rhythm brings praise and distinction to prose, as Cicero, the great Latin orator, teaches. It makes a rhythm that fits any passage: a long follows a short, a short a long, and add a long; or, the first syllable is short, the second long, the third long, the fourth short, and the fifth long. The orator Cicero, as many do, adorns the dochmiac.[8]

The same man writes as follows: the cretic and trochee—or a spondee at the end, it makes no odds—will be the measures to end sentences. To describe the same thing in different terms, you will have a trochee at the beginning, and a molossus ($---$) at the end. But suppose the ending is a bacchius[9] with the final syllable short; well, it makes no difference, according to the metrical practice of skilled poets, whether the final syllable is short or long. Or the Asian rhyme is nice, two trochees at the end; but the clausula is stronger if it ends with a spondee. The style of Demosthenes, the supreme orator, teaches this artifice.

More verses of Rufinus: Orators generally use the spondee for narrative, because it is slow and ponderous in depicting events. They fight battles with dactyls, because dactyls can race. We tell of outstanding exploits in the manner of Theopompus, and praise a noteworthy life with the art of Isocrates. The former style is more suitable for history, the latter for panegyric.

On the period, which the Greeks call *periodos:* Apollo and the muse bid me tell how many members an orator must use to make a period. You companions of Phoebus, do not forget these instructions, and let the artifice settle in your clever memories. Nature, who linked the two fair arts[10] by interchangeable laws, has not granted us a single load to carry. We observe that the orator forms a full period from four members; hence its name, "period," which means "circuit." You see the poet doing a corresponding thing in verses comprising four metrical units.[11]

---

8. The dochmiac admitted several variations, but this is probably not what Rufinus means by "adorns." He probably means that the dochmiac gains in prestige from Cicero's use of it in oratory.

9. Variously given as $--\cup$ or $\cup--$.

10. Poetry and oratory.

11. For the practice in oratory see Cic. *Orator* 222.

On forensic style (Greek, *peri tou dikanikou*): Cicero tells you that the paean is suitable for trials at law.

On deliberative style (Greek, *peri tou symbouleutikou*): If anyone is pondering a moot point, his weapon is the iambus. The dactyl is suitable for both forensic and deliberative oratory.

The same Rufinus says this, in sapphic metre, about Theophrastus:

Theophrastus invests orators with finery by sprinkling their speeches with the fair members of the dithyramb; the anapaest blossoms in that treatise. Because of his treatise the rhythm which that anapaest has given us has become more drawn out. From the anapaest orators develop passages of those fine dithyrambic measures.

Cicero has this to say about rhythm in oratory: "A period may end in several ways, but the one which Asia has most favored is called the dichoreus,[12] the last two feet being trochees, each consisting of a long and a short syllable; one has to explain this, since the same feet are now getting different names from different people. But in prose rhythm there is no greater fault than constant monotony. The dichoreus in itself has a glorious cadence, so we have all the more reason to beware an excess of it."

Treating of the rhythmical structure of Demosthenes, Quintilian says: "Hence the rhythm used by Demosthenes in *tois theois euchomai pasi kai pasais* and again in *kan mēpō ballēi mēde toxeuēi* (to which only Brutus, so far as I know, takes exception) is considered strictly correct." Elsewhere, he says: "Such rhythms as *pasi kai pasais* and *pasin hymin* are characteristic of Demosthenes, and occur throughout almost the entire opening section of his speech."[13] At another point: "The dochmiac also, consisting of a bacchius and an iambus, or of an iambus and a cretic, makes a firm and severe ending; so does the spondee, which Demosthenes so often used." Diomedes says in the second book of his treatise: "So the spondee, consisting of two long syllables, is suitable for

---

12. Cicero uses *choraeus* for our trochee, and *trochaeus* for our tribrach. Some Latin authors use the terms *trochaeus* = trochee, and *tribrachys* = tribrach.

13. *De corona.*

long clausulae of the kind Demosthenes particularly uses: *pasi kai pasais* and *kai pasin hymin*. For it has a weighty sound, it rounds off the sense, and makes a firm basis for the clausula, as in *reipublicae causa* and *arma sumpsi* and *esse pro nobis*. But it is weightier when a long syllable, rather than a short one, precedes it; for *arma sumpsi* ($-\cup--$) has a different sound from *esse pro nobis* ($-\cup---$)."

Cicero says in the treatise to Herennius: "*Hyperbaton*.[14] A transposition of this kind, which does not obscure the thought, will be very useful for periods, which have already been discussed. If periods are to take on a finished excellence and the very highest degree of polish, they must have their words arranged in something approaching poetical rhythm."

Concerning structure, that is, rhythm, or word arrangement within the period, Cicero has this to say: "The longest sentence, then, is one that can be reeled off in a single breath. Nature sets this limit, art another. Among the various metres, Catulus, your master Aristotle forbids the orator frequent use of the iambus and the tribrach. These come into our native speech naturally and spontaneously, but they have a very marked rhythm and their metrical units are too clipped. He suggests therefore that we use primarily heroic metres, in which one can safely proceed for two feet or a little more without falling into obvious verse or something close to it: *altae sunt geminae, quibus* ($---\cup\cup-\cup\cup$). These three heroic measures[15] fall quite nicely into the opening of a period. But the measure particularly recommended by the same master is the paean, of which there are two kinds; the one in which a long syllable is followed by three shorts, as in *desinite, incipite, comprimite,* and the one in *dormuerant* and *sonipedes*. That philosopher likes a sentence to begin with the former paean, and end with the latter. This latter paean, however, is almost the same as the cretic, not in the number of its syllables, but as the ear measures it, which is a sharper and more reliable test. The cretic

14. A Greek term; strict Latin is *transgressio*. In this figure the normal word order is deliberately disturbed to produce a desired rhythmical effect, e.g., *virtute pro vestra* ($--\cup---$) for the more normal *pro vestra virtute* ($-----\cup$).

15. A spondee plus two dactyls. Heroic verse admitted only spondees and dactyls.

consists of long, short, long; for example, *quid petam praesidi aut exequar? quove nunc?* Fannius opened a speech with this rhythm: *Si, Quirites, minas illius*[16] ($-\cup--\cup--\cup-$). Aristotle thinks this foot more suitable for the ends of clauses, which he wants terminated as a general rule with a long syllable."

Later in the same third book *On the orator* he says this: "But a speech should be frequently broken up into smaller units, although these units should each have their own rhythm. And do not let that paean or dactyl bother you; they will come into the speech of their own accord, actually muster themselves without being called on parade. But make it your practice in writing or speaking that the thoughts and words wind up together, and that the way those words are put together springs from noble and free rhythms, particularly dactyls or the first paean or the cretic. Their closes, however, should be varied and discrete, for simility is particularly obvious at closes. If the first and last feet are governed by this rule, the intervening ones can hide away, provided the period itself is not shorter than the ear anticipates or longer than your strength or breath holds out. But in my opinion sentence endings need even more attention than the preceding parts, because here above all is the test of finished workmanship. The beginning, middle, and end of a verse all get equal attention, and the verse is weakened by a slip at any point, but in prose few people notice the first words, although most notice the last ones, and since they are so conspicuous and the focus of attention, they must be varied, to avoid rejection by a critical mind or an ear bored with too much of the same thing. There are two or maybe three feet which should be reserved for endings and given prominence, provided that the preceding rhythms are not too short and choppy. These will have to be trochees or dactyls alternated with the second paean that Aristotle favors, or its equivalent, the cretic. If you ring the changes with these, you will make sure the listeners do not get bored with sameness, and that we do not seem to have made heavy weather of preparing for the task ahead."

---

16. Three successive eretics. The middle syllable of *illius* was generally short in Cicero's time, later usually long.

Later, he says this: "But just as the public spots a flaw in versification, so does it sense any lameness in our oratory. It does not excuse in the poet what it forgives in us, although no one fails to observe, although not perhaps in so many words, that what we said lacked neatness and polish."

Concerning the use of rhythm in short clauses, members, and periods (Greek: *kommata, kola, periodoi*)[17] Cicero has this to say in the *Orator:* "This has been established practice in Greece for the past four hundred years, but we have only recently recognized it." Afterwards, he says: "But if their ears are so uncultured and boorish, not even the authority of scholars will impress them. I say nothing of Isocrates and his pupils, Ephorus and Naucrates (although when it comes to constructing a speech, orators themselves should be the ultimate authorities), but who ever surpassed Aristotle in learning or intelligence, who ever was a keener critic or researcher? Who, for that matter, was a more bitter opponent of Isocrates? Well, Aristotle forbids the use of verse in a speech, but demands rhythm. His student, Theodectes, a highly accomplished writer and craftsman, as Aristotle often remarks, holds this same opinion and teaches this same thing, and Theophrastus is even more explicit on the same point. So who could put up with people who will not accept these authorities? Of course, they may be quite ignorant of the fact that these men made such recommendations."

Elsewhere, he says: "As a rule, the rhythm flows on from the beginning, faster when the feet are short, and slower when they are long; disputation demands speed, exposition a slow rhythm."

In another passage he says: "*Cur de perfugis nostris copias comparant contra nos?* Those first two[18] are what the Greeks call *kom-*

---

17. Cicero translated Gk. *komma* (pl. *kommata*) by *incisum* (pl. *incisa*); Gk. *kolon* (pl. *kola*) by *membrum* (pl. *membra*); Gk. *periodos* (pl. *periodoi*) variously by *circuitus, ambitus, circuitus verborum, amplexio, comprehensio* and *continuatio*. These technical terms, which can usually be translated as "short phrase," "clause," and "period," respectively, are retained in my translation. For Cicero's definition of them see the last paragraph of this treatise.

18. This refers to two phrases, *missos faciant patronos* and *ipsi prodeant,* which appear in Cic. *Orator* 222 but not in *Rufinus,* who begins this extract from Cicero with his example of a full period.

mata, and we call *incisa;* the third[19] they call *kolon,* we *membrum.*
The one that follows is a period complete in its members—not long,
since it has only two verses[20]—and it ends with spondees. Crassus
in fact usually spoke in this manner, and it is the style that I personally like best. But if *incisa* and *membra* are used, they must
have the most proper cadences, for instance, in my own works,
domus tibi deerat? at habebas: pecunia superabat? at egebas.
These were four *incisa.* What follows is a pair of *membra: incur-
risti amens in columnas, in alienis insanisti.* Then the entire passage is supported, as it were, on the foundation of a longer period:
*depressam, caecam, iacentem domum pluris quam te et fortunas
tuas aestimasti.* It ends in a double trochee (*aestimasti,* $-\cup--$); but
the previous one with spondees (*insanisti,* $----$); for in these
phrases which should be used like tiny daggers, their very short-
ness will make the feet freer. One must often use one, sometimes
two (and part of a foot can be added in either case) but hardly
more than three. A speech made up of *incisa* and *membra* is enor-
mously effective in real court cases, especially in passages where
one is proving or disproving a point, as in my second speech for
Cornelia: *o callidos homines, o rem excogitatam, o ingenia metu-
enda!* So far we have *membra;* then *diximus,* an *incisum,* then
testes dare volumus, another *membrum.* Finally comes a period
consisting of two *membra,* the shortest form possible: *quem,
quaeso, nostrum fefellit ita vos esse facturos?* There is no better or
sturdier style than to strike with two or three words, sometimes
with single ones, sometimes with just a few more, in the midst of
which comes at rare intervals the rhythmical period with a variety
of cadences."

19. The example in Cicero is: *cur clandestinis consiliis nos oppugnant?* It
does not appear in Rufinus. Note that what we call a sentence (*cur . . . oppugnant*) Cicero here calls a *membrum,* and that what we call a sentence is
not necessarily the same as the Latin period, although it may be.

20. He means *membra.* Rufinus' text is: *sequitur non longa, ex duobus
enim versibus, id est membris perfecta comprehensio est,* which I have attempted to translate. (The punctuation is, of course, Halm's). The sense
would be improved by transposing *est* (Lambinus' suggestion) and repunc-
tuating: *sequitur non longa, ex duobus enim versibus, id est membris, perfecta
est, comprehensio,* "a period follows, not a long one, for it is made up of two
verses, that is members."

The same man says this about Theophrastus: I agree with the notion of Theophrastus, who thinks that prose with any polish and pretensions to system must have rhythm, not strict rhythm, but a rather loose one. In fact, as he forecast, the anapaest, a more drawn-out metre, has since blossomed forth, and from it has flowed the freer and richer dithyramb, the limbs and feet of which, as the same critic says, are found in abundance in all sumptuous prose."

Likewise, Cicero says in the *Brutus:* "When those men I have just mentioned were old, Isocrates emerged, and his house was a school and workshop of eloquence open to the whole of Greece. He was a great orator and a master teacher, although he shunned the publicity of the law courts and within his own walls brought to ripeness such glory as no one, in my opinion, has since achieved. He himself wrote many very fine works, and taught others. He was more perceptive than his predecessors, but especially so in being the first to realize that even in prose, while verse should be avoided, a certain measure and rhythm should still be observed. Before him sentences had no structure and no rhythmical cadence, or if such existed, it was not manifestly the result of hard work; which may be a matter of praise, but the fact is that it happened at that time more by instinct and luck than by any rule or design."

Flavius Sosipater Charisius says about rhythm: "An example of bacchiac metre is as follows:

bacchare, laetare praesente Frontone
($--\cup/--\cup/--\cup/--\cup$)."

This seems to me suitable for prose. In fact, we use many feet in prose, although stupid people think that the language of prose should be free from the shackles of rhythm."

Cicero says this about rhythm: "For those old masters thought that in this prose style we should use something approaching verse, to wit, certain rhythms." Later he says: "Isocrates is said to have been the first to tighten up the artless oratorical style of the ancients with rhythms, designed, as his pupil Naucrates says, to charm the ear. For the musicians, who in those days were also the poets, invented the twin devices of verse and melody to give pleasure, the idea being to forestall boredom in the listener by the rhythm of the words and the modulation of the notes. These two things, then, namely vocal modulation and the arrangement of words in periods, they thought fit to carry over from poetry to oratory, so far as the severity of oratory would permit. Note this very important point: although it is a defect if the verbal arrangement in prose produces verse, we want that arrangement to have a rhythmical cadence like verse, to fit snugly in, and to be rounded off. The differences that mark off an oratory from an ignorant and inexperienced speaker are not many."

The same Cicero says in another passage: "For even the poets have raised the question of how they differ from orators. Once it seemed to be chiefly a matter of rhythm and verse, but now rhythm itself has become common in oratory. For whatever falls with any kind of measure upon the ears, even if it is a long way from being verse—verse being certainly a fault in oratory—is called rhythm. The Greeks call it *rhythmos*. For that reason I know that some people have thought that because the language of Plato and Demosthenes, although not in verse, nevertheless has vigor and is brilliantly figurative, has more claim to be considered poetry than has comedy, which is no different from ordinary speech, except that it is in a species of verse."

Victorinus says this about word arrangement: "They say that if a spondee or a trochee follows a cretic, which consists of long, short, long, it makes a good word arrangement: *Quo usque tandem abutere, Catilina, patientia nostra?* The last two feet are a cretic and a spondee." The same man says much about word arrangement and rhythm and poetical feet in oratory.

According to Cicero, the following were the Greek writers: Thrasymachus, Naucrates, Gorgias, Ephorus, Isocrates, Theodectes, Aristotle, Theodorus of Byzantium, Theophrastus, and Hieronymus. The following are some of those who wrote in Latin: Cicero, Victorinus, Eusebius, Terentianus, Varro, Probus, Charisius, Diomedes, Quintilian, Donatus, Victor, and Servius.

Likewise, Cicero says this about rhythm and word arrangement: "Isocrates' greatest admirers praise him most for being the first to introduce rhythm into prose. For when he saw that people listen to orators with grave attention, but to poets with pleasure, he is said to have sought rhythms for us to use in prose also, not merely for the element of delight but also to counter monotony with variety. What they say is certainly true to some extent, but not entirely. For it must be admitted that no one has shown more skill in this style than Isocrates, but the first to invent it was Thrasymachus, all of whose works display an excess of rhythm. As I said a little earlier, Gorgias was the first to discover the use of clauses with similar endings and antitheses, which by their very nature, without any effort on the writer's part, usually have a rhythmical cadence. But Gorgias rather overdid these devices. (That, however, as has been said already, is the second of the heads under the rubric 'word arrangement'). Both Thrasymachus and Gorgias were predecessors of Isocrates, so his superiority lies not in the discovery but in what he did with it. He is less violent in his use of metaphor and neologisms, and less hectic in his rhythms, while Gorgias is over-partial to this style and too bold in using what he himself considers 'graces.'[21] These were used with more restraint by Isocrates, although he was still a young man when he studied under the aged Gorgias in Thessaly."

In another passage he says: "But when I mention the use of these feet in clausulae, I am not speaking of the last foot alone; I include the next to last foot at least, and often the third from last. Even the iambus, consisting of a short and a long, or the tribrach with its three short syllables, equivalent to the trochee, but only in time and not in the number of its syllables, or even the dactyl, consisting of a long and two shorts, if it comes next to last, reaches the end of the period swiftly enough if the last foot is a trochee or a spondee; for it makes no difference which of these two comes in the final foot. But these same three feet make a poor cadence, if any of them is placed last, save when a final dactyl is used in place of a cretic; for it makes no difference whether the last foot is a dactyl or a cretic, because even in verse the length of the final syllable does not matter. So whoever claimed superiority for the paean in which the last syllable is long was not very perceptive,

21. *festivitates.*

since it makes no difference how long the last syllable is.[22] Because the paean has rather many syllables,[23] it is even considered by some people to be a rhythm, not a foot." The same Cicero has much to say in his dialogues *On the State* about orators of the Asian persuasion ending sentences with the double trochee.

Terentianus says this about the cretic or amphimacer: "It is an excellent foot for melic poetry and splendid prose. It will most become the speaker when it holds its right place in the penultimate position, if a dactyl or spondee—and I do not rule out a trochee—ends the sentence. Shun either variety of bacchius, but do not reject the tribrach, for the long syllable of the trochee is wont to be resolved into two shorts. Hence people actually give the name 'trochee' to what we call a tribrach. That matter is more fully dealt with in treatises on rhetoric."

Pompeius Messalinus says this about rhythm and metrical feet in oratory: "Cicero considers the spondee suitable for *incisa*, because, as he says, it makes up for the small number of feet with its natural weight and slowness. He thinks the dochmiac fits in anywhere, provided that it is put in only once, because a series of them destroys the smoothness of the rhythm; also that the double trochee is a glorious cadence; but among them all he gives first prize to the cretic." The same Pompeius says this about Sallust's word arrangement or rhythmical structure: "Now, if you please, let us examine the rhythms of a period by Sallust: *res popu* is a dactyl, *li Romani Marco* three spondees, *Lepido* an anapaest, *Quinto Catulo* a spondee and an anapaest, *consulibus* the first paean, *ac deinde* a dichoraeus or double trochee, *militi* a dactyl, *ae domi* a cretic, *gestas* a spondee, *composui* a choriambus, consisting of long, short, short, long."

Cicero says this about word arrangement in Demosthenes: "As if indeed Demosthenes came from Tralles! Those famous thunderbolts of his would not shiver with such power if they were not sped on their course by rhythm."

---

22. Quintilian 9.4.93 disagrees.
23. Later, Rufinus quotes Cicero more accurately: *quod plures habeat syllabas quam tres,* "because it has more than three syllables." See n.29.

Verses of the famous scholar, Rufinus, on rhythm and metrical feet in oratory.

"It will be the cretic or spondee or the fourth paean;[24] at hand, too, are the dactyl and trochee or the racing iambus, which is placed in any position but last. Their equivalents in time can replace all of these, depending on whether you prefer long syllables or to resolve them into shorts, with the addition of a syllable. The Asian orators like a double trochee at the end. The dochmiac serves you as an ornament at the beginning, middle, and end."

Cicero says this about *incisa* and *membra* and the period: "*O Marce Druse, patrem appello* has two *incisa*, each consisting of two feet;[25] then, *tu dicere solebas sacram esse rem publicam*, which is in *membra*, each *membrum* having three feet;[26] next, a period, *quicumque violasset, ab omnibus esse ei poenas persolutas*, which ends in a double trochee,[27] the quantity of the final syllable being irrelevant; then, *patris dictum sapiens temeritas filii comprobavit*, at which double trochee it was amazing what a roar went up from the crowd.[28] I put it to you that this effect was produced by the rhythm. Change the word order and make it *comprobavit*

24. He means that any of these three is suitable for the final foot. Cicero considered the iambus, tribrach, and dactyl poor cadences in themselves, but the iambus and tribrach (considered as a resolved trochee) could precede a final spondee or trochee. The dactyl could be used in the final position if it was thought of as taking the place of a cretic (possible only under his doctrine that the length of the final syllable is unimportant). The logic of this is poor, since any final dactyl could be thought of as taking the place of a cretic, so it is hard to see how the dactyl could under any circumstances make a poor cadence.

25. [O] Mārcĕ Drūsĕ, two trochees (if we discount the opening exclamation), and pātr(em) āppēllō, two spondees, the final syllable of *patrem* being elided.

26. Tū dīcĕrĕ sōlēbās consists of spondee, tribrach, spondee; sācr(am) ēssĕ rēm pūblĭcăm consists strictly of spondee, iambus, dactyl, but since Cicero frequently states that the quantity of the final syllable is unimportant (but see n.24), the dactyl could here be counted as having the force of the

27. Strictly, the ending is a trochee plus a spondee. desirable cretic cadence.

28. We may believe that ancient audiences were attuned to such graces, but it is more likely that the sentiment, not the rhythm, produced the uproar. The younger Drusus, an adherent of Gaius Gracchus, had recently been murdered when the tribune Gaius Carbo made this remark, quoted by Cicero.

filii temeritas. What do you have now? Nothing, although *temeritas* consists of three shorts and a long, the foot which Aristotle considers the best." Later, the same Cicero says this: "But there are a number of clausulae with pleasing and rhythmical cadences; for example, the cretic, which consists of long, short, long, and its equivalent, the paean, which takes the same length of time to pronounce, but has one syllable more. The paean is thought to fit very neatly into prose, since it has two varieties; either it consists of a long plus three shorts, which is a strong rhythm at the beginning of a sentence, but weak at the end; or it consists of the same number of short syllables plus a long, which the ancients consider the best cadence. I do not reject it out of hand, but I prefer others. Not even the spondee should be utterly ruled out. It may seem a trifle plodding and sluggish, consisting as it does of two longs, but it does have a kind of steady movement which is not without dignity, especially in *incisa* and *membra,* where its natural weight and slowness make up for the small number of feet."

Donatus says this about structures and rhythmical feet in oratory: "In the matters of adorning a sentence and constructing endings, Cicero variously favors the double trochee, or the first paean, which is suitable for the beginning of a sentence, or the fourth paean, which fits into the ending, or the dochmiac, consisting of short, long, long, short, long (he gives *amicos tenes* as an example), or the cretic. Sometimes again he praises dactylic, anapaestic, or dithyrambic rhythms."

Probus says this about rhythm in oratory: "A trochee plus the third paean will create that structure peculiar to Cicero, *esse videatur* ($-\cup\cup\cup-\cup$)."

Cicero says this about rhythm and metrical feet in oratory: "Because it has more than three syllables,[29] the paean is even considered by some people to be a rhythm, not a foot; in fact, all the ancients, Aristotle, Theophrastus, Theodectes, and Ephorus, agree that it is the one rhythm or foot most suited to the beginning and middle of a sentence. They think it suitable for the cadence also, but in my opinion the cretic fits that position better. But the doch-

29. See n.23.

miac, consisting of five syllables, a short, two longs, a short and a long, as in *amicos tenes*, fits in anywhere."

The same Cicero says this about feet and structures: "The iambus occurs most often in ordinary conversation, the paean in more elevated discourse, and the dactyl occurs in both; so in a long speech with various tones these rhythms must be mixed and blended."

In the rhetorical treatise to Herennius, Cicero says this about the *membrum*, that is, the *kolon:* "*Membrum* is the name given to that part of a sentence, which is short and complete in itself, but does not express the complete thought of the sentence, and is taken up in turn by another *membrum*, in the following way: *et inimico proderas;* that is one *membrum*, so-called; this must then be taken up by another *membrum* of the sentence; *et amicum laedebas.* This figure can consist of two *membra*, but it is neatest and most finished when it consists of three, in the following way: *et inimico proderas et amicum laedebas et tibi non consulebas.* Likewise: *nec rei publicae consuluisti nec amicis profuisti nec inimicis restitisti.*"

6. PRISCIAN THE GRAMMARIAN

Fundamentals Adapted from Hermogenes[1]

Translated by Joseph M. Miller

Priscian of Caesarea (fl.c.500) is probably the best known of the Latin grammarians who influenced the Middle Ages. Born in Mauretania, he taught in Constantinople. Although his most renowned work was his *Institutiones grammaticae*, which became a standard text in grammar for the next eight centuries, ranking with the *ars minor* of Aelius Donatus (fourth century), he also contributed to the study of rhetoric and prosody in some of his minor works. Of all his tracts, the only one with a primarily rhetorical focus was his translation-adaptation of the *Progymnasmata* of Hermogenes, arranged and simplified for use in the rhetorical schools of the sixth century.

The Fable

1. A fable is a composition made up to resemble life, projecting an image of truth in its structure. This is what orators first offer to children, because thus they can easily introduce impressionable young minds to the better things. The great authors of antiquity also used fables, men like Hesiod, Archilocus, Horace. Hesiod used the fable of the nightingale, Archilocus that of the fox, Horace that of the mouse. Some stories are called Cpyrian by their inventors, some Libyan, some Sybaritic,[2] but all have in

1. *Praeexercitamina Prisciani Grammatici ex Hermogene versa, RLM*, 551–560. Though Priscian's work is frequently identified as a "translation" of the *Progymnasmata* of Hermogenes, a careful comparison of the two works indicates that "adaptation" is a somewhat more accurate term.
2. Although both Hermogenes and Priscian list these three branches to the fable family, the terminology is not universally accepted. A cursory examination of standard classical reference works does not reveal other examples of its use.

common the label Aesopian, because Aesop was accustomed to use fables frequently among groups. This technique applies to the needs of life and becomes realistic if the things which happen to the subject are then related to the experiences of real men. For example, when one wants to talk about beauty, a peacock may be brought in; if it is one's purpose to treat of cleverness, let him tell about a little fox; if he wants to show how human beings are imitators, let that be the place for apes. Now it is also important to tell the story succinctly in some cases, at greater length in others. How can that be done? By telling a simple story one time, then at another giving speech to the participants, as for example: "The apes came together to discuss building a city, and agreed that they should start construction. But one old ape in the group prevented them from beginning by pointing out that they could be easily captured if they were hemmed in by walls." That is the succinct form. But if you want to develop it more, then do this: "The apes came together and had a council meeting about establishing a city. One of them stood before the group and proclaimed that it was important for them to have a city. 'For you see,' he said, 'that men who have cities have individual homes and an assembly hall for the whole tribe, they go to theatres where they enjoy themselves in pleasant sights and sounds of all kinds.'" And you may draw out the oration in this way by lingering over details, telling how the written vote was taken, and developing in the same way the speech of the old ape. In developing the fable, one should avoid circumlocutions and be more informal. But the statement which points out the moral of the fable, which we call *epimythion* (and which we can also call the *affabulation*) is placed at the beginning by some authors, but by most (and more reasonably) at the end. Be sure that you note how orators frequently use fables among their examples.

Narration

2. Narration is the presentation of an event as it happened or as if it happened: some, however, deal with the *chrēian,* which is the anecdote, before narration. But there are four kinds of narration: the fabulous, the fictional, the historical, the legal. The

fabulous relates to fables such as we examined above; the fictional is composed for use in tragedies or comedies; the historical is used to explain things that have really happened; the legal is drawn for use by orators in presenting cases. Now let us speak about a narration used for practice, which we can usually present in any of the different styles: through direct discourse, through indirect discourse, through accusation, through periodic style, through comparison. Through direct discourse: "Medea was the daughter of Aeetes; she stole from him the golden fleece," and so on. This is called direct because throughout all or most of the composition, the nominative case is used. The discourse is called indirect when the oblique cases are used, as in, "They say that Medea, the daughter of Aeetes, loved Jason," and so on; so that the story is told through the use of the cases. Accusation is the figure we use in argument, as: "What evil did Medea not commit? She not only did not love Jason, but did she not betray to him the golden fleece? did she not murder her brother?" and so on. The periodic narration goes this way: "Medea, daughter of Aeetes, betrayed the golden fleece, murdered her brother, Absyrtus," and so on. And contrast is this: "Medea, daughter of Aeetes, who should have preserved her chastity, betrayed it in an illicit affair; when she should have been the guardian of her brother's safety, she murdered him; when she should have protected the golden fleece, she sold it to a plotter." Direct discourse is most suitable to history, for it is plainer; indirect is best for rhetorical contests; accusation is most appropriate for argument; and periodic fits perorations and conclusions, for it is highly emotional and likely to move the heart.

The Anecdote

The anecdote, which the Greeks call *chrēian*, is the recalling of someone's words or acts or both together, which are suited to a quick explanation and can be offered as a lesson to some person or group. Some anecdotes are exclusively verbal, some deal with actions, some are mixed. The verbal deal only with a statement: "Plato said that the muses live in the hearts of geniuses"; those dealing with actions narrate only an act that was performed: "When Diogenes saw a youth behaving shamelessly, he struck the pedagogue with his stick"; the mixed would be if you added, "he struck him saying, 'Why have you taught him so?' " There is this difference between an anecdote and an episode: an anecdote is told quickly, but episodes, to which the Greeks give the label *apomnēmoneumata*, are longer. A *sententia* is also different because it is always proposed in direct form, while the anecdote may involve a question and answer; besides the anecdote is usually found in an action, while the *sententia* is in words only; in addition, the anecdote always involves a person who says or does something, while the *sententia* is proposed without being attributed to any specific person. Different kinds of anecdotes are handed down from the ancients; some are indicative, some interrogative, some argumentative. So now let us look at an instance which shows the workings and construction of an anecdote in its applicable parts. It should be put together thus: first, a brief statement of praise for him who said or did it, then the anecdote itself, then the application. For instance, "Isocrates said that the root of knowledge is indeed bitter, but the fruit is sweet." Praise first: "Isocrates was a very wise man," and step by step bring out how wise he was. Next follows the telling of the anecdote itself; nor is it wise simply to state it by itself, but you should develop it at some length. Finally, the explanation: "For the greatest of things become perfect only through labor, but when they are perfected they bring joy." Next you might make use of a contrast: "Now the basest of things need no labor and come to an offensive end, but the most precious things are exactly the opposite." After this, develop it by a comparison: "Just as it is necessary for farmers to labor at the soil in order to harvest its fruits, the same thing is also true for those who seek eloquence." Then offer an example: "Demosthenes shut himself up in a small room to study, and after much labor he finally received the fruits, his crowns and public recognition." Afterward you may argue from the authority [of others], as, "Hesiod has said [*Works and Days*, 287]:

The sweat of virtue occupies a long day,[3]

3. Two points are worth noting about this citation: the Latin text is far removed from the Greek of Hesiod, *Tēs daretēs hidrōta Theoi proparaithen ethēkan,* and the line is inaccurately given as 287; actually it is 289 (Loeb edition, p.24).

and another poet has said, 'The gods sell us all our benefits for our labor'."[4] Then, after all this, you may bring in your exhortation that it is advisable to comply with the advice of him who said or did [what the anecdote was about].

The Sententia

3. A *sententia* is a composition offering a general maxim urging us to a certain action or calling on us to refrain or demonstrating what something is. It calls on us to refrain, as in the Homeric line [*Iliad* 2.24]: "It is not fitting for a man who serves as counsellor to sleep the night away," or the line of Vergil. . . .[5] An exhortation to do something is: "One who is fleeing poverty must swim the widest ocean, climb the highest mountains"; a demonstration of what something is would be: "It would be dishonorable for those whose deeds are honored foolishly to agree to an opportunity for acting wickedly." Moreover some *sententiae* are true, others are apparently true, some are simple, others are made up of parts,

It is wicked to expect the gods to do anything against their wills;[6]

and some are statements of superlatives. True ones are like, "The man cannot be found who does not have a problem," or
those which appear to be true are like this: "If one converses freely with evil persons, ask not what manner of man he is, for you know that he is just like those with whom he keeps company," or

Those who are conquered have one refuge: not to seek any refuge.[7]

Simple *sententiae* are like this: "Riches can make men compassionate," and

Oh cursed greed for gold! To what lengths do you not
Drive the hearts of men?[8]

---

4. Epicharmus, quoted by Xenophon, *Memorabilia* 2.1.20.
5. The line is missing from the Halm text, though the textual note suggests *Aeneid* 2.402, which is actually quoted later in the paragraph (see n.6).
6. This is the line from Vergil's *Aeneid* (2.402) suggested for insertion above (see n.5).
7. *Aeneid* 2.354.
8. *Aeneid* 3.56.

Compound may be like this: "It is not good that there be many kings; let there be one king only," and

Compliance makes friends; truth only engenders enmity.[9]

The superlative *sententia* is like this: "Earth produces nothing so dangerous as man," or

Rumor is an evil more swift than any other.[10]

The application of the *sententia* is very much like the workings of the anecdote, of which we have already spoken above. It begins with a short tribute to the one who said it, then moves through an unadorned statement, to an explanation, to contrast, to comparison, to example, to the opinions of others, to a conclusion. As an example, let us look at this *sententia:* "It is not fitting for a man who serves as counsellor to sleep the night away."[11] First you should praise the one who said it; then express the thought in a simple statement, like, "It is not proper that a man who sits in a place of power, governing many, should be overcome by sleep from the setting of the sun until it rises again"; then explain: "A chieftain should be ever watchful, but sleep destroys the vigilance of anyone." A contrast based on the difference between king and private citizen as against the difference between sleep and wakefulness: "Just as no harm results if a private citizen sleeps the whole night through, so it would be unforgivable for a king not to spend sleepless vigils considering the safety of those who depend upon him." Then use a comparison: "Just as governors must keep watch over the common good while others are sleeping, so an emperor must look after his territories." An example might be: "Hector, watching and awake all night, sent Dolon as a spy among the ships of the Greeks."[12] The opinion of others: "Sallust also agrees with this saying, 'Many men, wholly given to greed sloth, pass like ignorant and untrained vagrants through life'."[13] The conclusion contains an exhortation

9. Terence, *The Woman from Andros* 1.1.41. Actually, this citation is incorrect. The line in question is 69 (Loeb edition, p.10).
10. Vergil, *Aeneid* 4.174.
11. Homer, *Iliad* 2.24.
12. *Ibid.* 12.314 et seq.
13. Sallust, *De bello Catilinae* 2.8.

for many, as "So it behooves us, when we undertake necessary
tasks, to take thought over them with very great care and
watchfulness."

Refutation, which the Greeks call Anascuen

5.[14] Refutation is the disproving of a proposition; confirmation,
on the other hand is the bringing in of additional proof. Now
those things which are unchallenged need no rebuttal or no
substantiation; such are the fables of Aesop or obviously false
history; rather we look for refutation or confirmation regarding
topics which leave room for opposing views. You can refute an
argument from the standpoint of its uncertainty, its incredibility,
its impossibility, its lack of consistency, its impropriety, its in-
convenience. From its uncertainty: "It is unclear just when
Narcissus is supposed to have lived." From its incredibility: "It is
beyond belief that Arion would wish to sing when he was so
beset with troubles."[15] From its impossibility: "It is impossible
that Arion could have been saved by a dolphin." From its inconsistency, on the grounds that it involves a contradiction: "It is a
contradiction for a man who once preserved liberty to wish now
to destroy it." From its impropriety: "It was not fitting that Apollo,
being a god, should seek union with a mortal woman." From in-
convenience, when we see that it does not suit our convenience
to consider these things. You may confirm arguments by using
the reverse of these.

The Commonplace

6. The commonplace, has the purpose of emphasizing something already known, as if the arguments are finished. In using
it we do not ask whether the accused man is a blasphemer[16] or
a hero, but we magnify the importance of the thing already established or proved, that the punishment or reward determined by

14. The numbering in the Halm text.
15. Herodotus, *Historiae* 1.24.
16. Although "blasphemer may be too mild a word to catch the full
implication of the Latin *sacrilegus* (one who violates the sanctity of the
gods), yet it seems to be the best one-word translation in this context.

law may be seen as due to him. It is called a commonplace because it can be applied to every blasphemer, for example, or to every hero, if you prefer. It is best then to proceed thus, through the investigation of a contrary act, to the exposition of the deed in question, then to a comparison, followed by a *sententia;* after that, you might offer a hypothetical account of the early life of the evildoer, basing it on his present actions; finally, you should erase every feeling of pity through the portions which are spoken in concluding, dealing with need, justice, equity, honor, and other such topics through the delineation of the act itself. But remember that you never find principles for building a commonplace in the abstract; instead they are always found in terms of a particular formula. And to make this clear to you, let me use as an example the commonplace regarding the blasphemer. First you state your principles, like this: "It is only right, oh judges, that you hold in abhorrence all men who are evildoers; but you should especially despise those who dare to attack the gods." Secondly, you offer a quasi-principle: "Therefore, if you want to be sure that others will do things even worse than this, let this man go; however, if that prospect is not appealing to you, then decree for him the punishment he deserves." Third: "It may seem that the defendant is the only one in danger, but the fact is that you also have reached a crisis; I am not sure that contempt for the law and violation of a sacred oath deserve any less punishment than sacrilege." Then, after this presentation of principles, before getting to the particular case, it is necessary to deal with the opposite behavior, pointing out how the laws very wisely demand that we propitiate the gods with altars, dedicate temples to them, bedeck shrines with votive offerings, honor them with sacrifices on feast days, celebrate their epiphanies. And you must indicate also your approval of all this by treating of the explanation which these laws so justly support: "When the gods are honored, the safety of the republic is protected by their providence; when they are dishonored, it is destroyed by their anger." Then move on to the proposition: "In the face of this, who would dare to offend them?" And explain what has happened, not as though proving it, but emphasizing that it has harmed the entire city and the welfare of the community and the private citizens alike, and that "it is to be feared that such a crime may render our fields barren and may cause us to be crushed by the armies of our enemies," and so on. After this, you should make the comparison that this is a much worse crime than homicide: "How great the difference is we may understand from the identity of the injured party. Homicides, after all, act only against men, but the blasphemer displays his foolhardy malice against the gods themselves. This man is like a tyrant—but not just any tyrant, rather the very worst of tyrants; those whose crime is the most vicious because they pillage the sacred treasures from the very temple itself." However, you should make your comparison seem to be of a great crime to a lesser one by your comments, lest you seem to minimize the evil deed, as "Is it not most wicked above all else to burden the thief or the brigand with punishment while forgiving the blasphemer?" And it is permissible to accuse the early life of a man on the basis of the present, maintaining that he began with little things and progressed to this most vile of crimes: "So you have to deal with a man who is not only a blasphemer but also a thief, a burglar, an adulterer." Then you may strike off a *sententia* to the effect that only a person unwilling to work like a free man or to obtain his food by cultivating the land wishes to acquire riches through sacrilege. Next, deal with the consequences, that through this man the majesty of the temple was profaned, the priests defamed, the citizens rendered unwilling to offer gifts at the sacred shrines. Try to remove every vestige of mercy also. Mercy should be removed in your concluding sections, by showing that it would be honest, realistic, effective, and proper [to impose punishment], and by a description of the crime itself: "Do not pay any attention to him as he stands here beside me, weeping before your eyes; see him rather as contemptuous of the gods, breaking into the temple, pulling down the doors, carrying off the sacred votive offerings." And, after all this is done, you may present your peroration, concluding, "But why should I take any more of your time? What do you think of this man who is, it seems, already condemned by all the citizens?"

Praise

7. Praise is an explanation of the good qualities which are found in a man, either general or particular. It is either general, like praise of a man, or particular, like praise of Socrates. We can also praise concepts like justice, and dumb animals like a horse, and even trees and seeds and mountains and rivers and things like that. Notice that praise and obloquy fall into the same demonstrative category, so that both can be built on the same commonplaces. But what is the difference between these two and the commonplaces themselves? They certainly seem to be very much alike in some ways. The difference is this: when we speak of a man in a commonplace, we speak according to a plan, to obtain for him a reward; but praise has as its goal only to bear witness to his virtue. Now the places of praise or of abuse are these: race, like Latin or Greek; citizenship, like Roman or Athenian; lineage, like the Aemilian family or the Alcmaeonides. You might also note whether anything spectacular happened on the occasion of his birth, like dreams or signs or other omens. Then you might mention his diet, as how Achilles, for instance, was nourished with the marrow of a lion's bones; or in speaking about Chiron, where he was educated, how he was taught. And do not forget to treat of the qualities of soul and body, and to develop each of them by division. You may say, for instance, of the body that it is beautiful, that it is large, that it is swift, that it is strong; of the soul you might point out that it is just, that it is moderate, that it is wise, that it is vigorous. Afterward you may praise people according to their life work; that is, because a man has followed the calling of philosophy or rhetoric or arms. In these cases, though, be most careful to stress the man's accomplishments; in dealing with military life, for instance, tell what deeds of valor he performed. You may also praise a person or blame him because of one special characteristic, like his relatives, his friends, his fortune, his family, his lineage, and such things. You can also base your argument on how long he has lived, whether a long or a short time, for each of these can offer an occasion either for praise or

for obloquy. After this you may wish to refer to how he died, for example, in fighting for his country, and to whether anything marvelous occurred in connection with his death or even in reference to the one who slew him, as in the case of Achilles who was slain by Apollo, for instance. You should also investigate what happened after his death: whether games were held in his honor, like those held by Achilles in honor of Patroclus or those in honor of Anchises sponsored by Aeneas; whether any prophecy was made over his bones, as was made over those of Orestes and Palinurus; whether he had sons of great merit, as Achilles had Pyrrhus. Comparisons supply a great opportunity for this kind of oration; you can bring them in anyplace when the opportunity presents itself. Likewise you may praise dumb animals in any way that is convenient: they may be praised because of the place from which they come, or because of the gods in whose care they rest, like the dove which belongs to Venus or the horse which is called sacred to Neptune. Moreover you may indicate how the animal is fed, what kind of spirit it displays and what kind of body, how necessary it is, what it can do, how long a life it lives; and do not fail to use comparison as well as all the places of accident.[17] You may also praise a thing because of its inventors, as when you say, "Diana and Apollo invented hunting," or because of those who made use of it, as by saying, "Many of the heroes practiced hunting." An especially effective tool in encomiums of this kind is the examination of those who made use of the activity, to determine what they were like in mind and body; for example, hunters are strong, daring, clever, well-built. From this step you must not fail to recognize how you ought to be praising the gods. In the same way, you can praise trees because of the place where they grow, and because of the god in whose care they rest, like Minerva's olive and Apollo's laurel, and because of the food with which they are fed; and if they require a great deal of attention, you may marvel at this, but if they need only a little,

17. By "places of accident" Priscian means those commonplaces which are based on what he earlier called "the non-essential character."

you may praise them for this also. You may speak about the trunk of the tree, its massiveness, its beauty, its fruit (if, for instance, it is an apple tree), what use it has, and how long it will live. In all of these, comparisons can be made. You may also develop without difficulty the praises of cities from the same sort of places: you may speak of their origin, that they are peculiar to one place; of their food, saying that they were nourished by the gods. You may, in short, treat a city exactly as you treat an individual: what is its structure, what profession does it follow, what has it accomplished?

Comparison

8. Comparison is the bringing together of similar things or different things, or a cross reference of greater things to lesser or of lesser things to greater. We may also use them in a commonplace, increasing the seriousness of a crime by comparison; it can be used for the same purpose in praise or obloquy also. But since the most learned of orators have often used this as a basic technique in itself, let us speak of it here from that standpoint. Proceeding, then, through the commonplaces of praise, we may compare one city with another city from which men come, or one race to another, or food to food, or professions to professions, or accomplishments to accomplishments, or characteristics which are not essential, or the different ways of dying, or the things that follow death. Likewise if you compare trees, you may bestow primacy on the basis of their tutelary divinities, their places of origin, their fruits, their uses, and so forth. If you compare activities, you may say who were the first to discover them, and you may examine those figures as to the qualities of their own minds and bodies. As to the rest, always let this principle guide you: be sure that the things you are comparing are alike in everything, or at least in most things. It is a fact that when we criticize one member, we praise the other, as in a comparison between justice and wealth. Also compare your theme to something greater; for instance, if you want to praise Ulysses, you should compare him to Hercules in order to make the lesser of the two seem like the

greater in his virtues. But the use of this kind of commonplace demands a superior orator, eloquent and fluent, so that he can make his transference easily.

Impersonation

9. Impersonation is the imitation of speech accommodated to imaginary situations and persons; for example, one might compose a speech such as Andromache would have spoken over the dead Hector. This becomes personification, which the Greeks call *prosōpopoiian,* when the speaker is given a personality contrary to its true nature; for example, Cicero gives speech to the fatherland and to the republic in his invectives.[18] There is also another part of this kind of figure, one that the Greeks call *eidōlopoiian,* when words are put in the mouths of the dead, as Cicero in the *Pro Caelio* has Appius Caecus speak against Clodia.[19] Speeches of impersonation can be addressed either to particular persons or to indefinite ones; an example of a speech to an indefinite person would be the use of the kind of speech anyone might address to his family when he is ready to leave the fatherland, while an example of the particular kind would be the words Achilles might address to Daedamias as he prepares to set out for the Trojan war. There are simple forms of impersonation, as when one creates a speech as though he were speaking to himself; and there are double impersonations, as though he were speaking to others. A speech to one's self might be to compose the words Scipio would use when returning victorious; a speech to others might be the words he spoke to his army after the victory. Always, however, be careful to preserve the character of the persons and times being imagined: some words are appropriate to the young, some to the old, some to the joyful, some to the sad. Moreover, some impersonations have to do with manners, some with passions, and some with a mixture of the two. Those dealing with passions are speeches in which emotion, particularly overwhelming sorrow, is the focus, as in the imagining of the words Andromache might

18. See, for example, the *First Catilinarian Oration* 7.18.
19. *Pro Caelio* 34.

speak over the dead Hector; those dealing with manners are speeches in which the speaker's way of life takes hold, as in the words a country bumpkin might speak when he first beholds a sailing ship; those which use a mixture of the two are speeches having both elements, as in the words Achilles might use over the slain Patroclus. This last contains both the passion of a grieving friend and the manner of one planning war. But the development must include three temporal elements: it begins in the present, recalls the past and presages the future. Always, however, adhere to a style suited to the imaginary speaker.

Description

10. Description is a presentation which gathers together and lays out before one's eyes that which it deals with. There are descriptions of people and of events and of times and of a situation and of places and of many other things. A description of persons might be like Vergil's

Having the face and raiment of a maiden, the weapons of a daughter of Sparta.[20]

A description of events would be of a battle on foot or of a naval battle; one of time would be of spring or summer; one of a situation would be of the state of peace or of war; one of places would be of a seashore, a meadow, mountains, cities. The portrayal can also be mixed, as when one describes a nocturnal battle, bringing in at the same time both the time and the event. We might also try to describe an event by beginning with the acts which went before, and then describing what happened or what was done in the course of the event; thus if we are giving a description of a war, we ought first to say what kind of men were recruited, the cost of outfitting them, and which of them was afraid, then the clashing of armies, the carnage, the deaths, the victories, the praises of the conquerors, the tears of the defeated troops, their slavery. And if we describe places or times or people, we will have some narration, such as we talked about earlier, and an explana-

20. *Aeneid* 1.315.

tion from the standpoint of the good, the useful, the praiseworthy. Now the real power of a description is particularly in its
plainness and its realism or exactness of expression. After all, it is
the duty of the speaker about an event to make that event live
before the eyes through his appeal to the ears, and to make the
style of his presentation worthy of the dignity of the event. If the
event is striking, let his presentation be the same; if the event is
subtle, then the quality of the language should be adapted to it.
It should be noted that some do not include description among
the basic exercises, because they give all their emphasis to the
fable and to narration, holding that in these we do describe places
and rivers and people and events; however, since many of the
most eloquent treat it as one of the fundamentals, it is not out of
order for us to follow their lead.

The Abstract Situation (*Positio*)

11. *Positio* is the consideration of some general question which
relates to no particular person or other circumstantial consideration, like a debate over whether sailing or getting married or
studying philosophy is good, without asking for whom; it simply
investigates an issue on its own terms and in light of its own
conditions. For example, if we are asking. whether something
should be done, we ask only what the act itself would mean to
the doers and what its implications would be. But if we assume
that a particular person is involved and debate the question on
that understanding, then it is not an abstract situation at all, but
an hypothetical case (*suppositio*), which is rather the subject of
a *controversia* than a topic for deliberation. Now some abstract
considerations are civil, others are private: the civil are those
which relate to the common good and to matters of the state, like
whether rhetoric should be taught and the like; non-civil or
private, on the other hand, are those which relate to particular
areas and to those who work in such areas, like whether the earth
is shaped like a pillar, or whether there are several worlds, or
whether the sun is made of fire. All of these questions are the
purview of philosophers, for orators are trained in other matters.
Some call the former (civil questions) active and the latter in-

spective or intellective, for the former can actually be brought to reality, while the goal of the latter can be only inquiry for understanding. Now this is the difference between the commonplace and the abstract situation, that the commonplace gives emphasis to a proven and well-known event, while the *positio* is the discussion of a matter open to doubt. Some considerations are simple, while others are comparisons with something else and are thus considered double. For if we debate whether wrestling should be practiced, our consideration is simple; but if we ask whether wrestling should be preferred over farming, it is twofold: for it necessarily follows that as we urge the one, we are also dissuading from the other. Considerations are also divided into sections which are called conclusions, that is: the just, the useful, the possible, the fitting. For example, "it is just for a man to get married and pass on the life he received from his parents"; it is useful because "many consolations flow from marriage"; it is possible because "from many other cases we draw a conclusion not to be doubted"; it is fitting "not to live like brute beasts." In this way you may establish your contention; and you may refute a contention by the opposite arguments as well as by wiping out related objections. In the peroration you should use both exhortations and the common habits of all men.

Proposal of a Law

12. Some place proposal of a law in the category of fundamentals. And since, in a real case, both the proposing of laws and the making of accusations affect the question,[21] they say that this is the difference: that in a real case there is a pertinent circumstance, but in a rhetorical exercise there is not. For example, "Someone proposes that honors be sold, without adding anything about time or other circumstantial considerations." This can be argued on the grounds of obviousness, legality, justice, usefulness, possibility, propriety: obviousness, as when Demosthenes says, "It can easily be seen and understood by all that the rights given

---

21. Although the Latin text is extremely corrupt here, yet all the suggested readings have approximately the same meaning. Cf. *RLM,* 559,n.

by law are clear and evident";[22] legality, if we say that it is against
the old laws; justice, as when we say that it violates nature and
human values; useful, as when we say that it is harmful both now
and in the future; propriety, when we say that it is disgraceful.

22. *In Lept.* 93. Although Priscian's Latin is not an exact translation of
the Greek of Demosthenes, it catches the full spirit of the original. Cf. Loeb
edition, p.552.

7. ANICIUS MANLIUS SEVERINUS BOETHIUS

An Overview of the Structure of Rhetoric[1]

Translated by Joseph M. Miller

No figure of the later Roman period towers more completely over medieval education and culture than Boethius (*c*.480–524). Nearly every major commentator on civilization who wrote between the sixth and the sixteenth century quotes him with a respect reminiscent of the homage paid Cicero; Rabanus Maurus, Bernard of Clairvaux, John of Salisbury, Dante—all recognize him as master.[2] He was a senator of Rome and a philosopher (not a rhetorician), a pagan who was venerated as a saint; Dante places him in the Heaven of the Sun, along with Albertus Magnus, Dominic, Thomas Aquinas, Solomon, Isidore of Seville, Bede, and others.[3]

Although not a rhetorician, Boethius composed a number of works directly or indirectly influential in the development of rhetorical theory. Among these are several commentaries on the rhetorical works of Aristotle and Cicero, as well as treatises on the various elements of logic; outstanding to the work of the rhetorician are two little known tracts dealing specifically with the theory of the persuasive art: *An Overview of the Structure of Rhetoric* (*Speculatio de cognatione rhetoricae*), here reproduced in its entirety, and *An Examination of the Rhetorical Places* (*Locorum Rhetoricorum Distinctio*). These latter works appeared for the first time in print in Migne's *Patrologia Latina*, vol.64, where they are identified as "unedited opuscula." The contributor,[4] in an unsigned introductory essay, explains how he discovered

1. *Speculatio de cognatione rhetoricae Boethii, PL* 64.1218–1225.
2. Among the translators into English of his most important work, *De consolatione philosophiae*, were King Alfred the Great and Queen Elizabeth I.
3. *Paradiso* X.103 ff.
4. On the title page of *PL* 63, the first of two volumes comprising the works of Boethius, four sources are identified as contributing to the collec-

them in "an extremely old codex"; even in the formal Latin he com-
municates a sense of the excitement he felt at his discovery. In addition, he offers proof of the authenticity of the documents, thus fore-
stalling the objections and suspicions which might otherwise have
tarnished the moment.

1. It is not easy to analyze the strength of the structural bond
which holds rhetoric together; the listener can hardly ever recognize it, and it is certainly not easy to describe. The angry disputes which center about the rules governing each of its parts
may lead to a serious error: [Readers] may investigate each of
the separate parts of the act and ignore the final product. It is this
treatment of the whole, heretofore neglected, to which we now
address ourselves as best we can. So we shall treat of the genus
of the art, its species, its parts, its tools and the parts of the tools,
the duty of its practitioners, and its goals. With this general outline of what is to be covered, we conclude the exordium of this
investigation.

2. By genus, rhetoric is a faculty; by species, it can be one of
three: judicial, demonstrative, deliberative. It is clear that the
genus is what we have said. What we have said about the species,
moreover, is true because rhetoric deals with all these processes.
There is one special kind of rhetoric for judicial matters, based
upon their special goals; there are other kinds for deliberative
and demonstrative purposes. These species of rhetoric depend
upon the circumstances in which they are used; all cases deal
either with general principles or with the specific application of
those principles, in either case using one of the three species we
have already identified. For example, judicial rhetoric can treat
either of general topics like rendering just honor or demanding
satisfaction, or of individual cases, like paying honor to Cornelius
or demanding satisfaction of Verres. Likewise, cases which involve

---

tion. The fourth citation is to "The Illustrious Cardinal Mai, who is responsible for certain unedited works." Apparently, then, the anonymous contributor was Cardinal Angelo Mai (1782–1854), editor of *Spicelegium
Romanum*, 10 vols. (Rome, 1839), and an avid classical scholar. The essay
in question occupies four columns of *PL* 64.1215–1218.

deliberation fall under the heading of deliberative rhetoric in the same way: they may deal with general topics like war and peace or with specific issues like the Pyrrhic war and the peace which followed. Similarly, in demonstrative oratory, we deal with what deserves praise or blame; we may do this either in a general way, as when we praise bravery, or in a particular case, as when we praise the bravery of Scipio.

3. The subject matter for the faculty is any subject at all which can be proposed by speaking; it is usually a question of civil importance. On such a matter, the three species of rhetoric act as molds which shape the topic to themselves; as soon as one of these forms is applied to the question, it is held to that particular structure, as will be evident in what follows. Thus, when a question of public interest which has not yet been given a form is directed at a specific goal, it immediately becomes part of one of the species of rhetoric. So a civil question can take any of the forms: when it seeks the ends of justice in a court of law, it becomes judicial; when it asks in an assembly what is useful or proper, then it is a deliberative act; and when it proclaims publicly what is good, the civil question becomes demonstrative rhetoric. So the category into which the material falls comes from the rhetoric; otherwise the faculty would be unable to work with the topic which requires special parts of its own; for when those other parts are not present, then rhetoric itself is missing.

4. But since we are treating of the species of rhetoric and how those species relate to the case being dealt with, we must make clear that they apply to every kind of business which can arise in civil matters. Anything seeking justice for its goal is judicial; anything dealing with what is useful or proper in public action is deliberative; and anything treating of the propriety, justice or goodness of an act already performed in a matter of public interest is demonstrative. But enough of this.

5. And now we must treat of the parts of rhetoric. Rhetoric has five parts: invention, disposition, style, memory, and delivery. These are referred to as parts because if an orator lacks any one of them, then his use of the faculty is imperfect. And clearly it is not absurd to call those elements of the faculty of rhetoric its

parts when, if taken together, they make the faculty itself complete. But, since these are the parts of the faculty of rhetoric and since they comprise the whole of that faculty, it is absolutely necessary that wherever rhetoric is to be used, they must be present as well. Now if rhetoric is completely present in each of its species, then all these parts must be present in each of the species. Therefore they all must be used in treating any public business when the issues are clearly assigned to one of the above-mentioned species of rhetoric. It makes no difference whether the matter is treated in a judicial manner, in a deliberative manner, or in a demonstrative manner, invention, arrangement, style, memory, and delivery must all be present.

6. Since nearly every faculty must use a tool to accomplish what it can do, we must look for some tool here. That tool is the oration, which is sometimes of a civil nature, sometimes not. We are speaking now of the [rhetorical], which deals with some such question or is designed to expedite a solution to such a question. When that kind of oration treats an issue of civil importance, it moves forward without a break in continuity; when it does not deal with matters of public concern, it is developed through questions and answers. The former is rhetoric, the latter is called dialectic. They differ because the former treats of civil hypotheses, the latter of theses; the former is an unbroken oration, the latter is interrupted; the former needs both an adversary and a judge, the latter has for a judge the same person who acts as adversary.

7. The rhetorical oration has six parts: the introduction or exordium, the argument,[5] the partition, the proof, the refutation, and the peroration. These therefore are the parts of the tool of the rhetorical faculty, and since rhetoric is completely present in each of its species, these also must be present in each of them. Nor can they be any more present than to accomplish what they are intended for. And so the structure of introduction and narration and of all the other parts of the tool is necessary in the

---

5. In this list of the parts of a speech, the text uses the word *ratio* rather than the traditional *narratio* to indicate the second part. This may be a corrupt reading, since the ms. is unedited; at any rate, all subsequent references are to *narratio*.

judicial type of rhetoric, just as it is all necessary in the deliberative and demonstrative types. Now it is the duty of the faculty of
rhetoric to teach and to move;[6] the same duty falls no less to the
lot of these six elements, which are the parts of the oration. Now
the parts of rhetoric, being parts of a faculty, are themselves
faculties; therefore the tools which work in the entire oration must
also function in each part of the oration, and so they must be
present in order to work. For unless the previously mentioned
parts of rhetoric are present, that is, unless the author discovers
suitable material, clothes it in a good style, arranges it properly,
remembers it and delivers it well, he accomplishes nothing. And
the same is true regarding the parts of the tool: unless all parts
of the oration have them [the parts of rhetoric], they will be useless. And, in conclusion, the practitioner of this faculty is the
orator, whose duty it is to speak in such a way as to persuade.

8. The orator must look for his goal both in himself and in his
audience. In himself, because he must be able to say upon com-
pletion of the act that he has spoken well—that is, that he has
spoken in a way calculated to persuade; in his audience, because
he must in truth have persuaded them. For if a deficiency in any
of those qualities which are expected of orators causes him to fail
to persuade, then, even though the act of speaking be complete,
the goal is not attained. And also, one who is truly wrapped up
in his work and tied to it, will succeed when the task is done, but
one who is unconcerned usually will not succeed. Nor does an
orator lessen the dignity of his oratory because he seeks to attain
his goal. And all of these factors are all bound together in the
same way that rhetoric is complete in each of its species, and each
species is a complete piece of rhetoric. Now the parts of cases are
known as the *status;*[7] and we must now make a detailed examina-

6. For some reason, the text omits the traditional third function: Cicero's
delectare (to please).

7. At this point it becomes quite difficult to translate Boethius's explanation. The reason for this is that he uses two terms which should be synonymous, *status* (Quintilian's word for "issue") and *constitutio* (the word used
in *Ad Herennium*); at times he seems to consider them synonymous, but at
other times he seems to maintain that *status* is the "case" being discussed
and *constitutio* the individual issues. Because of this confusion, I shall not
attempt to translate the two words, but shall use them as Boethius did.

tion of them. How can they be considered parts of a case if "parts of a case" means the same things as "species of a genus"? And how is it possible that in one case there should be many *constitutiones?* The answer is that the species are very closely bound in with one another. There are indeed many *constitutiones* in a case; but they are no more "parts of cases" than *status* is "part of the species." This is all the more clear because no species strengthens another species opposed to itself insofar as content is concerned; however each *constitutio* adds strength to every other *constitutio.* Besides, it is impossible that there should be as many parts of cases as there are parts of an entire oration. Nothing composed of one part can be whole and entire, but a single *constitutio* can be enough to build a whole case.

9. Then what is there to be said about this? It is clear to one who thinks it out. No *constitutio* can be called a "part of the case" in which it figures, because it is the subject of the dispute and the status establishes it as an issue. This is especially true when we consider that a *status* which is added to the case after one *constitutio* has been settled is not considered principal, but subsidiary. Besides, in one affair there are as many points to be argued as there are *constitutiones,* and there are as many cases as there are points to be argued; and, even granted that one piece of business may need to consider all of them, yet the cases themselves are different, despite the fact that they are so closely related to one another. For example, if a husband sees a young man coming out of a brothel, and a few minutes later sees his own wife coming out of the same place, he may accuse the young man of adultery. This, then, is the one matter to be decided; yet there are two cases: one is a conjectural one, if the young man denies that he has done anything; the other is a case of definition, which hinges on whether an act of intercourse in a brothel can be considered adulterous. But for the man who denies having done anything wrong, the conjectural *status* is not part of the controversy; to the one who is arguing definition, the definition is not part of the controversy: it is the whole controversy. Of course, I am not speaking now of "a case" in the generic sense of that word, but of an argument based on a particular *constitutio.*

10. The *constitutiones* are, however, parts of the case as a genus in this sense. For if every case were conjectural, and if there were no other status to be investigated, then the conjectural *status* would not be just a part of the case, but would be the very case itself, without exception. But since every case depends partly upon the conjectural, partly upon the end, partly upon the quality, and partly upon objection,[8] the *constitutio* is part of the case—not of the one particular case on which it imprints its mark, but of the case generically, because it is one of the alternative approaches which can be used independently of the others, like cutting one member off from the others. The *constitutiones* are, therefore, parts in the sense of species of the genus case, but they are not parts of any given case in which they function as necessary to the structure.

11. In summary, then, the faculty of rhetoric is a genus of which the species are judicial, demonstrative and deliberative. The subject matter is any question of civil importance, called "a case." The parts of this subject matter are the *constitutiones*. The parts of rhetoric are invention, arrangement, style, memory and delivery. The tool used is the oration, and the parts of the tool are the exordium, the narration, the division, the proof, the refutation, the peroration. The function of the oration is to teach and to move. The practitioner is the orator, his duty is to speak well, and his goal is to have spoken well and to persuade.

12. All rhetoric is contained in each one of its species; and the species exercise final control over the content, so that they truly make it their own. We can understand this from the fact that each of the species controls completely all the material which it contains. Thus you may find four *constitutiones* in judicial rhetoric, and in deliberative or demonstrative rhetoric you may expect to

8. In identifying these four questions, Boethius ignores the approach of *Ad Herennium*, to which he has adhered thus far, and returns to the *staeseis* as identified by Hermagoras: (1) Conjecture, "Did it happen?"; (2) Definition, "Was it really theft?"; (3) Quality, "Did circumstances justify it?"; and (4) Objection, "Does this assembly have the right to judge?". It seems, moreover, that the text of Boethius' list is corrupt, since it reads, *"partim conjectura, partim sine, partim qualitate, partim translatione,"* while the customary Latin words would have been *conjectura, fine, qualitate,* and *tralatione.* See M. L. Clarke, *Rhetoric at Rome* (London, 1953), pp.26–27.

find the same four. From this we may conclude that if each of the species has all the parts of a case, speaking generically, that is of a civil question to be decided, then the case is the combination of all those parts. The entire case itself, then, which is the civil question, is determined by the species. It is much like the way a word comes to the ears of many people at once, complete in all its parts, that is in its syllables; for the whole case with all its parts comes under the different species at one time.

13. But when the species asserts itself over the subject matter, which is the civil question, and imposes itself upon the subject with all its parts, then it brings with it into the question the faculty of rhetoric, and also, in consequence, all the parts of rhetoric. Therefore the parts of rhetoric are necessary in each of the *constitutiones*. But when rhetoric is given authority over the material, it brings in its tool with it: it applies the oration, with all its peculiar parts. So there will be in each *constitutio* an exordium, a narration, and so on. And when the instrument is brought into play, it in turn adds its own function to the civil question; it will, therefore, teach and persuade concerning each *constitutio*. But none of these elements can enter the picture unless there is someone to move them, like an operator or an architect. This person, then, is the orator, who comes into the case and makes it his own project. Therefore he must speak well in every manner of case and in every *constitutio*. The orator also must seek his goal, both to speak well on every *constitutio* and to persuade as well.

We have treated in this discussion, now, everything about rhetoric in general terms. Later, if it is possible, we shall go into greater detail about each item separately.[9]

THIS CONCLUDES THE OVERVIEW OF THE STRUCTURE OF RHETORIC.

9. Whether Boethius carried out this promise is not certain. There are no extant tracts about the subjects he has discussed; however, we do have his short treatise on the rhetorical places, as well as tracts on some of the works of Aristotle and Cicero.

8. FLAVIUS MAGNUS AURELIUS CASSIODORUS

Institutiones Divinarum et Saecularium Litterarum, II. 2: "On Rhetoric"

Commentary

Flavius Magnus Aurelius Cassiodorus Senator (c.480–575), confidant and counselor to Theodoric the Great and a leading force in the Ostrogothic Kingdom from his youth till his old age, was one of the most distinguished scholars of his time as well. In his most important work, *Institutiones Divinarum et Saecularium Litterarum*, he produced the first Christian handbook which attempted to reconcile Christian and pagan cultures, a work which would be perfected in the next century with Isidore's *Etymologiae*. Cassiodorus spent the last thirty years of his life in retirement, founding two monasteries and establishing himself as a spiritual director. During these years he composed much of the material for which he is remembered, including the *Variae*, a twelve-volume collection of his writings, and *De orthographia*, completed shortly before his death, in which he laid down rules of spelling and punctuation to aid monks who were copying and transcribing ancient manuscripts.

The *Institutiones* is made up of two books; the first deals with sacred literature and the second with secular learning. In the first, Cassiodorus studies the Scriptures in an effort to demonstrate that the *artes liberales* were planted in man's culture from the beginning by God; his position is that secular teachers received these inspired principles from God's own hand and then reduced them to a system of rules. In the second book, he attempts to lay out the rules for each of the arts—grammar, rhetoric, dialectic, arithmetic, geometry, music, astronomy. The second book is far less incisive and thoughtful than the first, being business-like and efficient rather than convincingly enthusiastic; this is, perhaps,

77

an indication of the comparative value the author assigned to sacred
subjects and profane.

To the rhetorician, the chapter "On Rhetoric" will seem flat and
mechanical. It relies heavily on Fortunatianus and Cicero, and includes
a few references to Quintilian and the *Ad Herennium*, but adds nothing
original to the field. Cassiodorus first defines the words "rhetoric" and
"orator," using the words of Fortunatianus, then distinguishes function
and purpose before moving to a rapid consideration of the five parts
of rhetoric, status, kinds of argument, elements of a case, parts of a
speech, the syllogism and the enthymeme, and memory. The work is
neither so clear as the *Speculatio* of Boethius nor so complete as the
Three Books of Fortunatianus, on which it is principally based. As a
matter of fact, Cassiodorus contributes more insight into the field in
his discussion of the Psalms in Book I, where he insists on a rhetorical
analysis of the Bible as essential to the increase of man's learning.

The influence of the *Institutiones* on subsequent educational com-
pends is attested by the fact that Isidore took much of the material and
transferred it bodily into Book II of his *Etymologiae*, which is reproduced next in this volume. For the student who wishes to examine the
work first hand, there is an excellent translation with a thorough introduction and set of notes: *AN INTRODUCTION TO DIVINE AND
HUMAN READINGS by Cassiodorus Senator*, trans. with notes by
Leslie Weber Jones (New York: Columbia University Press, 1946), a
publication in the series *Records of Civilization: Sources and Studies.*

9. ISIDORE OF SEVILLE

The Etymologies, II. 1-15: "Concerning Rhetoric"[1]

Translated by Dorothy V. Cerino

What Augustine had been to the early fifth century, Boethius to the early sixth, and Cassiodorus to the later sixth, Isidore of Seville (c.560–636) was to the early seventh century: the outstanding scholar whose influence would pass from generation to generation, shaping the thoughts and cultural values of multitudes. His brother, Leander, who raised Isidore after the early death of their parents, became Archbishop of Seville in 579; Isidore, predictably impressed by the spiritual focus of his older brother's life, decided to undertake himself a life dedicated to the service of the Church and the preservation of learning. He entered a monastery, where his cell soon became a gathering place for princes, prelates, and sages, men who came to hear Isidore's discourses and to discuss scholarly and spiritual matters under his guidance. When his brother, Leander, was near death in 599, he called Isidore and urged him to prepare to succeed to the Archbishopric of Seville; even when a unanimous vote of the king, the bishops, and the nobles of the province supported Leander's summons, Isidore refused the office; finally he was taken from his cell by force and installed as archbishop, a post he filled until his death. Pope Benedict XIII proclaimed him a Doctor of the Church in 1725. Isidore, like his three brothers, Leander, Fulgentius, and Florentinus, is venerated as a saint.

Into his master work, the *Etymologiae*, Isidore attempted to put all the knowledge of his age; his purpose was to preserve for future generations both the factual information and its application available to him. It included not only an outline of each of the liberal arts, but an epitome of universal history and a continuation of Jerome's "chronicler's

---

1. Dorothy V. Cerino, "The *Rhetoric and Dialectic* of Isidore of Seville: A Translation and Commentary," M. A. thesis, Brooklyn College, 1938. The translated material occupies pp.53–74.

literary historiography." To appreciate the importance of this labor, we must realize that even at the end of the Middle Ages an English reader could still write on a codex leaf:

> This booke is a scoolemaster to those that are wise,
> But not to fond fooles that learning despise,
> A Juwell it is, who liste it to reede,
> Within it are Pearells precious in deede.[2]

To call it, then, a mere compilation or to agree with Dr. H. D. Taylor's opinion[3] that Isidore has nothing to teach us now is to ignore the tradition of encyclopaedism in which Isidore worked.

Book II of the *Etymologiae* deals with both rhetoric and dialectic. The material presented here comprises the first fifteen chapters, all the material up to the point where Isidore begins to deal with style. The chapters omitted (16–21 dealing with style and stylistic devices, and 22–31 dealing with dialectic) continue in the same mode as those here included: selection of terms and identification. The technique is typical of the encyclopaedic approach in that it offers little in the way of practical advice to the reader.

The footnotes are the work of the translator, unless otherwise indicated.

I. Concerning rhetoric and its system of nomenclature.[4]

    1. Rhetoric is the science[5] of speaking well: it is a flow of eloquence on civil questions whose purpose is to persuade men to do what is just and good. The word rhetoric comes from the Greek phrase *apou tou rhētorizein;* that is, a command of expression. For the Greek word *rhēsis* means expression, and *rhētor* means orator.

2. Quoted by Ernest R. Curtius, *European Literature*, p.455.
3. Cerino, *"Rhetoric and Dialectic,"* p.2.
4. This first chapter of Isidore's *Rhetoric* is almost a verbatim copy of Cassiodorus, I (p.495 in *RLM*). (Ed. note: The actual numbering of the section in question is Book II, cap. 1; it occurs on pp.148–149 of the Jones translation.)
5. It is helpful here to know that, by a science, Isidore means a body of knowledge through the mastery of which a student is enabled to evolve a method; and by an art he means either a performance based on artistic principles and rules, or one of the seven liberal arts (cf. *Etymol.* I.1–2; II.1). At times, however, his use of the terms is somewhat loose.

2. Rhetoric goes hand in hand with the art of philology. In philology we teach the science of correct speaking, while in rhetoric we show how to make use of the knowledge we have taught.[6]

II. Concerning the founders of the art of rhetoric.

1. The foundations of this subject were laid by the Greeks, Gorgias, Aristotle, and Hermagoras, and translated into Latin by Cicero, as everyone knows, and by Quintilian, with such wealth of detail, such variety of treatment, that while it is easy for the reader to marvel at it, it is impossible for him to grasp it.

2. For as long as he holds the manuscript, the order of the words clings to his mind, as it were, but as soon as the book is laid aside, all memory of it fades.[7] A perfect knowledge of this subject makes the orator.

III. Concerning the title of orator and the parts of rhetoric.

1. The orator is the good man skilled in speaking.[8] The good man, as we know, is formed by nature, by his habits, and by his actions. Skill in speaking results from studied eloquence. It has five parts: invention, disposition, elocution, memory, and utterance.[9] Its purpose is persuasion.[10]

2. Skill in speaking depends upon three things: natural ability, training, and practice. Nature furnishes the bent; training, the knowledge; and practice, the skill.[11]

6. It is obvious that rhetoric, in Isidore's time, still retained its essentially practical nature; that is, it was a method of performance rather than criticism (which belonged rather to *grammatica*, or philology).

7. This remark furnishes the only clue we receive as to why Isidore found it necessary to compile his work on rhetoric. The works of Cicero and of Quintilian were obtainable in but few places; the manuscripts were unreliable; and there were few persons capable of reading the originals with understanding.

8. Isidore quotes Cicero's definition, which had long been accepted as the standard in Roman rhetoric.

9. The conventional five parts of classical rhetoric.

10. Isidore sees persuasion as the end of rhetoric, as did Aristotle.

11. In his statement of the relative importance of natural ability, training, and practice in the formation of the orator, Isidore follows Cicero and Quintilian.

These three things are required of the orator, to be sure, but no less of every creative person who wishes to accomplish anything.

IV. Concerning the three kinds of cases.[12]

1. There are three kinds of cases: deliberative, demonstrative, and judicial. A deliberative case is one which is argued on the basis of expediency; that is, what ought or ought not to be done.[13] A demonstrative case is one in which a person is shown to be praiseworthy or the opposite.

2. A judicial case is one in which a sentence of punishment or of reward is passed upon the act performed by an individual. A judicial case is so called because it *judges* a man, and by the sentence shows whether he is worthy of praise and reward or is to be condemned or to be acquitted through the mercy of the court.

3. A deliberative case is so called because it weighs both sides of some matter. There are, here, two types: suasion and dissuasion; e.g., Shall we hold our ground or shall we break and run? Shall we do this thing or not?

4. Hortatory speeches are divided into three classes: the good, the useful, the feasible. They are somewhat different from deliberative speeches (of the suasive type) in that the hortatory speech must necessarily concern another person, whereas the deliberative speech may sometimes concern itself alone. In hortatory locution two motives are very useful: hope and fear.

5. A demonstrative case is so called from the fact that it has an object which it either extols or criticizes adversely. This type has two variations: the speech of praise and the speech of condemnation. The speech of praise recognizes three temporal divisions: before, during, and after the event.

6. Here is an example of praise before the event:

12. Chap. IV is reproduced almost exactly from Cassiodorus, III (p. 495 in *RLM*).
13. Cf. Aristotle, I. 3 (p.18 in the Lane Cooper translation, 1932).

Happy is the age that bore you![14]

During the event:

O wretched land and shameful toils of Troy![15]

And after the event:

As long as rivers run down to the sea,
As shadows converge on the mountains,
As long as the hollow Pole feeds the stars,
Even so long will your fame and your name
and your praises resound.[16]

7. The same temporal divisions must also be observed in criticizing a person adversely: before, during and after the event. This commonplace also belongs to the demonstrative speech of condemnation, which nevertheless differs in some respect from criticism. For the speech of adverse criticism, whose opposite is the speech of praise, is especially suited to the acts of a particular person.

8. In fact this commonplace is generally preferred in a criminal case. It has the name, commonplace, because, in the absence of the defendant, the case is argued not so much against the criminal as against the crime. For all evil is not found in one man alone, but it is common to many.[17]

V. Concerning the twofold status of cases.[18]

14. Vergil, Aeneid I. 605.
15. Ibid., I. 597.
16. Ibid., I. 607 ff.
17. Later, in chap. XXX, Isidore treats of topoi. Obviously, however, he did not understand that the Latin translation of the Greek word topoi was communis locus—commonplace. This rather ingenious explanation, therefore, originates with him and has no foundation in classical rhetoric. It is a good example of the type of thinking familiar to the medieval mind, based on misunderstanding and supported by supposition.
18. Isidore's chap. V is closely modelled on Cassiodorus, IV, V, and VI (pp.496–497 in RLM). Cassiodorus and Isidore both are indebted to Cicero's De Inventione, Book II, for their materials. Isidore, however, has misunderstood the classical concept of status; for, whereas Cicero and Quintilian specifically state that there may be more than one issue in a case, Isidore believes that there is only one possible.

1. Among rhetoricians the term, "the status of a case," is applied to that point on which the case rests; that is, the issue. The Greeks use the word because a controversy exists. In Latin, however, the word not merely implies the contention on which the adversaries argue the proposition, but includes also the fact that both sides depend on it. It arises out of the prosecution and the defense.

2. There are, however, two types of status: syllogistic and legal. The syllogistic type gives rise to conjectural inference, explanation, condition,[19] version. There are two types of explanation, one relating to questions of law, and the other to questions of fact. In questions of law there are the total and the partial defenses.[20] In affirmative or partial defense the attorney may use a plea of mitigation,[21] a counterclaim,[22] a retort,[23] a defensive comparison of the crime with a good motive.[24] The plea of mitigation may take the form of a prayer for pardon[25] or a justification.[26]

3. The status is conjectural when a fact which is alleged by one party is flatly denied by another. The status is absolute when it is held that the act under charges is not that specified, and when its true nature is proved by definition. The status is conditional when the nature of the act is the point at issue; and since such a case is concerned with the real meaning and classification of the business in question, it is called a *general* point at issue.[27]

19. Cicero, *De Inventione*, Book I.
20. *Ibid.*, I. 11; II. 24.
21. *Ibid.*, I. 11, 15; II. 31, 94.
22. *Ibid.*, II. 29, 86; II. 30, 91.
23. *Ibid.*, I. 11, 15.
24. *Ibid.*
25. *Ibid.*, I. 2, 34.
26. *Ibid.*, I. 11, 15.
27. Brehaut says, in *An Encyclopaedia of the Dark Ages*: "This is the general heading under which all the subheads classified under *finis* should have been placed. Isidore made a mistake in copying from Cassiodorus, in whom the classification is correct."

4. A case of version is one which hinges on one of these arguments: that it is not the proper person who brings suit, or that it is not brought before the proper tribunal, or at the proper time, or under the proper law, or that it does not charge the proper felony, or demand the proper retribution. It is a case of version when the suit seems to require a reciprocal opposition and an interpretation.

5. A question of law is one in which the purpose is to discover the nature of legal and equitable remedy, and the abstract grounds of punishment or of reward. A civil case is one which is argued on the basis of common law and equity.[28] An affirmative case offers in itself no satisfactory grounds on which to base the defense, but assumes the counterplea on something extrinsic.

6. In a plea of mitigation the criminal does not defend his action, but asks that he be pardoned, for this, we have shown, indicates penitence. In a counteraccusation the defendant tries his utmost to exculpate himself and to incriminate somebody else.

7. In a retort one party claims that there is justification because the second party had committed a wrong previously. In a defensive comparison it is pleaded that another act of the defendant was either honorable or beneficial, and that the act named in the charges was committed for its accomplishment.

8. In a justification the fact is admitted but criminal intent is denied. Three reasons may be advanced here: absence of forethought, mischance, need. A prayer for pardon takes the form of the defendant's admitting the deed with malice aforethought, and yet asking that he be pardoned: a rare occurrence, indeed.

9. In legal status these matters also arise: the conflict between the letter and the spirit of the law, laws at cross-purposes, ambiguity, recapitulation, or legal rati-

28. Cicero, *De Inventione* I. 11, 14.

ocination and explanation.[29] The conflict between the
spirit and the letter arises when the very words of the
law are shown to be at variance with the author's
meaning. The condition of laws at cross-purposes occurs when two or more laws are known to present
discrepancies.

10. There is a case of ambiguity when the written matter
seems to admit of two or more interpretations. An explanation or ratiocination occurs when the written law
is shown to apply to cases not specifically mentioned
in the statutes. In a legal definition the point at issue
is the exact force of a word in the context.

11. There are eighteen types of status, then, both syllogistic
and legalistic. Some authorities, following Cicero's
works on rhetoric, make it nineteen, because he determined status by the transposition of syllogisms. Cicero
himself disapproved of this, and hence applied the
concept to legal status.

VI. Concerning the tripartite division of controversies.[30]

1. The tripartite division of controversies, according to
Cicero, is either simple or complex. If it is complex it
must be considered whether the complexity arises out
of many questions, or out of a comparison. A simple
controversy contains one question and only one, as:
Shall we declare war upon Corinth or not?[31]

2. A complex controversy asks many questions and requires many answers, in this fashion: Should Carthage
be destroyed, or should it be returned to the Carthaginians, or should a colony be established on this spot?[32]
In a comparison the question centers around the relative merits of the suggestions, thus: Would it be better
to send reinforcements into Macedonia against Philip,

29. These matters are frequently treated in classical rhetoric, cf. Cornificius, Ad Herennium, Book I, p.17 (Teubner text, 1856).
30. Chap. VI follows closely on Cassiodorus, VII (p.497 in RLM).
31. The archaic character of these illustrations is a hint as to the state of
rhetoric in Isidore's time.
32. See footnote 8.

or should the troops be kept in Italy to augment our defenses against Hannibal?

VII. Concerning the four parts of an oration.[33]

1. According to the art of rhetoric[34] an oration is divided into four parts: The introduction, the narration, the argument, the conclusion. The first captures the attention of the audience; the second sets forth the facts; the third wins assent by offering proof; and the fourth ties up all the threads of the speech.

2. We must begin, then, in such a manner as to make the audience indulgent, docile, and attentive.[35] We make them indulgent by supplicating them, docile by instructing them, and attentive by exciting their interest. We must state our case as briefly and as plainly as we can. We must argue first to establish our case and then to destroy that of our opponent. We must conclude so as to leave the minds of our audience full of what we have said.

VIII. Concerning the five kinds of cases.[36]

1. There are five kinds of cases: honorable, strange, lowly, dubious, and obscure. An honorable case is one which the audience immediately favors, without any speech from us to influence them. A strange case is one which alienates the sympathies of the audience. A lowly case is one which leaves the audience indifferent.

2. A dubious case is one in which the decision is doubtful, or is influenced by honesty or by dishonesty, so that there is no chance either of making the audience indul-

33. Whereas Isidore lists only four divisions of a speech: the exordium, the narration, the argument, and the conclusion, Cassiodorus lists six: the exordium, the narration, the partition, the confirmation, the rebuttal, the peroration. Isidore has simplified this division.

34. Cf. footnote 2. Isidore there refers to rhetoric as a science.

35. Cf. Cornificius, *Ad Herennium*, pp.7–8 (Teubner text, 1856).

36. Chap.VIII closely resembles Cassiodorus, VIII (p.497 in *RLM*), but both Isidore and Cassiodorus are indebted to the *De Inventione* and the *Ad Herennium* for the substance of the chapter. Cf. *Ad Herennium*, p.6, line 13 ff. Note that the basis for these distinctions between cases is the audience reaction.

gent or of forfeiting their sympathies. An obscure
case is one in which either the audience is dull-witted,
or else the case concerns matters very difficult to
comprehend.

IX. Concerning syllogisms.[37]

1. The Greek syllogism is the Latin *argumentatio*—the
adducing of proof. The word argumentation seems to
have been derived from the expression: *argutae mentis
oratio*—the speech of a lively mind, and this hypothetical derivation we should probably find to be true. The
syllogism is, thus, the sum total of a proposition, an
assumption, and an argument; and it is either doubtful
for lack of proof, or confirmed by means of proof.

2. It consists of three parts: the proposition, the assumption, the conclusion. The proposition may be: What is
good cannot be put to evil uses. The audience con-
senting, the speaker proceeds with the assumption:
Money is put to evil uses; and the conclusion is: Therefore money is not good.

3. The syllogism is used not only by rhetoricians, but
also and particularly by dialectitians; for example, the
Apostle often made propositions, assumptions, confirmations, and conclusions; and these, as we have said,
are appropriate to the art of dialectic as well as to that
of rhetoric.[38]

4. Two principal kinds of syllogisms are distinguished by
rhetoricians: induction[39] and ratiocination. The inductive process has three parts: first, the proposition; next
the logical inference, which is called the assumption,
and thirdly, the conclusion.

5. Induction is a process which, in certain matters, wins
the assent of him for whose benefit it is employed,

37. Chap.IX resembles Cassiodorus, XI-XV (pp.495–500 in Halm, *RLM*).
38. This observation is particularly interesting, not only because the example departs from the classical usage, but also because it illustrates the uses
that the Church made of rhetoric and dialectic.
39. He means by induction exactly what we mean by the deductive
syllogism and he uses this terminology throughout.

whether it is used among philosophers, rhetoricians, or sermonizers. The proposition[40] of the induction is the means whereby, the similarity of the objects being admitted, the consequences are shown necessarily to to apply to one or more of them.

6. The logical inference[41] which is called the assumption, introduces the object in question, for whose sake the similarity has been adduced.[42] The conclusion of the induction either confirms the inference of the minor premise, or states the results of it. Ratiocination is a speech which establishes a fact in question.

7. Now, as for the enthymeme, which is considered by the Latins to be a mental concept, the grammarians are wont to call it an imperfect syllogism. For the form of this type of argumentation has only two parts; and furthermore, it uses material outside the domain of syllogism, for the purpose of winning belief; for instance: If you cannot bear a storm at sea, you must not go a-sailing. The conclusion, here, is established in one proposition alone; wherefore the enthymeme is thought better fitted for the use of the rhetorician than of the dialectician.

8. There are two kinds of ratiocination: first, the enthymeme, which is an incomplete rhetorical syllogism, and second, the epicherema, which is a fuller rhetorical syllogism.

9. The parts of the enthymeme are five: 1) the convincible; 2) the plausible; 3) the sentential; 4) the paradigmatic; 5) the compendious.

10. The convincible is that which wins the judges over to the plan advanced, as Cicero did in *Pro Milone:* "Then

40. I.e., Major premise.
41. I.e., Minor premise.
42. Cf. "The minor premise relates some particular instance of the phenomenon under question to the generalization stated in the major premise, and the conclusion is then drawn regarding this particular instance." J. M. O'Neill and J. H. McBurney, *The Working Principles of Argument* (New York: The Macmillan Company, 1932), p.139.

will you seat the avenger of the death of a man whose life you would not wish restored, even if you thought you could do it?"[43]

11. The plausible is that which clinches the matter by demonstration, like Cicero's in *In Catilinam:* "But he lives, he lives! Nay more, he even enters the Senate!"[44] The sentential is that which is revealed by a popular saying, as Terence's "Flattery begets friends; truth begets hatred."[45]

12. The paradigmatic is that which, through a comparison of the present case with a previous example, threatens a similar outcome; to wit, Cicero's *In Philippicum:* "I wonder, Antony, that you do not fear the fate of those whose example you are following."[46]

13. The compendious is that which summarizes all the arguments, as, for instance, Cicero's sentence in *Pro Milone:* "Then he whom Milo would not kill when his death would have brought thanks, him he chose to kill when the murder brought him enemies. Whom Milo did not dare to molest under the protection of the law, in an auspicious place, on the right occasion, him he did not hesitate to slay outside of the law, at another time, under peril of his life!"[47]

14. Furthermore, according to Victorinus[48] there is another definition of the enthymeme, consisting of a single proposition, as has already been mentioned, which goes somewhat like this: If you cannot bear a storm at sea, you must not go a-sailing. There is another definition which makes the enthymeme consist of a single assumption, like the following: There are some who claim that the world moves without divine guidance.

43. Cicero, *Pro Milone,* 79.
44. Cicero, *In Catilinam* I. 2.
45. Terence, *Andrea,* 68.
46. Cicero, *In Philippicum* II. 1.
47. Cicero, *Pro Milone,* 41.
48. Marius Victorinus, whose work on *Hypothetical Syllogisms* Isidore mentions, XXVIII, 25; and XXIX.

15. Yet another definition would have it consist of a single conclusion, as: Therefore divine feeling is true. Or there is another which says it consists of a proposition and an assumption: If he be your enemy, he will kill you; and he is your enemy. Since the conclusion is wanting here, it is called an enthymeme.

16. Next comes epicherema, which is derived from ratiocination, a fuller and more expanded rhetorical syllogism, broad in the area it covers, a syllogism for the construction of discourses in dialectics, because it is the tool of rhetoricians. It may be constructed in three ways: (1) the three-part; (2) the four-part; (3) the five-part epicherema.

17. The three-part epicherematic syllogism has three members: the proposition, the assumption, the conclusion. The four-part type has four members: first, the proposition; second, the assumption and a combination of proposition and assumption; third, the proof thereof; and fourth, the conclusion.

18. The five-part epicherema has five members, i.e.: first, the proposition; second, the proof of it; third, the assumption; fourth, the proof of it; and fifth, the conclusion. Cicero demonstrates it thus in *Ars Rhetorica:* "If the deliberative and the demonstrative are kinds of speaking, they cannot properly be held to be parts of the same type of speaking. The same thing can be a type of one thing and part of another, but it cannot be type and part of the same thing . . ."[49] and so forth, until the members are complete.

X. Concerning Law.[50]

1. Law is the citizen's constitution, which our forebears ratified with the people. For what a king or an emperor decrees is called a constitution or edict. The institution of equity is twofold, sometimes existing in laws, some-

---

49. Cicero, "Ars Rhetorica," *De Inventione* I. 12.
50. Brehaut, p.110, states that this chapter on the history and the nature of law is an original contribution by Isidore to textbooks on rhetoric.

times in customs. Between law and custom there is this difference, that law is written. Custom, indeed, when long-tested is common law, or unwritten law; for *lex* (law) is so called from *legendo* (to be read); that is, from the fact of its being written.

2. Though custom is of long standing, common law based on these customs extends equally far back. Common law is civil law established by custom, and it is accepted in the place of statutory law when a statute does not exist. It makes no difference whether the law exists in theory or in writing, since theory is the foundation of the written law.

3. Furthermore, if the law is consistent with the theory, it will be consistent throughout, as long as it agrees with divine law and is consonant with civic discipline, for this is favorable to civic well-being. Common law is so called because it is in common use.

4. All law, however, either permits an action, e.g., that a brave man should seek a reward; or forbids an action, e.g., that anyone should be allowed to ask the hand of one of the Vestal Virgins in marriage; or imposes a penalty on an action, e.g., decapitation for murder.

5. Laws were made that human temerity might be bridled by the fear of them, that innocence might dwell in safety amid the wicked, and that the opportunity of doing harm might be checked in the wicked by fear of punishment. Law regulates human life by means of rewards and of punishments.

6. If a law is to be beneficial, just, enforceable, natural, conforming to the custom of the country, suitable to the time and place, necessary, useful, and clear as well, it must contain nothing sophisticated by reason of obscuration, nothing for the convenience of the few, but it must be drawn up for the common use of all citizens.

XI. Concerning Apothegms.

1. An apothegm is an impersonal saying, like: "Flattery

begets friends; truth begets hatred."[51] If a personal name be added thereunto, it becomes a chria (a sentence proposed as a theme for rhetorical exercise), thus: "Achilles offended Agamemnon by speaking the truth; Metrophanes won Mithradates' gratitude by fawning."

2. Between the chria and the apothegm there is this distinction, that the apothegm is composed without proper names, whereas the chria is never coined without proper names. Wherefore, if a proper name be added to an apothegm, it becomes a chria; if it be eliminated, we have an apothegm.

XII. Concerning Proof and Disproof.

1. Proof is the confirmation of the proposition, and disproof is its opposite. Disproof means the denial that the fact alleged ever existed, or now exists, or was ever begun or done or said; as, for example, denying or confirming the existence of the Chimera.

2. Between proof and disproof and tnesis [sic for thesis] there is this distinction, that tnesis may be used on either side of a controversy in which the decision has not yet been reached; that is, either in support or in rebuttal. Proof and disproof, however, find their chief uses in those matters which are unsubstantiated, but which are advanced as true.

3. Disproof is the first division; and it is useful in handling matters irrelevant or fallacious. Irrelevance is of these varieties: the dishonest and the pointless. Dishonesty, too, may be classified as dishonesty of word or of deed. Dishonesty of word would be present in cases of improper remarks or of speeches contemptuous of the truth; as, for instance, the libelous statement that Cato the Censor encouraged youth to be wicked and self-indulgent.

4. An instance of dishonesty of deed would be the case of

51. Terence, *Andrea,* 68.

a person who committed an act inconsistent with his own dignity; e.g., the story of the adultery of Mars and Venus. Fallacious reasoning is of three kinds: first, the incredible, wherein the act is not given credence; as for example, that a boy standing on the seashore in Sicily saw ships landing in Africa.

5. The impossible is the second type: "that Clodius carried out a plot to kill Milo but was himself killed by Milo." The rebuttal is: "If Clodius carried out his plot, he killed Milo. But, as he himself was killed, he did not carry out his plot." This method of resolution into opposites produced the transposed proof. It will be helpful, however, so to arrange our main arguments that we shall be in a position to say either that the audience must respect the authority of the ancients, or that it should pay no attention to fables.

6. And, finally, in disproof we may have recourse to the following type of remark, in case those who devised the story should wish to force its significance; we may state, for example, that Scylla was not a sea monster girdled with dogs, but merely a fishwife who was somewhat greedy and ungracious to visitors.

XIII. Concerning Personification.

1. Personification is the figure which endows inanimate objects with personal character and with the power of speech. For example, refer to Cicero in *In Catilinam:* "Even in my country, which is much dearer to me than life itself, should speak to me saying . . . , etc."[52]

2. So we endow mountains, rivers or trees with the power of speech, awarding a personal character to objects which have not the ability to speak. This method, so popular among dramatists, is often found in orations.

XIV. Concerning Ethopoeia.[53]

52. Cicero, *In Catilinam,* I. 27.
53. Cf. Aristotle's *Rhetoric,* three-dramatic characterization, 3. 7. Also cf. Quintilian, 3. 8. 49, for a discussion of ethopoeia (called prosopoeia therein), or dramatic consistency.

1. We call that figure ethopoeia, in which we achieve the expression of a man's character, age, interests, rank, pleasures, sex, habits, courage. When the character of a pirate is portrayed, the speech will be bold, abrupt, and daring; when the speech is likened to a woman, the oration should be consistent with the sex. A different character must be assumed for the youth, for the old man, for the soldier, for the emperor, for the parasite, for the farmer, for the philosopher.

2. Sometimes the speaker appears to be transported with joy; again, he seems cut to the heart. In this type of speaking these points must always be borne in mind: Who is speaking? In whose presence? About what? Where? When? What will he lose; what will he be required to do; what will he suffer, if he should disregard this advice?

XV. Concerning the kinds of questions.[54]

1. There are two kinds of subjects, of which one is finite and the other infinite. The Greeks call the finite kind *hypothesis;* the Latins call it *causa,* the case, since here the controversy is concerned with a definite person.

2. The infinite, which the Greeks call *thesis,* is *propositum,* the proposition, in Latin. The proposition is not concerned with a particular person, nor need it be confined to definite circumstances; that is, neither the person nor the place need be mentioned. In the case all these facts are definite, so that a part of the case is already established.

54. Cf. Quintilian, 3. 5. 5. Both prosopoeia and theses and hypotheses were prominent traits in the Second Sophistic in Greek rhetoric.

10. THE VENERABLE BEDE

Concerning Figures
and Tropes[1]

Translated by Gussie Hecht Tannenhaus

One of the greatest of English scholars, Bede (c.673–735) was the author of the first history of England, *Historia Ecclesiastica Gentis Anglorum* (*An Ecclesiastical History of the English People*), as well as of more than thirty other works dealing with history, grammar, science, theology, etc., and a volume of sermons. He composed the *De schematibus et tropis* in 700 or 701 for the pupils at the Northumbrian monastery of Yarrow, where he was a deacon. In the *De schematibus* he adhered to the contention of Augustine that Scripture offered the best possible variety of examples for all rhetorical figures and tropes.[2] The form he adopted was identical with that of the fourth-century grammarian, Aelius Donatus,[3] and the encyclopaedists, Cassiodorus and Isidore of Seville, reflecting the influence of Martianus Capella and Aquila Romanus: a catalogue listing of technical terms, each followed by a definition and an example to clarify. (In the case of Bede, the examples all come from Scripture rather than from pagan authors,[4] in the tradition of Augustine, Jerome, and Pope Gregory I.)

The significance of the *De schematibus* lies in its position as the first treatise on rhetorical style composed in England; in its elimination of invention, disposition, and memory from consideration, it anticipates

---

1. Latin text: *RLM*, 607–618; translation: Gussie Hecht Tannenhaus, "Bede's *De schematibus et tropis*—A Translation," *Quarterly Journal of Speech*, 48:3 (Oct., 1962), 237–253. Reprinted with permission.

2. Cf. Augustine, *De doctrina christiana*, IV.8–9.

3. Bede's dependence on Donatus is evident from the fact that they follow the same order of presenting terms, with a single exception (*Homoeopton* precedes *Homoeoteleuton* in Donatus, follows it in Bede), and in that Bede takes nineteen of his definitions directly from Donatus.

4. There are three exceptions to this rule: one line is quoted from the Christian poet Sedulius, another from the *Moralia* of Pope Gregory I, and a third from an anonymous source, probably a Christian.

a peculiarly English attitude of the next eight centuries: the equating of rhetoric with style. Thus it also looks forward to the dichotomy proposed on the continent in the sixteenth century by Peter Ramus and Omer Talaeus, the total separation of stylistic rhetoric from dialectical logic (which included invention and disposition).

On Figures

It is quite usual to find that, for the sake of embellishment, word order in written compositions is frequently fashioned in a figured manner different from that of ordinary speech. The grammarians use the Greek term "schema" for this practice, whereas we correctly label it a "manner," "form," or "figure," because through it speech is in some way clothed or adorned. Metaphorical language is also quite commonly found when, either from need or for adornment, a word's specific meaning is replaced by one similar but not proper to it.[5] The Greeks pride themselves on having invented these figures or tropes. But, my beloved child, in order that you and all who wish to read this work may know that Holy Writ surpasses all other writings not merely in authority because it is divine, or in usefulness because it leads to eternal life, but also for its age and artistic composition, I have chosen to demonstrate by means of examples collected from Holy Writ that teachers of secular eloquence in any age have not been able to furnish us with any of these figures and tropes which did not appear first in Holy Writ.

There are to be sure many varieties of figures, but the following are the more prominent: prolepsis, zeugma, hypozeuxis, syllepsis, anadiplosis, anaphora, epanalepsis, epizeuxis, paronomasia, schesis onomaton, paromoeon, homoeoteleuton, homoeoptoton, polyptoton, hirmos, polysyndeton, and dialyton.

Prolepsis, anticipating or taking up in advance, is the name of a figure in which those things which ought to follow are placed ahead, as in the Psalms (87:1–2):

---

5. Cf. *Ad Herennium,* trans. Harry Caplan (Loeb Classical Library, 1954) iv.14.21.

His foundation is in the holy mountains.
The Lord loveth the gates of Zion.[6]

The word "His" is used first, and thereafter it is made clear that
the reference is to the Lord. And in another place (Ps. 22:18):

They have parted my garments among them,
And upon my vesture they have cast lots.

This in place of "they will part" and "they will cast." Ezekiel
begins thus without any further introduction (1:1):

And it came to pass in the thirtieth year.[7]

He has used a connective word [and], yet put nothing ahead of it
to which the word might be joined.

Zeugma, a joining, is the name for the figure in which many
ideas depend upon one word or are enclosed in one utterance.
The following is an example of the former. The Apostle says
(Eph.4:31):

Let all bitterness, and wrath, and anger, and clamor, and railing,
be put away from you.

And the following is an example of the latter. The Psalmist points
out (15:2):

He that walketh uprightly, and worketh righteousness, and
speaketh truth in his heart, et cetera.

Finally he ends thus:

He that doeth these things shall never be moved.[8]

Hypozeuxis is just the opposite of the figure mentioned above,
and occurs where separate words or thoughts are joined each to its

6. The Psalm numbers here used correspond throughout to those of the
King James text. In the case of Douay translations after Psalm 18, the reader
must lower each Psalm number to correspond with the Douay text. The
following Bible texts were used: Holy Bible, ed. American Revision Committee (New York, 1910); Douay Bible, ed. Richard Coyne (Dublin, 1840).
7. Translation by Tannenhaus.
8. Both precept and illustration are used by Cassiodorus (*PL* LXX, cols.
109–111).

own special clause. Words so joined occur in the Psalm (145:6–7):

> And men shall speak of the might of thy terrible acts:
> And I will declare thy greatness.
> They shall utter the memory of thy great goodness,
> And shall sing of thy righteousness.

And the Apostle says (I Cor. 13:8):

> Whether there be prophecies, they shall fail; whether there be
> tongues, they shall cease; whether there be knowledge, it shall
> vanish away.

Thoughts so joined (Ps. 27:3):

> Though a host should encamp against me,
> My heart shall not fear;
> Though war should rise against me,
> Even then will I be confident.

Syllepsis occurs when words which do not agree in number are
used together to constitute a single thought, for example (Ps. 78:2):

> *Adtendite populus meus legem mean* (Give ear, O my people, to
> my law).[9]

And again (Ps. 149:7):

> *Ad faciendam vindictam in nationibus, increpationes in populis*
> (To execute vengeance upon the nations, and punishments upon
> the peoples).[10]

For he says *ad faciendam,* which is singular in number, and then
adds *increpationes,* which is plural. There may also be a Syllepsis
in the sense, when a singular noun is used in place of a plural, or
a plural in place of a singular. An example of singular for plural
(Ps. 78:45):

---

9. *Adtendite* is plural, *populus meus* is singular. Augustine in *Enarrationes*
in *Psalmos* points to this use of a plural verb with a singular noun as a rare
occurrence in Holy Writ. He explains, however, that a people is composed
of many men and so the Psalmist is not incorrect in his usage. See Augustine,
VIII. 366.

10. This is a parallel construction; the second half should be singular
(*increpationem*).

> He sent among them a beastly fly and it devoured them, and a
> frog and it destroyed them.[11]

For he did not send one fly or one frog to wipe out the Egyptians,
but a multitude of them. An example of plural for singular
(Ps. 2:2):

> The kings of the earth set themselves,
> And the rulers take counsel together against the Lord.

The Apostles believed that the word "king" referred to Herod,
and "rulers" to Pilate.[12] See the Acts of the Apostles.[13]

In *Anadiplosis* a word used at the end of one verse is repeated
at the beginning of the following verse, for example (Ps. 122:2):

> Our feet are standing within thy gates, O Jerusalem.
> Jerusalem that are builded as a city.[14]

And Jeremiah (2:13):

> They have forsaken me, the fountain of living waters, and hewed
> them out cisterns, broken cisterns that can hold no water.

Anaphora, or reduplication, occurs when the same word is used
at the beginning of two or more verses, for example (Ps. 27:1-3):

> The Lord is my light and my salvation; whom shall I fear?
> The Lord is the strength of my life; of whom shall I be afraid?

And below:

> Though a host should encamp against me, my heart shall not fear;
> Though war should rise against me, even then will I be confident.[15]

Anaphora may also be found at the beginning of several phrases in
the same verse, for example (Ps. 29:4-5):

11. Translation by Tannenhaus.
12. See Cassiodorus (*PL* LXX, col. 36) for a similar explanation of the
verse.
13. Acts 4:26. Augustine, XI, 70, after commenting in a similar fashion on
this verse, also refers the readers to Acts. Cf. also Cassiodorus (*PL* LXX, col.
36).
14. Both precept and illustration are used by Cassiodorus (*PL* LXX,
col. 910).
15. Precept and illustration, cf. Cassiodorus (*PL* LXX, cols. 188–189).

The voice of the Lord is powerful; the voice of the Lord is full of
majesty;
The voice of the Lord breaketh the cedars.

This figure is most common in the Psalms. Some call it epanaphora.
In *Epanalepsis* a word used at the beginning is repeated at the
end of the same verse, for example (Phil. 4:4):

Rejoice in the Lord always; again I will say, Rejoice.

And in the Psalm (82:1):

Douay trans.: O God, who shall be like to thee? Hold not thy
peace, neither, be thou still, O God.[16]

Epizeuxis is the reiteration of the same word in the same line
without any intervening words, for example (Isa. 40:1):

Comfort ye, comfort ye my people, saith your God.

And again (Isa. 51:17):

Awake, awake, stand up, O Jerusalem.

Still another example (Isa. 38:19):

The living, the living, he shall praise thee.

And in the Psalm (19:2):

Unto day, day uttereth speech, and unto night, night showeth
knowledge.[17]

Sometimes the repetition of the same word is called pallilogy.
Paronomasia, or wordplay, is the figure in which the words used
closely resemble one another in sound but differ in meaning; the
letters or syllables have obviously been changed, as in Psalm 22,
following the Hebrew version (verse 5):

In te confisi *sunt, et non* confusi (They trusted in thee, and were
not confounded).

---

16. Precept and illustration, Cassiodorus (*PL* LXX, col. 596).
17. I have chosen the reading in MS. Bambergensis, *nox nocti,* which
appears in all three Psalter revisions as well, in preference to Halm's reading,
non nocti. Precept and illustration, Cassiodorus (*PL* LXX, 138).

And when the Apostle says (Phil. 3:3–4):

> *Videte malos operarios, videte* concisionem; *nos autem* circum-
> cisio, *qui spiritu deo servimus* (Beware of evil workers, beware
> of mutilation; for we are the circumcision, who worship by the
> Spirit of God).

The prophet Isaiah used this figure very skillfully in his own
tongue when he said (5:7):

> I looked for justice, but behold oppression: for righteousness, but
> behold a cry.

In Hebrew the word for justice is "mesphath," and the word for
oppression "mesphaa"; righteousness is "sadaca," and cry "saaca."
By adding or changing a letter, the Psalmist arranged the similar
words in such a beautiful fashion that he might say "mesphaa" to
correspond with "mesphath," and "saaca" to correspond with
"sadaca."[18]

Schesis onamaton is a series of synonymous phrases; groups of
words that differ in sound but are alike in meaning are linked
together, for example (Isa. 1:4):

> Ah sinful nation, a people laden with iniquity, a seed of evildoers,
> children that deal corruptly.

And in the Psalm (106:6):

> We have sinned with our fathers, we have committed iniquity,
> we have done wickedly.[19]

Paromoeon, or alliteration, occurs when different sounds are
formed from the same letters. Since this figure depends upon the
position of the letters, it is doubtless better to look for it in the
language in which Holy Writ first appeared. However, even in
translation we have an example to offer. The Psalmist says
(118:26–27):

18. See Claude Jenkins, "Bede as Exegete and Theologian," in *Bede,* ed.
A. H. Thompson (Oxford, 1935), p.163. Jenkins remarks that this passage is
simply an abbreviation of Jerome. The passage comes from *Commentaria in
Isaiam Prophetam* (*PL* XXIV, col. 79).

19. Precept and illustration, Cassiodorus (*PL* LXX, col. 757).

Benediximus vobis de domo domini: deus dominus, et inluxit nobis (We have blessed you out of the house of the Lord. God is the Lord, which hath showed us light).

And again (Ps. 58:4):

Ira illis secundum similitudinem serpentis, sicut aspidis surdae (Their poison is like the poison of a serpent; they are like deaf adders).

Homoeoteleuton is a figure built on similar endings, that is, when the middle and final sections of a verse or thought end in the same syllable, as (Eccles. 6:9):

Melius est videre quod cupias *quam desiderare quod* nescias (Better to see what you may desire than to desire what you cannot know).

And again (Eccles. 7:5):

Melius est a sapienti corripi *quam stultorum adulatione* decipi (Better to be rebuked by a wise man than to be deceived by the flattery of fools).

Poets and orators often make use of this figure; poets in the following manner:

Pervia divisi *patuerunt caerula ponti* (The dark blue passages of the divided sea have opened). Sedulius, *Paschal.Carmin.* I.1.138.[20]

Orators use it thus:

Beatus Job deo soli sibique cognitus in tranquillitate ad nostram notitiam perducendus tactus est verbere, ut odorem suarum virium tanto latius spargeret, quanto more aromatum melius ex incensione flagraret (Blessed Job known to God and himself alone in his tranquillity, when he was to be brought before our notice, was smitten with a rod in order that he might scatter more widely

20. One of three examples used by Bede which do not come from Scripture [Ed. note].

the odor of his strength, the more sweetly he gave forth his scent, as spices from burning). Gregory I, *Moralia*, 23.[21]

Blessed Father Gregory, author of the above passage, is found to have used this figure quite often. I believe this is the type of address which Jerome refers to as the elegant declamations of orators.[22]

Homoeopototon[23] is a figure in which several words end with like sounds, for example (Psalm 98:4):

Cantate et exultate et psallite (Make a loud noise, and rejoice, and sing praise).[24]

And Ezekiel says (18:10–13):

Quod si genuerit filium latronem, effundentem sanguinem . . . in montibus comedentem et uxorem sui proximi polluentem, egenum et pauperum, contristantem, rapientem rapinas, pignus non reddentem et ad idola levantem oculos suos, abominationem facientem, ad usuram dantem, et amplius accipientem, numquid vivet? Non vivet (And if he beget a son that is a shedder of blood . . . but even hath eaten upon the mountains and defiled his neighbor's wife, hath oppressed the poor and the needy, spoiled by violence, hath not restored the pledge, and hath lifted up his eyes to idols, hath committed abomination, hath given forth upon usury, and hath taken increase: shall he live? He shall not live).

Polyptoton occurs when the discourse is varied by the use of different case endings; for example, the Apostle says (Rom. 11:36):

Quoniam ex ipso et per ipsum et in ipso sunt omnia, ipsi gloria in saecula saeculorum (For of him and through him and in him are all things, to whom be glory for ever).

21. Translation from *A Library of Fathers* (Oxford, 1847) III.2.1. [Ed. note: the second non-Scriptural example in the tract.]
22. See Jerome, Preface to *Commentaria in Isaiam Prophetam* (*PL* XXIV, col. 281).
23. This and the previous figure are reversed from the order with which Donatus discussed them. This is the only example where Bede does not follow Donatus exactly [Ed. note].
24. Precept and illustration, Cassiodorus (*PL* LXX, cols. 689–690).

And in the Psalm (68:14–16):

Nive dealbabuntur in Selmon. Montem *dei* montem *uberem;*
mons *coagulatus,* mons *pinguis. Ut quid suspicitis* montes *uberes?*
Mons *in quo bene placitum est deo habitare in eo (Douay trans.:*
They shall be whitened with snow in Selmon. The mountain of
God is a fat mountain, a curdled mountain, a fat mountain. Why
suspect ye curdled mountains? A mountain in which God is well-
pleased to dwell).

Hirmos, or connected sequence, is a figure in which the train of
thought in a speech remains unbroken to the very end; neither
the substance nor the subject is in any way altered, as in the Psalm
(54:1–2):

Save me, O God, by thy name, et cetera,

right up to the point where the Psalmist says:

They have not set God before them.[25]

The Prophet begs to be freed by the aid of the Lord, the Savior,
from the persecution of his enemies.[26]

Polysyndeton is discourse woven together by many conjunctions; for instance, in the Psalm (41:2):

The Lord will preserve him and keep him alive, and purify his
soul on earth, and will not deliver him into the hands of his
enemies.[27]

Dialyton, or asyndeton, is just the opposite of the figure mentioned above, since in it all conjunctions are omitted; for example,
in the Psalm (66:1–3):

Make a joyful noise unto God, all the earth;
Sing forth the glory of his name; make his praise glorious.
Say unto God, how terrible are thy works!

25. Precept and illustration, Cassiodorus (*PL* LXX, col. 382).
26. This explanatory note is also in Cassiodorus (*PL* LXX, col. 382).
27. Translation by Tannenhaus.

On Tropes

A trope is a figure in which a word, either from need or for the purpose of embellishment, is shifted from its proper meaning to one similar but not proper to it. There are thirteen tropes which Latin custom and usage recognize: metaphor, catachresis, metalepsis, metonymy, antonomasia, epithet, synecdoche, onomatopoeia, periphasis, hyperbaton, hyperbole, allegory, homoeosis.

Metaphor is a transference of qualities and words, and is effected in four ways:

    (a) from one animate creature to another animate creature
    (b) from one inanimate object to another inanimate object
    (c) from an animate creature to an inanimate object
    (d) from an inanimate object to an animate creature.

An example of transference from one animate being to another (Ps. 2:1):

    Why do the nations rage?

Again (I Sam. 17:37):

    The Lord that delivered me out of the paw of the lion, and out of the paw of the bear.

Still another example (Ps. 139:9):

    If I take the wings of the morning.

Men, beasts, and birds are animate creatures. An example of transference from one inanimate object to another (Zech. 11:1):

    Open thy doors, O Lebanon.

Again (Ps. 8:8):

    Whatsoever passeth through the paths of the seas.

Here there is a transference from a city to a mountain and from the land to the sea, neither of which is an animate creature. An example of transference from an animate being to an inanimate object (Amos 1:2):

Douay trans.: The head of Carmel is withered.

Men and not mountains have heads. Of transference from an inanimate object to an animate being (Ezek. 11:19):

I will take the stony heart out of their flesh.[28]

A stone is not animate but a people is. We use this trope in a great many ways when we speak of the Lord. An example of transference from birds (Ps. 17:8):

Hide me under the shadow of thy wings.

Of transference from beasts (Joel 3:16):

The Lord will roar from Zion.

Of transference from parts of the human body (Isa. 40:12):

Who hath measured the waters in the hollow of his hand, and meted out heaven with the span?

Of transference from the inner organs of man (Acts 3:22):

I have found David, the son of Jesse, a man after my heart.

Of transference from human emotions (Ps. 2:5):

Then will he speak unto them in his wrath.

Again (Gen. 6:7):

For it repented me that I have made them [man].

Again (Zech. 8:22):

I am jealous for Zion with great jealousy.

There are countless other examples of this sort. Of transference from insensible objects (Amos 2:13):

Douay trans.: Behold I will press you in your place as a cart presseth that is full of sheaves.

---

28. Both precept and illustration are used by Julian of Toledo (Lindsey, p.26).

This trope is very common even in ordinary conversation, as when we say the corn crops wave, the vines sparkle, youth is blooming, and grey hair is milk-white.[29]

Catachresis is the inexact use of a noun or adverb in order to identify an object which lacks a proper name, for example (Exod. 25:26):

Put the rings in the four corners that are on the four feet thereof.

Again (Exod. 26:9):

Double over the sixth curtain in the forehead of the tent.[30]

Again (Ps. 76:4):

There he broke the horns of the bows.[31]

Again (I Kings 7:26):

The lip of a cup and the flower of a lily.[32]

This trope differs from metaphor in that metaphor bestows another name to an object which already has a name; catachresis makes use of another name because the object lacks a specific name. Feet, forehead, horns, and lips belong exclusively to human beings and living creatures and not to insensible objects as well. If Holy Writ had not assigned these names to the objects mentioned above it would not have had proper names by which to refer to them. The following line illustrates this trope (John 5:2):

Est autem Hierosolymis probatica piscina (There is in Jerusalem a sheep-pond).[33]

---

29. See Beeson, "The Ars Grammatica of Julian of Toledo," in *Studi e Testi,* 1937–38, p.58. Beeson remarks that Donatus does not give any of these examples. Isidore (Lindsay, i.37) mentions only "blooming youth" and "the corn crops wave" as illustrative of metaphor, though in a later book (xi.2) he quotes "milk-white grey hair" in explaining the etymology of "canitie." Julian has all four examples used by Bede; see Julian (Lindsay, p.26).

30. Translation by Tannenhaus.

31. Translation by Tannenhaus.

32. Translation by Tannenhaus.

33. Translation by Tannenhaus. The word *piscina* (literally a fish-pond) was used for any pool of water.

The pond gets its name from the fish although it was by no means filled for their sake, but in order to wash the sheep destined for sacrifice; hence the name of "sheep-pond" was applied in addition.

In *Metalepsis* the true meaning of a word becomes apparent only gradually; one must reach the end of the thought before a word used earlier in the verse is completely understood, for example (Ps. 128:2):

Thou shalt eat the labor of thy fruits.[34]

The word "labor" is used in place of those goods which are acquired through labor.[35]

Metonymy is a kind of substitution of names. There are many types of this trope; for example, when the name of a container is used to designate its contents (Gen. 24:20):

Douay trans.: Pouring the pitcher in the troughs.

Or (Luke 16:7):

Take thy letter.[36]

The pitcher is not poured, but rather that which it contains; and it is not the letter that is taken, but the paper upon which it is written. Again (I Sam. 6:8):

And send it away, that it may go.

Not the ark but only the cart in which the ark was contained, and the cattle which were leading the cart were able to move. Metonymy often reveals the effect of an action through its cause and, conversely, the cause of an action through its effect.

Antonomasia is the use of an epithet in place of a proper name. One can clearly identify a particular person by means of his distinguishing traits. This is effected in three ways by means of:[37]

34. Translation by Tannenhaus.
35. The figure is not named in Augustine, VIII. 610; nevertheless a similar explanation of the passage is given.
36. Translation by Tannenhaus.
37. This threefold identification is a commonplace, especially in rhetoric; see, e.g., *Ad Herennium,* iii.6.10.

(a) his qualities of character
(b) his physical attributes
(c) external circumstances.

An example of identification by character (Isa. 51:9):

Douay trans.: Hast thou not struck the proud one?

By physical attributes (I Sam. 17:4):

A man base-born . . . whose height was six cubits and a span.[38]

The devil is identified by his haughty disposition and the giant by his huge body. When external circumstances are used they can be divided into various categories. For example, they may rest upon birth (I Sam. 22:7):

Will the son of Jesse give every one of you fields?

They may be connected with a particular place (Acts 24:5):

Douay trans.: A mover of insurrections . . . of the sect of the Nazarenes.

They may proceed from a particular action (Matt. 26:48):

He that betrayed him gave them a sign.

They may come from the result of an action (John 21:7):

The disciple therefore whom Jesus loved.

With the aid of this trope even the Lord himself is described:
(a) by His birth (Matt. 21:9):

Hosanna to the son of David.

(b) by His place of abode (Ps. 80:2):

Thou that sittest above the cherubim, shine forth.

(c) by His activities (Job 7:20):

38. This is an artificial example of antonomasia. Actually, Goliath is named in the Vulgate.

> I have sinned, what do I unto Thee,
> O thou watcher of men?

An *Epithet* is a descriptive phrase preceding a proper name. Whereas antonomasia takes the place of a name, an epithet is never used unless the proper name is given, for instance (Ecclus. 45:1):

> *Douay trans.:* Moses, beloved of God and men.

Again (Ps. 110:4):

> The Lord, gracious and full of compassion.

Again (II Pet. 2:7):

> Righteous Lot, sore oppressed.

An epithet is also used in three ways. With it we may describe (a) character, (b) physical attributes, (c) external circumstances. We may censure, identify, or praise a man by means of these two tropes.

Synecdoche is a designation allowing full understanding of a thing although saying that it is quantitatively either more or less than it is in actuality. It either designates the whole by means of a part, thus (John 1:14):

> The Word became flesh.

Again (Acts 27:37):

> And we were all in the ship two hundred threescore and sixteen souls.

Or a part by means of the whole (John 19:42):

> There then because of the Jews' preparation (for the tomb was nigh at hand) they laid Jesus.

In *Onomatopoeia* a word is formed from its sound, for instance (I Cor. 13:1):

> The tinkling of cymbals.[39]

39. Translation by Tannenhaus.

Again (Num. 10:7):

> The clangor of trumpets.[40]

Again (Amos 8:3):

> The hinges of the temple creaked.

Some believe that this trope is illustrated by the "roaring" of lions, the "bleating" of sheep, the "rumbling" of asses, the "hissing" of serpents, the "whistling" of pigs and of shrew-mice, and the mingled cries of other animals—which are in fact quite often used in Holy Writ,[41] for example (Job 4:10):

> The roaring of the lion and the voice of the fierce lioness.

And (Job 39:24):

> Frothing and growling he walks the earth.

Periphrasis is a circumlocution, and is used either to embellish and expand a simple idea or to avoid the direct mention of an unpleasant subject. An example of periphrasis used to embellish a simple idea is the following (II Cor. 5:1):

> For we know that if the earthly house of our tabernacle be dissolved, we have a building from God, a house not made with hands, eternal in the heavens.

An example of periphrasis used to avoid direct mention of an unpleasant subject (Rom. 1:26):

> For this cause God gave them up into vile passions: for their women changed the natural use into that which is against nature: and likewise also the men . . . against the men.[42]

Hyperbaton is a kind of transposition of words which upsets their natural order. There are five varieties: hysterology, anastrophe, parenthesis, tmesis, and synchysis.

---

40. Translation by Tannenhaus.
41. The same idea is expressed in Isidore (Lindsay, i.37), but the examples differ.
42. Both precept and illustration are used by Julian (Lindsay, p.31).

Hysterology is *hysteron proteron* or putting the "cart-before-the-horse"; it is an inversion of the thought brought about by changing the natural word order (Ps. 24:5):

He shall receive a blessing from the Lord and righteousness from the God of his salvation.

God first pardons wickedness with his compassion and thus rewards righteousness with his blessing.[43]

Anastrophe is merely a reversal of word order, for example (Job 5:8):

Quam ob rem deprecabor dominum (Wherefore I shall beseech the Lord),[44]

instead of:

ob quam rem.

In *Parenthesis* one interrupts a thought by inserting a reasoned explanation, for example (Gal. 2:8–9):

When they perceived the grace that was given unto me (for he that wrought for Peter unto the apostleship of the circumcision, wrought for me also unto the Gentiles), James and Cephas and John . . . gave to me and Barnabas the right hands of fellowship.

Tmesis is the separation of a compound or simple word by interposing one or more words. This type of trope is not easily found in Holy Writ as translated from the Hebrew or Greek. However, it is something like the following:

Hiero quem genuit Solymis, Davidica proles (Whom the descendant of David has brought forth for Jerusalem).[45]

The word is of course Hierosolymis.

Synchysis is a completely perplexing hyperbaton, for example (Ps. 68:13):

43. Cf. Cassiodorus (*PL* LXX, col. 173).
44. Translation by Tannenhaus.
45. Translation by Tannenhaus. Both precept and illustration appear in Julian (Lindsay, p.33). I am unable to find the author of this hexameter. In the text as presented by Migne (*PL* XC, col. 183), Bede says that this verse comes from a Christian poet.

Douay trans.: If ye sleep in the midst of the lots, wings of a
dove silvered with snow shall be whitened in Selmon.

In this verse, as Augustine says,[46] we must first examine the order
of the words and how the thought ends, for it certainly is sus-
pended with the words "if ye sleep." Then again we do not know
if it is "these wings," or "O ye wings," so that the Psalmist seems
to be addressing the wings themselves; whether the thought ends
with the words which have preceded, so that the order would be:

The Lord shall give the word to men preaching the Gospel with
much virtue, if ye sleep in the midst of the lots, O ye wings of a
dove covered with silver;

or whether with the words which follow, so that the order would
be:

If ye sleep in the midst of the lots, the wings of a dove silvered
with snow shall be whitened in Selmon.

In other words, the wings themselves shall be whitened if ye
sleep in the midst of the lots so that the Psalmist may be understood to say this to those "who are divded for the beauty of the
House, as if they were spoils."[47] That is, if ye sleep in the midst
of the lots, "O ye who are divided for the beauty of the House,"
through the manifestation of the Spirit unto profit, so that "to one
indeed is given through the Spirit the word of wisdom, and to
another the word of knowledge according to the same Spirit, and
to another faith, to another the grace of healing in the same Spirit,
and so forth, if then ye sleep in the midst of the lots, then the
wings of a dove silvered with snow shall be whitened in Selmon.
It may also read as follows:

46. The entire discussion which follows is a condensation of Augustine's
treatment of Psalm 68:14; see Augustine. VIII, 290.
47. Earlier in his discussion of the Psalm, Augustine explains that the
House is the Church. Christ has made the Church beautiful by depriving
Satan of his followers (as if they were spoils stripped off from conquered
foes), and then by dividing these men amongst the various duties in the
Church, making some apostles, others pastors, and so on.

If ye being the silvered wings of a dove sleep in the midst of the lots, with snow they shall be whitened in Selmon.[48]

According to this reading, those men are understood who through grace receive a remission of their sins, since even of the Church Herself it is said in the Song of Songs (3:6):

Who is she that goeth up whitened?

For this promise of the Lord is held out through the Prophet (Isa. 1:18):

Though your sins be as scarlet, they shall be as white as snow.

The passage may also be interpreted in the following manner: where the words "wings of a dove covered with silver" appear, we may understand "you shall be," so that the meaning of the passage would be the following:

O ye who are divided like spoils for the beauty of the House, if ye sleep in the midst of the lots, wings of a dove covered with silver shall ye be.

That is, you shall be lifted up into higher places, clinging, however, to the bond of the Church. I think that no other dove covered with silver can be thought of more appropriately than that dove of which it has been said (Song of Sol. 6:9):

My dove is but one.

She is silvered because she has been instructed in divine sayings: the words of the Lord in another place are described (Ps. 12:6):

As silver tried in a furnace on the earth, purified seven times.

And so it is a great blessing to sleep in the midst of the lots, for some have thought the lots to signify the two Testaments; therefore to sleep in the mist of the lots is to rest on the authority of those Testaments, to accept, that is, the evidence of either Testa-

48. This is a paraphrase of I Cor. 12:7.

ment so that whenever anything is presented from them and proved, all strife is ended in peaceful agreement.

Hyperbole is a statement passing beyond the bounds of credibility, and made for the purpose of magnifying or minifying. An example of hyperbole used for the purpose of magnifying (II Sam. 1:23):

> They were swifter than eagles, they were stronger than lions.

For the purpose of minifying (Lev. 25:36):

> The sound of a shaken leaf shall chase you.

Again (Lam. 4:8):

> Their visage is blacker than a coal.

Allegory is a trope in which a meaning other than the literal is indicated, for example (John 4:35):

> Lift up your eyes and look on the fields, that they are white already unto harvest.

In other words: Understand that the people are now ready to believe. This trope has many varieties, of which seven are prominent: irony, antiphrasis, enigma, euphemism, paroemia, sarcasm, and asteismos.

Irony is a trope by means of which one thing is said while its exact opposite is intended, for instance (I Kings 18:27):

> Cry aloud; for he is a god; either he is musing, or he is gone aside . . . or he sleepeth and must be awakened.

Without the aid here of impressive delivery, the speaker will seem to be admitting what he really intends to deny.

Antiphrasis is irony expressed in one word, as for example (Matt. 26:50):

> *Douay trans.:* Friend, whereto art thou come?

Irony and antiphrasis differ in the following respect: irony, from the manner of delivery alone, indicates what it wishes to be understood; antiphrasis does not express a contrary thought through the vocal intonation, but merely through words used with a meaning contrary to their true, original meaning.[49]

Enigma is a figure in which the meaning of a statement is hidden by the use of obscure analogies, for example (Ps. 68:13):

> The wings of a dove covered with silver, and her pinions with yellow gold.

This may mean that the statements of Holy Writ are filled with divine illumination but their deeper significance glows with the even greater beauty of heavenly wisdom. It may also mean that although the life of the Holy Church on earth rejoices in the wings of virtue, the life which awaits us in heaven shall enjoy everlasting splendor together with the Lord.

Charientismos, or euphemism, is a trope which uses a mild word to express something harsh, as for example (Gen. 29:25):

> Did I not serve with thee for Rachel? Wherefore then hast thou beguiled me?

By using the one, very mild, word "beguiled" he has in a restrained manner designated the very grave injustice he suffered.

Paroemia is a proverb applicable to events and circumstances, as for example (II Pet. 2:22):

> The dog turning to his own vomit again.

Another illustration (I. Sam. 10:12):

> Is Saul also among the prophets?

We use the first of these proverbs when we see a person who has just done penance lapse back into sin. We use the second when an ignorant man takes up the task of teaching, or practices some other skill which he has not learned. This trope is in widespread

---

49. This distinction between irony and antiphrasis is found in Augustine, "On Christian Doctrine," II, 567, and in Isidore (Lindsay, i.37).

use; there is, for example, the Book of Solomon which, following the Hebrews, we call *Parables*,[50] but which among the Greeks retained the name *Paroemiai*,[51] or *Proverbs*.

Sarcasm is hostile derision, laden with hate, for instance (Matt. 27:42):

> He saved others; himself he cannot save. He is the King of Israel; let him now come down from the cross, and we will believe on him.

Asteismos, or urbanity, is a trope of great and inestimable power. Every expression which is free of rustic simplicity and has the polish of urbane elegance is considered an instance of asteismos, as for example (Gal. 5:12):

> I would they were even cut off which trouble you.

It is surely worth noting that allegory uses facts at one time and words at another. An example of factual allegory (Gal. 4:22):

> For it is written that Abraham had two sons, one by the handmaid, and one by the free woman.[52]

These, the Apostle explains, are the two covenants. An example of verbal allegory (Isa. 11:1):

> And there shall come forth a shoot out of the stock of Jesse, and a branch out of his roots shall bear fruit.

This signifies that from the house of David, the Lord our Savior would be born through the Virgin Mary. Sometimes one and the same idea is expressed by both verbal and factual allegory. An example of factual allegory (Gen. 37:28):

> They sold Joseph to the Ishmaelites for twenty pieces of silver.

The same idea is expressed by verbal allegory thus (Zech. 11:12):

---

50. The Douay version gives Parables as an alternate name for the Book of Proverbs.
51. The Septuagint gives Paroemia as the name for the Book of Proverbs.
52. Both precept and illustration are used by Augustine, II.587.

They weighed for my hire thirty pieces of silver.

Another example of factual allegory (I Sam. 16:12):

> Moreover he [David] was ruddy and withal of a beautiful
> countenance, and goodly to look upon . . . and [Samuel] anointed
> him in the midst of his brethren.

Of verbal (Song of Sol. 5:10):

> My beloved is white and ruddy, the chiefest among ten thousand.

In both cases it has been indicated in a mystical manner that the
Mediator between God and Man was indeed adorned with wisdom and virtue, but was ruddy-colored because of the flow of
blood, and likewise that he was anointed by God, his Father,
with the oil of gladness in the midst of his comrades. In the same
way a factual or verbal allegory may now denote a historical fact,
now have a figurative meaning, now a tropological or moral interpretation, and still again an anagogical explanation leading us
figuratively to higher things.[53] A historical event is represented
through an account of facts, as when the creation of the first six
or seven days (in Genesis) is compared to the same number of
generations of this world. A historical fact is represented through
a word; for example, when Jacob the patriarch says (Gen. 49:9),

> Judah is a lion's whelp; from the prey, my son, thou art gone up,
> et cetera,

he is talking about the kingdom and victories of David. A spiritual
meaning about Christ or the Church can also be derived from this
same speech of the patriarch when it is faithfully understood to
represent the suffering and resurrection of the Lord. In a like
manner, factual allegory designates a tropological, or moral, perfection; for example, the coat of many colors which Jacob the
patriarch made for Joseph his son signifies the beauty of the many
virtues with which God our Father has always clothed and in-

---

53. See Harry Caplan, "The Four Senses of Scriptural Interpretation and
the Mediaeval Theory of Preaching," in *Speculum*, IV (1929), 282–290, for
an explanation of these exegetical methods.

structed us and endowed us until the end of our lives. Verbal
allegory points to this same perfection of morals, as for example
(Luke 12:35):

> Let your loins be girded about, and your lights burning.

Factual allegory indicates an anagogical interpretation, leading us
to higher things, for instance:

> Enoch the seventh descendant of Adam has been carried out of
> the world.[54]

This signified figuratively the Sabbath of future bliss reserved in
the end for the elect after they have performed the good works of
this world, which will be completed in six life-spans.[55] Verbal
allegory in the same way expresses the joys of the heavenly life,
for example (Matt. 24:28):

> Wheresoever the carcass is, there will the eagles be gathered
> together.

Where the Mediator of God and Man is in the flesh, there indeed
even now spirits are raised to the heavens, and when the glory of
the resurrection has been celebrated, also the bodies of the just
will be gathered together once more. Frequently by one and the
same word, or historical event, mystical sense concerning Christ
or the Church, the tropological, and the anagogical are all at the
same time figuratively designated. According to historical fact

---

54. Cf. Ecclus. 44:16.
55. See Charles Plummer's edition of the *Historica Ecclesiastica* (Oxford,
1896), p.xli. Plummer remarks that this doctrine of the six ages of the world
which Bede borrowed from Isidore became such a favorite that he introduced it into almost all his later works. A more recent discussion of the six
ages can be found in C. W. Jones, *Bedae Opera de Temporibus, passim,*
especially pp.134–135. The six ages may be described as follows: "The first
age is from the creation to the Flood; the second from the Flood to Abraham;
the third from Abraham to David; the fourth from David to the Captivity of
Judah; the fifth from the Captivity to the Birth of Christ; the sixth lasts until
the day of Judgment, and its duration is known to God alone. These six ages,
during which the faithful labour for God in this world, correspond with the
six days of God's labour in the world of Creation. The seventh age, answering
to his Sabbath rest, is that in which the souls of the faithful, separated from
their bodies, rest from their labours in the unseen world."

the temple of the Lord is the house which Solomon built; allegorically, it is the body of the Lord, about which He said (John 2:19):

Destroy this temple and in three days I will raise it up.

Or it is his church, which was addressed as follows (I. Cor. 3:17):

For the temple of God is holy, and such are ye.

Through the tropological interpretation it signifies some one of the loyal men, who are addressed as follows (I Cor. 3:16):

Know ye not that ye are a temple of God and that the Spirit of God dwelleth in you?

Through the anagogical interpretation it signifies the joys of the heavenly dwelling for which that man longed, who said (Ps. 84:4):

Blessed are they that dwell in thy house:
They will be still praising thee.

In a like manner (Ps. 147:12–13):

Praise Jehovah, O Jerusalem.
Praise thy God, O Zion.
For he hath strengthened the bars of thy gates; he hath blessed thy children within thee.

This passage can be properly interpreted as a reference to the nations of the earthly Jerusalem, the Church of Christ, any elect soul, and the heavenly fatherland, in accordance respectively with the historical, allegorical, tropological, and anagogical interpretations. My discussion of the Church in accordance with the allegorical interpretation has followed the example of that most scholarly commentator, Gregory, who in his *Moralia*, while he did not apply the specific name of allegory to those deeds or words about Christ or the Church, nevertheless interpreted them figuratively.

Homoeosis, or resemblance, is the description of a less familiar object through something similar but more familiar. There are three varieties: icon (simile), parabole (analogy), and paradigma (exemplification).

Icon, or simile, is a comparison of persons or of things which may happen to persons, as for example (John 1:14):

> We beheld His glory, glory as of the only begotten from the Father.

Again (Luke 20:35):

> They neither marry, nor are given in marriage: for neither can they die any more: for they are equal unto the angels.

Parabole, or analogy, is a comparison of things which differ in kind, as for example (Matt. 13:31):

> The kingdom of heaven is like unto a grain of mustard seed.

Again (John 3:14):

> And as Moses lifted up the serpent in the wilderness, even so must the Son of man be lifted up.

Paradigma, or exemplification, is the use of an example for the sake of encouragement or restraint. Encouragement (Jas. 5:17):

> Elijah was a man of like passions with us, and he prayed fervently that it might not rain; and it rained not on the earth for three years and six months.

Again (Matt. 6:26):

> Behold the birds of the heaven, that they sow not, neither do they reap, nor gather into barns; and your heavenly Father feedeth them.

Restraint (Luke 17:31):

> In that day he that shall be on the housetop, and his goods in the house, let him not come down to take them away: and let him that is in the field likewise not return back. Remember Lot's wife!

11. ALCUIN

The Dialogue of Charlemagne and Alcuin concerning Rhetoric and the Virtues[1]

Commentary

During the reign of Charlemagne, the first renaissance of learning took place within the monasteries of Europe. Having first encountered the scholar, Alcuin, at Parma in 781, Charlemagne made him *Magister* of the royal school; under this patronage and leadership, the school assumed a position of great importance in Europe. Alcuin's precise scholarship and Charlemagne's recognition of its importance earned for the latter a quite justified reputation as the chief protector of learning during the period.

Alcuin's friendly relationship with Charlemagne and their mutual respect for one another went beyond the typical patron–protégé bond into deep personal affection. The personal esteem in which each held the other is evident in the *Dialogue concerning Rhetoric and the Virtues* which Alcuin composed in 794, obviously with the full cooperation of the monarch. The *Dialogue* is basically a compendium of ideas and commentaries from earlier sources, particularly Cicero's *De inventione* and the *Ars rhetorica* of C. Julius Victor (late fourth century), and elucidated in a question–answer form not unlike that of Fortunatianus. The *Dialogue*, like the treatises of Cassiodorus and Isidore of Seville, did not contribute many original insights, though it is much more complete than either of the earlier works. It goes beyond the mechanical definition of terms to include practical advice on how rhetoric and the virtues could influence the daily life of the sovereign and his subjects.

1. Latin text and English translation are available in Wilbur Samuel Howell, ed. and trans., *The Rhetoric of Alcuin and Charlemagne* (New York: Russell & Russell, 1965; reprint of 1941 edition).

In his preface to the "first English translation ever printed," Wilbur S. Howell points out the importance of the work not only to rhetoricians but also to historians, jurists, and philosophers among others; the popularity of the translation since its appearance indicates that Professor Howell did not overestimate the value of the original and that he contributed something of almost equal value in making it available to non-Latinists.

12. RABANUS MAURUS

On the Training of the Clergy, III.19[1]

Translated by Joseph M. Miller

Rabanus Maurus Magnentius (c.780–856)[2] was one of the brightest lights of the Carolingian renaissance. He studied under Alcuin, acquiring the breadth of interest which later enabled him as abbot to establish a renowned school and library in the monastery at Fulda. From his election in 822 until his retirement in 842 he devoted himself to ruling the abbey and writing theological and ascetical works; in 847 he accepted the office of Archbishop of Mainz, and served for the remaining nine years of his life as a pillar of the German church. His writings are encyclopedic collections of works from earlier days rather than original commentaries; the *De clericorum institutione*, as its title indicates, proposes a course of study for aspiring clerics.

All material relating to rhetoric and oratory in the *De clericorum institutione* appears in the last part of Book III; none of it is original. Chapter 19, *De rhetorica*, is a summary of the first three chapters of *De doctrina christiana*, IV; chapters 28 to 36, which apply rhetorical principles to preaching, are almost verbatim transcripts of entire sections of Augustine's tract.

Rhetoric is, as the ancients have told us, skill in speaking well concerning secular matters in civil cases. However, although this definition does apply to earthly knowledge, the topic is not for that reason foreign to ecclesiastical discipline. After all, any orator or speaker who wishes to treat the divine law adequately and skillfully in his teaching, or one who wishes to compose a literate and polished statement needs this skill; nor should one be con-

---

1. Rabanus Maurus, *De clericorum institutione*, III. 19, PL 107.395.
2. His name is also spelled Rhabanus and Hrabanus.

sidered a sinner who studies the art at the proper time and who observes its precepts in writing or speaking. The fact is that he is doing something very worth while if he studies it diligently so that he may be fitted to preach the word of God. Since rhetoric can be used to convey either truth or falsehood, who would dare to maintain that the defenders of truth should come unarmed against liars? that those who wish to support what is false should know how to win attention, good will, and acceptance from an audience, while their opponents remain ignorant of these matters? The former could lie succinctly, clearly, and convincingly; the latter would speak the truth in such a way as to tire the listener, confuse the issues, and make belief impossible. The former would defeat truth with fallacy and would assert lies, while the latter would be able neither to defend right nor to refute error. The former would frighten, move, elevate, and inspire the hearts of their listeners, leading them into error and compelling them by sheer eloquence; the latter would put them into a long cold sleep for the sake of truth. Who would be so silly as to demand this?

Since therefore the faculty of eloquence is the key which makes possible the winning of many either to virtue or to vice, why not tie it in with the study of the virtues, so that it can battle for truth just as the wicked now make it serve iniquity and error by supporting ends that are perverse and evil? But, whatever the observations and conclusions about this may be, anyone who adds a consistent habit of practice to a natural gift for words and figures of speech will develop eloquence and fluency; therefore those who can easily do so should set aside the time to learn such matters quickly while they are still young. For even the greatest of the Roman orators did not hesitate to say that one who does not master this art in his youth will never master it at all.

On the other hand, we do not consider these things so important that we would wish them to be carried over for teaching to the mature or even to the elderly. This is a matter for youth. And we do not desire it for all candidates for the ecclesiastical life, but only for those to whom more urgent and more necessary tasks do not supersede this subject. After all, if a strong desire to learn is not present, then eloquence is more likely to come to those who read or listen to eloquent discourse than to those who study the principles of rhetoric. Moreover, there are ecclesiastical writings other than the Scriptures, preserved in the citadel of authority; these a man may master by reading. And if he does not look for them, but devotes himself solely to that first source [the Scriptures] and the style in which it is presented, he will be filled with that style even as he studies it. Thus he will gain by impression and even by imitation the ability to write, to dictate, and eventually to speak what he knows by virtue of his devotion and his faith.

But this is enough about rhetoric for the present. A little later we will discuss the application of its rules to the act of speaking.

In the next eight chapters (20–27), Rabanus deals with the study of the other arts he deems necessary to the training of a cleric. Finally, in chapter 28 he returns to the treatment of rhetoric and applies it to preaching, devoting the remainder of his work to that subject (chapters 28–39). None of the material is original; he merely takes large chunks of Augustine's *De doctrina christiana*, IV, and reproduces them almost verbatim, sometimes rearranging sections, but never altering the text. For example, chapter 28, "What the Catholic teacher ought to do in speaking," is identical with chapters 4–5 of *DDC*, IV; chapter 30 of *De institutione*, III, takes *DDC*, IV.10 from the beginning of the third sentence of section 24 to the middle of the sixth sentence of section 25, where Augustine's comma is replaced by a period, and the discussion ends. One who wishes to read Rabanus, then, will do well to return to Augustine.

13. WALAFRID STRABO

Verse on the Five Parts of Rhetoric[1]

Translated by Joseph M. Miller

Walafrid Strabo (*d.c.*849) was a monk of the abbey of Fulda, where he studied under the direction of the great Rabanus Maurus. His cognomen (*strabo* is the Latin word for squinting or cross-eyed) seems to indicate a prominent physical deformity, though this conclusion is not easily proved. Walafrid wrote numerous exegetical and spiritual works, none of which are superior to the standards of the age; he also composed many short verses on miscellaneous subjects, including the following five-line piece of doggerel taken from a collection titled simply, *Verses which he Composed on Various Subjects after the Fifteenth Year of his Life.*[2]

The first of rhetoric's parts is the wise choice of matter,
And clearly the second is proper arrangement of thoughts;
The third, a difficult task, demands the use of appropriate
   language;[3]
Memory's fourth—be master of what you would say.
Then, fifth, be eloquent; this makes the system perfect.

1. *De quinque partibus rhetoricae, PL* 114.
2. *PL* 114.1104 *et seq.*
3. The line appears in Migne's edition: *Tertia condignis sequitur pars angusta duobus,* with the note, "Corrupt text." The translation is, therefore, hypothetical.

14. AL-BÂQILLÂNÎ

Rhetorical Figures in Poetry and Qur'an[1]

Commentary

As the Bible in the West came to represent not only perfect theology, but also perfect style (following the norms of excellence supplied by Jerome and Augustine), so in Islam a long debate ensued about whether the miraculous uniqueness of the Koran as a theological document was equalled by its perfection of prose style. Arab critics argued that, while the Christian document suffered contamination through translation from Hebrew and Greek to Latin, the Koran represented God's word in the original tongue, uncontaminated by human interference.

In order to understand this position, it is necessary to understand the background of Arab rhetoric. The theory of rhetorical style among the successors of Muhammad deals almost exclusively with poetry and artistic prose, rarely with oratory.[2] Indeed the term which comes closest to the meaning of rhetoric is *balāgha,* applied indiscriminately to poetry, artistic prose, and oratory. Though a theory of oratory existed in the Arab tradition, it had little chance to develop: it seems to have contributed nothing to the art of *balāgha,* and to have disappeared almost entirely under the influence of Islam ritual. By the year 132/750,[3] what passed for rhetorical criticism was generally grammatical or lexicographic analysis, dealing more with the nature of language than its effective use.

1. G. E. von Grunebaum, A *Tenth-Century Document of Arab Literary Theory and Criticism* (Chicago: University of Chicago Press, 1950).
    2. The development of this thesis makes up most of the content of S. A. Bonebakker, "Aspects of the History of Literary Rhetoric and Poetics in Arabic Literature," *Viator: Medieval and Renaissance Studies,* ed. Lynn White, Jr., I (Berkeley: University of California Press, 1970), pp.75–95.
    3. Two dates are given; the first refers to the Muslim computation, the second to the Christian.

A somewhat more literary approach to the study began with the appearance of the *Kitāb al-Badī'* (*Book of Ornate Style*) composed by Ibn al-Mu'tazz (*d.c.*296/908), and the *Kitāb Naqd ash-Shī'r* (*Book of the Criticism of Poetry*) of Qudāma ibn Ja'far (*d.c.*320/932), which delved into questions of poetic technique and the proper use of figures of speech. During subsequent centuries there appeared several works of the same type, similar to the encyclopaedic commentaries of Isidore of Seville and Cassiodorus: long compilations in which each chapter followed the same pattern of naming a technical element, defining it, and presenting whatever examples seemed necessary.

Whether the traditional western concept of rhetoric influenced this broadening of treatment is uncertain; nevertheless it is clear that Aristotle's *Rhetoric* did become available in an Arabic translation by Isḥāq ibn Ḥunayn (*d.c.*299/911), though many scholars in Arabic cultural history agree that it exercised little influence. They take the position that neither the *Rhetoric* nor the *Poetics* offered much salient material to those authors who felt that specific rules of style were dependent upon the purity of the language used, and that there was no need to develop a different rule for prose and poetry.

For this reason it seems that there is little connection between the development of Arabic rhetorical theory and medieval western rhetoric. To the student of the latter, the former have interest only as curiosities; Arab commentators on rhetoric were simply not talking about the same field as were their western counterparts. For a discussion of these works, however, and for a translation of one treatise which discusses the Koran as a rhetorical production, using rhetoric to support the argument that the Koran is inimitable in stylistic perfection, see G. E. von Grunebaum, *A Tenth-Century Document of Arabic Literary Theory and Criticism* (Chicago: Chicago University Press, 1950), which includes a translation of al-Bâqillânî's "Rhetorical Figures in Poetry and Qur'an."

15. ALBERIC OF MONTE CASSINO

Flowers of Rhetoric[1]

Translated by Joseph M. Miller

The system of rhetoric known as *ars dictaminis* (the art of letter writing) is a peculiarly medieval development; it grew out of the needs of administrative procedure, and was primarily intended to furnish principles and models for the composition of official letters and documents. Although discussions of the art of letter writing had appeared in rhetorical context in the appendix to C. Julius Victor's fourth-century *Ars rhetorica*, and although model letters (*formulae*) were already in existence during Merovingian and Carolingian times, there had been little effort to systematize the theory for broad application until a more complicated international pattern began to emerge in the tenth and eleventh centuries.

That rhetoric became the art of letter writing is certainly not surprising. Collections of letters by Pliny, Sidonius, and Cassiodorus had prepared the way and Felix Ennodius (*c*.500) had used the phrase "*epistolaris sermo* (epistolary discourse)" to mean artistic prose. And as royal, imperial, and papal documents took on greater importance, a sense of style and beauty demanded greater understanding of the uses of the written word. The resultant field of endeavor took its name, *dictamen*, from the fact that such documents were dictated aloud.

Alberic of Monte Cassino, teacher in one of the oldest of all Benedictine monasteries, thus became a pivotal figure in the history of medieval rhetoric. In about 1087 he produced the first work formally linking the ancient art of discourse and the new art of correspondence, *Flores rhetorici* (or *Dictaminum radii*).[2] This work deals primarily with

1. Alberici Casinensis *Flores Rhetorici*, ed. D. H. Inguanez, H. M. Willard (Montecassino, Miscellanea Cassinese, 1938). The text occupies pp.31–59 of the monograph.
2. Although the edition from which this translation was made appeared under the former title, James J. Murphy indicates that the latter would be more correct. "Alberic of Monte Cassino: Father of the Medieval *Ars Dictaminis*," *American Benedictine Review*, XXII: 2 (June, 1971), 139.

rhetorical ornament in composition, while Alberic's later work, *Breviarium de dictamine,* actually prescribes rules for correspondence.[3]

It is worth noting that Alberic does not exhaust any of the topics comprising the *Flores.* Indeed his discussions are frequently cryptic, his conclusions abrupt; this seems to indicate that the work is primarily a set of notes concerning ideas previously presented orally and already familiar to the reader. Of further interest is the frequency with which Alberic refers to such pagan authors as Cicero, Sallust, Ovid, Lucan, Terence, and especially Vergil: in this foretaste of renaissance learning we may see some hint of the role the monks of Monte Cassino had played in the preservation of the ancient traditions.

I

Until now we have nourished, as it were, the minds of infants with the milk of our instruction; but now it is time to strengthen the minds of grown men with bread. Until now we have rehearsed our hearers[4] in the preliminary training of grammar; now that the period of practice is over, we must lead them to the battlefield of composition. After all, if we have omitted so much up to this point regarding the incredibly wide choice of words and regarding the appreciation of their melody as well, what else can we call our work but the milk of learning, the training of a child? Thus far we have looked at the rudiments of education; now we move into the full manly power of knowledge. The first is infancy; the second is adulthood. Any art one can think of must proceed in ordered stages; that is, one must move from basics to comprehensiveness. Therefore, let the sincere soul develop, let it eat and drink and grow from within, let flaws and triviality vanish, let the juices not be drawn too soon; at last, touched by the rod of Phoebus, the mind will bear fruit. Here Alberic soars high, expects to gain the palm of victory; now his adversary becomes silent, mute, agape, stunned with admiration; here integrity and de-

---

3. A partial text of the *Breviarium* appears in Ludwig Rockinger, *Briefsteller und Formelbucher des eilsten bis vierzehnten Jahrhunderts,* 2 vols. (Munich, 1863; Reprinted in New York, 1961), I, pp.29–46.

4. This use of the word *auditores* seems to indicate that the text is an adaptation of notes from a lecture or series of lectures by Alberic.

pendability thrive. We will put into a few brief words a discussion
that is far from brief; by wiping away confusion, we will become
effective. What figures there are and how they fit together in
complex as well as simple matters will be clear. And now let us
move to the topic itself; let us begin weaving the fabric of our
proem.

II

1. Anyone who is preparing to decorate his work with a prologue, or (to put it more accurately) to enhance the beauty of the
other members by means of a beautiful face, must observe the
proprieties and use the suitable figures. First, the prologue must
be drawn from the subject of the work as from the very womb of
its mother. For example, if you intend to treat of the virtues and
the vices and the strife between them, you will outline fittingly
from that area what you intend to offer. Augustine begins in this
way: "We must address ourselves to you in love, my brothers, concerning that which is dangerous to your salvation and that which
will bring you new life, that with which you will rise with the
living, without which you will sink with the dying." Vergil
begins (*Aeneid* I.1):

> I sing of arms and the man . . .

Boethius writes (*De Consolatione Philosophiae* I.1):

> I who once wrote verses in the passion of youth
> Begin now weeping to use a mournful strain . . .

You see that the messengers sent before are born of the thoughts
that will follow, that authors foreshadow the story that is to come
by giving to the mind a preview. Indeed if you would offer any
other kind of beginning, it would be the same as giving a stone
to one to whom you have promised gold. It should also be noted
that in such a beginning a response is often made to unspoken
objections, so that it will be clear that the work should not be
considered the product of insufficient effort. Therefore the author
should set as the purpose of his preface to render the mind of the
reader attentive, receptive, and open. This will be the light and

beauty of the work as the eye is of the head. But concerning some of the figures which will be dealt with later, it is best to be silent at this juncture. It is sufficient that you tie together the elements of the prologue with brevity. For it is foolish to wax eloquent in the proem and then prune the history. But since we will deal later with the quality of brevity, let us for the present draw to a close. Let us now set sail into an account of narration.

2. At the beginning you should look over the entire work with an unbiased eye; you should search out what is clear, what is obscure, what is insignificant, what is important, what adds nobility, and what adds vileness; you should examine it and afterward you should judge what you consider essential to the overall effect. If a thing is obvious, do not complicate it with circumlocutions: project your thought in a few words, since it is clear even if you say nothing. On the other hand, if the matter is obscure, do not hesitate to take time so as to let the light of words make the point clear that is inherent in your topic; otherwise you make the obscurity worse by your silence. Furthermore, let all things be kept in proportion: do not treat trivial things too seriously nor momentous things with contempt, nor vice versa. When you have subjected a theme to diligent attention, then decide where and how you should begin speaking. What a Narrative ought to be. It is narrative that puts at the beginning what is best suited for that; it also puts at the heart what is more appropriately placed there. One who begins in the middle drives a wedge between the nobility of his topic and the enjoyment which art and labor should add to it. First of all, the author should take particular care not to begin in such a way as to render his topic confused, but should begin rather in a way that will shed greater light. For this reason it is essential that you choose to begin at a place where you can easily bring your hearers to understanding so that it will be clear from the very beginning that no part of the narrative is missing, so that the readers will grasp the heart of the story immediately, because they are fully aware of the beginning, so that all will be clearly defined as in sort of a mirror.

3. No less caution is needed to insure that you treat carefully in its proper place everything you bring up for consideration. I am

certain that some things ought to be reserved for later treatment, although not so that you can compress everything into one heap at the last moment nor, on the other hand, so that you may somehow scatter, as it were, the seeds carelessly in badly plowed furrows. So it is of the utmost importance that you begin very cautiously with certain topics, that you keep all in their places with equal caution. There are many examples of what I mean: Vergil is a master of the art, and Terence is outstanding also.

4. There is another way also for giving advance information about the subject we are going to treat. Sometimes it happens that something may arise quite far removed from the original purpose of the work, yet necessary for the full realization of that purpose. In that situation, do not let your style become weighted down in confused explanation, and do not let a sudden digression interrupt the work that is in progress; rather, explain in the beginning whatever will be necessary for what follows. This kind of approach is illustrated by the way Sallust wrote the [historical monographs] *Conspiracy of Catiline* and *War Against Jugurtha*.

5. So, as regards all introductions, let us offer this general principle: first, let your composition move at a steady pace both at the beginning and as it proceeds through the middle toward the conclusion; avoid sudden transitions; do not drag in a thousand little rags to be sewn onto the fabric. For it is a defilement of the composition if one wanders too far from the theme proposed at the beginning, if he smears a perfect piece of cloth by dipping it into pots of dye. After all, what can you call it but a stain to defile and violate the simple narrative structure expected in the manner of one who deforms a body by attaching all manner of superfluous members to it? Let your thought, therefore, move gracefully along, confining itself to its own content; let not the vileness of an unnatural rape multilate it when its own beauty is great enough to illuminate it from within. A narrative is so strong of itself that you should be able to carry it through to the end so long as you do not violate its integrity. And so never deviate from simplicity. Therefore from the beginning through the middle to the very end, let nothing be brought in very suddenly, let nothing irrelevant be added to the fabric. And do not give any less atten-

tion to the dignity of the composition; unless you are fully aware of the dignity of the work you are writing, you will be unable to judge the appropriate style. There are three kinds of histories, as we know: there are those which deal with noble topics like wars and the acts of the gods, those which deal with the ordinary subjects like flowers and trees and the physical elements, and those which deal with such low themes as the games of youth and the dalliance of lovers. Let the author's own caution warn him as to what level or degree is involved in whatever he writes, so that he may prudently adapt the level of his style to the level of the topic. And if you seriously analyze your theme at the very beginning, the words will follow after—not words which are badly chosen or silly, but words which will flow most fittingly as from a pure and lovely fountain. After all, what can I call a well-planned story but a sort of beautiful fountain from which there flows like a living stream the vibrant richness of the thought? But if you do not know the kind of theme you are going to write about, then you are indeed ignorant of what and how to write.

III

1. Now we must examine with the most careful scrutiny the rhetorical division of the whole oration. It has an exordium, a narration, an argument, and a conclusion. The exordium is the very same thing that we have already spoken of above as the proem. We spoke a little about its *colores* earlier; at that time we promised to develop the subject at greater length later on, so let us proceed to keep that promise. I would say that its *colores* are those which serve to earn good will, acceptance, and attention. So if you want to render your reader attentive, you ought to offer him words which are true, honorable, and useful. For if you suggest things that are false, degraded or not likely to be of value to your listener, you will make him turn a deaf ear; even worse, you will create an attitude that what is to follow will be contemptible and vicious. But in order to confirm the truth of this, let us go to the authority of Sallust in his *War Against Jugurtha* (2.1): "What separates human desires from the brute beasts is that it (the human mind) distinguishes its goals by noting the

difference between those of the mind and those of the body."[5] The fact that one attempts to prove some things are true and others false, that some are transient, others permanent—for what reason does one do this but to assure that the subject he is going to treat will be greeted with the kind of attention its importance or dignity entitles it to? Through this approach, he makes people want to know, and by that wish he arouses their attention. If you want to lay the groundwork for good will, then you must follow the procedures which are designed to gain attention. Sometimes you may add a reminder of your own dignity, and sometimes you may use a style of exhortation. This is why Terence both pays tribute to himself and adds beauty to his work, at once exhorting his reader and reminding him of the poet's stature (*Heautontimorumenos* Prol. 28, 35, 48–50):

> Make sure you come with an open mind.
> If ever I greedily put a price on my
> art and gave it the highest value . . .
> it was to serve your convenience.

Then there remains agreeableness, from which path one should never wander if he has time for preparation at all; let him seek brevity and rid himself of obscurity.

2. In some narration it is fitting that the adornment of elegant language be used: it should follow the path of brevity and be guided along the highway of aptness. But as to how elegance and briefness can be brought together (for they seem to be mutually exclusive), this we shall explain later in its own place.

3. Next comes the argument, which has a place in the course we would follow if we intend to strengthen our own position first and then weaken the position of our adversary. Yet it is important to note that this approach is not always and everywhere called for, but only when the subject in hand is one to which serious objections might be raised.

4. The conclusion follows, which has the effect of turning the

5. Although the text indicates that this is a direct quotation, it is actually a very free paraphrase of chapters 1–2 of Sallust's *Bellum Jugurthinum*.

audiences' attention once more to what you have said. When this
fits well with all the other parts, then especially it adds new
beauty, new attractiveness through its conciseness. Indeed, since
many demand this technique as necessary, useful, or ennobling,
no matter what norms of judgment we follow, we must sense the
needs of the readers.

5. [Salutation]. First we must consider the identity of the
sender and of the person to whom the letter is sent;[6] we must
consider whether he is noble or common in rank, a friend or an
enemy, and then what kind of person he is and of what background. The next consideration is the thing dealt with: is it a just
or unjust matter, and is it serious or minor? Next the writer should
ask himself what attitude he wishes to project: proud or humble,
harsh or forgiving, threatening, flattering, stern, or that of a trusted
friend. When you have examined the person, the topic and the
goal, then you must weigh each according to its importance.
If you write to an exalted person, use a style that is exalted; to a
simple person use a style that is simple; to a friend use a friendly
style; and to an enemy use a style that is bold. If a learned man
is writing to one who is educated poorly or not at all, he should
govern his words according to the powers of his correspondent.
You must address a prelate in one way, a subject in quite another;
you should address a gentle person quite differently from a demanding one; portray each one strictly according to his own character, balancing the subject with the goal you are seeking. If you
are seeking justice in some matter, you must speak the more confidently, you must appeal to the law, you must remind the judge,
you must warn him that God is the avenger of all unfair judgments,
as you do this, you must always keep in mind both the person and
the purpose. If you do not have justice on your side, then you
need to choose clever words. And so it is in all things. If a person
thinks haughtily or harshly, let your language be elevated that it
may pour forth rather than in ordinary patterns. If your goal is
mild and just and pleasant, then you must use pleasantries and

6. Although the word *epistola* (letter) does not actually appear in the
text, the phrases *persona mittentis* and *persona cui mittitur* make clear that
the composition referred to must be a letter.

familiar terms, not timid ones, in your style. Never should you neglect showing proper respect both for the person and for the subject. Generally you should cultivate attitudes toward people, showing openness and frankness toward the rich and noble, being reserved and grave toward the common folk. One man trusts in the protection of the law, another in his wealth; one depends on God, the other on man. Therefore, when you have weighed all these considerations, fashion your salutation from the topic, the person, and the purpose; this will be a most expedient technique if you do not wander too far from it.

6. After the salutation, begin the exordium; after the exordium, move into the narration, which will be quite good if it is short and clear. The accurate use of logic will, if necessary, establish what I have called the argument. Finally, the conclusion recalls to the memory the principle point and locks it there. And logic should not stagger on (like) a widow bereaved of the support of examples; therefore, I propose that you follow these suggestions. One's work should be brilliant with examples, both original and drawn from other sources. For example, one who wishes to regain the friendship of a former companion ought to call to mind the outstanding examples of this, saying, "To one whom I long to call a friend once more, as he was in days gone by, that he may be to me like a brother to a brother, like Orestes to Pylades." One may say this in many different ways, according to what his own reputation suggests, his dignity and well-being demand, according to what is appropriate for the securing of his life and friendship; also, one can look at the friend and his needs, what seems best for him or for his well-being or for his reputation. For example: . . . "Nothing is weaker than a man. Blindness is almost always a part of human nature: the wise directing of human life limps, staggers, falls, even dies because it neither knows how to ward off dangers with the shield of foresight nor considers or plans how to protect its good fortune with proper caution. And so, my brother, be generous to my foolishness, blame my slips on a flaw of nature. I was at fault; I blush to admit that I was at fault. I broke faith with you; I wounded your love. But what my lapse has brought on, the depth of my sorrow has wiped away. If I were the only

one who had ever been wrong, I would think that such a fall had
no right to expect mercy. But it is human to err, and it is more
than human to refrain from condemning one who is trying to
atone for his sin. If pardon had not followed crime, I make bold
to say, we would not have had Peter as Prince of the Apostles or
Paul as an Apostle: the former denied Christ, the latter sinned in
that he persecuted the Church of Christ. Yet both now sit on
thrones to judge the Church. So consider compassion, my friend
so dear, and do not carry with you the memory of my failing; for
a long time now, I have already endured the punishment of
remorse."

There you have an example you can imitate in developing the
divisions mentioned above; you may also confirm this lesson by
studying the works of the pagan authors. Sallust, for instance,
keeps the same order as that indicated above when he says
(*Jugurtha* 14. 1–5, 28):

Fathers of the Senate, when my father Micippa, was dying, he
ordered me to consider myself only as a viceroy for the kingdom
of Numidia, while the power to make and impose laws remained
with you, at that same time I was to use my household and my
army in every way possible to assist the Roman people. . . .
While I was carrying out this trust of my father, Jugurtha, the
wickedest man on the face of the earth, sneered at your empire
and robbed me, the grandson of Masinissa, me, a friend and
supporter of the Roman people from my infancy, of my throne
and my fortune. And I, Fathers of the Senate, having reached
this depth of wretchedness, wanted to ask your assistance because
of the services I had rendered you myself, rather than because
of those of my father. . . . But since integrity does not always
serve as its own best advocate. . . . I have turned to you, Fathers
of the Senate, and with the greatest reluctance have been forced
to become a burden to you before I have been an ally. Other
kings have received your friendship after being vanquished in
war, or they have sought your support in their own time of
danger; my family, however, established a bond of friendship
during the Carthaginian war, at a time when it was Rome's
future promise that attracted rather than any present fortune.
. . . Fathers of the Senate, I implore you by your own honor, by
your children, by your parents . . . aid me in my distress, take
action against injustice; do not allow the kingdom of Numidia,

which belongs to you, to fall in the face of crime and bloodshed directed against my family.[7]

So you see how he makes the proem short, how he works the narration in, how he adapts the argument, how he fits the conclusion in with the rest. One should note, though, that these elements do not always fall together in the same way. Sometimes for instance, the prestige of the persons interferes; sometimes the need for haste or the triviality of the theme. Even in the example given above, we see that the style is mixed; where we call it simple, we make it simple by eliminating all rhetorical adornment from the pure unembellished text. Here, then, let us append some more examples. Sallust writes in his *War Against Jugurtha* (9.2):

> The courage of your Jugurtha in the Numantine war was truly outstanding, as I am sure you will be glad to hear. Because of his merits he is dear to us, and we shall make every effort to see that he is equally dear to the senate and people of Rome. We congratulate you as a friend; you have in him a man who is worthy of yourself and your grandfather Masinissa.[8]

Likewise, in his *Plot of Catiline* (44.5), the same author writes:

> Who I am you will learn from the messenger I send you. Keep in mind how serious your danger is, and remember that you are but human. Think about what your plans demand; seek help from all, even from the meanest.[9]

There you have the simple style, making the point clearly, without any embellishment at all, using clarity as its only decoration.

IV

1. To these rules already given, let us add another: in shorter compositions always be careful of your choice of words, and be brief. Granted, then, that you have applied all these principles, both general and specific, in composing epistles of either mixed or simple style to the extent that brevity allowed, let us now direct

7. Condensed from a speech which Sallust puts in the mouth of Adherbal as he pleads for help from the Roman Senate.
8. A letter purporting to be from Scipio to Micipsa.
9. A letter which Lentulus is said to have sent Catiline.

our attention to what follows: let us examine, as we earlier promised to do, the variety of rhetorical tropes. First of all, the discriminating man must cultivate a facility for using words accurately; one who flounders for words will not clearly be sure of how to make clear the essence of his thoughts. Nor can he hope to plant his foot firmly on the path of good usage unless he first shuts off the by-paths of bad. By "bad usage," then, I mean whatever leaves a disfiguring stain on one's eloquence; this would include barbarisms, solecisms, and such things. One must avoid both the barbarism, which is the serious misuse of one word, and the solecism, which is the serious misuse of a group of words. Both are improprieties of style which can be recognized as "malapropisms."[10] For example, one might say "hope" when he really means "fear," or "floral" for "florid." In this category falls cacophony, a harsh combination of words in which the similarity between the end of one and the beginning of the next causes syllables to clash. Nor should one be less anxious to avoid the pleonasm, which is the use of more words than necessary. When this appears in a phrase, it is a blot on eloquence; for example, "the stars in heaven," or "he said with his mouth." Even Vergil is guilty of this (*Aeneid* I.546–547):

> If the fates preserve that man; if he feeds on the breezes
> Of the air and lies not still in shadows dark.

Beware too of *tapinosis*, by which one demeans the solemnity of his theme by the crudeness of his language. And do not overlook the tricky problem of ambiguity (*amphilologian*), where one's words act as though they are drunk, unable to establish a firm basis of understanding. This can result from the case of the word, as (Ennius, *Annales* 179):

> I say to you Acida, that you the Romans shall overcome;[11]

---

10. Although the English word "malapropism" is anachronistic in an eleventh-century treatise, yet it most accurately translates the idea of Alberic's *dictio impropria*.

11. The ambiguity results from the use of two nouns in the accusative case, one to be the subject of the infinitive, the other its direct object.

or it can result from the placement of the word, as (*Aeneid* I.263):

> *Bellum ingens geret Italia;*[12]

Or it can result from the use of a word with two different meanings, as in the sentence, *Osculatur Cato; criminatur Cicero.*[13] These are faults which destroy good style and extinguish the light of composition. If you cannot avoid them, flee from them, despise them, then you should not pretend to be a writer.

V

1. Let us move on, then, to that which enhances propriety and embellishes the composition.[14] Let us, I mean, move on to those techniques which good Latin usage recognizes as figures. Granted that they are not of themselves necessary at all, yet by virtue of their own properties they add a degree of nobility, since they enhance, develop, improve, and illumine good style.

2. First, adornment is added to a piece of writing in this way, when an idea is repeated for effect in one sentence. This will be clear in an example (Vergil, *Aeneid* X.149):

> He approaches the king; he makes known to the king his name and his family.

3. There is also another source from which a brilliance by no means negligible attaches itself to a composition; indeed it is as splendid in its effect on a work as is Lucifer who shines more brightly than the heavens. This technique is called repetition, and there is no doubt that it takes many different forms. Sometimes it involves one word, sometimes it involves several. Sometimes it brings the words together at the end of one line and the

---

12. No English translation can catch the ambiguity here. The phrase can be translated, "He shall wage a great war in Italy," "Great Italy shall wage war," "A great man shall wage war against Italy," etc.

13. As above, the phrase can be translated, "Cato kisses, Cicero is accused," "Cato is kissed, Cicero is accused," etc.

14. Alberic's use of the word *orationem* (here translated as "composition") immediately after he has mentioned usurping the name of writer (*scriptoris nomen non usurpaveris*) indicates that he equates the concept of rhetoric with that of letter writing.

beginning of the next, sometimes it appears at the beginning of several consecutive lines, sometimes in the middle; sometimes it occurs in several lines, sometimes only in one. Examples follow which illustrate each method:

At the end of one line and the beginning of the next, it goes like this (Vergil, *Bucolics,* Eclogue VIII. 55–56):

> Let owls battle swans, let Tityrus become Orpheus—
> Orpheus in the forests, Orion among the Dolphins.

In consecutive beginnings (Ovid, *Metamorphoses* I.504–505):

Nymph, I beg you, daughter of Penea, stay! I am not an enemy who follows you;
Nymph, stay. . . .

It occurs within a line either by interposition or immediate reduplication. Interposition is (*Metamorphoses* I. 504–507):

Nymph, stay! Thus the ewe lamb flees from the wolf, thus 'scapes the fawn from the lion,
Thus on quivering wings doves fly before pursuing eagles,
All avoid their foes. . . .

Immediate reduplication, as (*Metamorphoses* I. 519):

> Sure is this arrow of mine; mine not so sure as another's. . . .

or (Vergil, *Aeneid* IV.660):

> Yes! Yes! I rejoice to enter the shadow land.

In several consecutive lines (Ovid, *Metamorphoses* II. 580–581, 584–585):

> I stretched out my arms toward heaven;
> My arms began to sprout black down. . . .
> I tried to beat my naked breast with my hands
> And found that I had neither hands nor naked breast.

In one line it occurs like this (*Metamorphoses* I. 480):

She cares not what Hymen means, what Amor means, what marriage is.

Sometimes it involves one word, sometimes several. How it works with one word only is evident in the foregoing examples; how it works with combinations of words will be clear from the following (*Metamorphoses* I.481–482; IV. 306–309):

> Often her father said, "Daughter, you owe me a son-in-law."
> Often her father said, "You owe me grandchildren, my girl."
> Take the lance or the painted quiver, Salmacis,
> And mix with the labors of the hunt your period of rest;
> But she takes not the lance nor the painted quiver,
> Nor mixes she with the labors of the hunt her period of rest.

But why say any more? All books (books that are worth while, I mean) abound in this kind of device. So study this sort of thing very diligently; after studying it, practice it; as you practice, learn to keep a tight rein on it—a tight rein, so that it does not take over control of what you are writing, with the result that the ensuing saturation of imagery engenders its own boredom in the hearts of readers. It is important to note here that this kind of speaking carries within it its own brilliance always, but it is especially effective when it is worked into the phrase. It may be used at times for anger, at times for admiration; now in joy, now in sorrow; first to add new meaning, later to embellish what is already clear. Note for example how Persius uses it not only in the ways already mentioned, but also by repeating a word in different cases (*Satira* 3.84):

> From nothing, nothing can come; to nothing nothing can return.[15]

And again (*Satira* 5.79–81):

> What!! Even at the word of Marcus do you refuse to believe?
> . . . Marcus said so, it must be true! Here, Marcus, sign the papers.

There is also another kind in which words have a similar sound but very different meanings, as in *obire an abire te convenit* (you must either die or come forth). But this kind of repetition seldom occurs in written matter.

---

15. In this example and the following one, the effect of using the same word in many different cases is partially lost in translation.

4. Another technique like this occurs when one uses a series of nouns without conjunctions, like (Isidore, *Etymologies* I.36.13):

> Clouds, snow, hail, storms, lightning, winds.

Or, "He is famous for wisdom, noted for virtue, of no mean estate, eloquent of speech, renowned for learning, trustworthy, friendly, generous, good-natured." We find something very like this in the use of several verbs together, without connectives being inserted. Cicero did this (*2 Catil.* 1.1): "He departed, he fled, he vanished." So did Terence (*Phormio* I.2.53–54): "We came, we looked about, we were pleased." And the latter author does the same thing when he says (*Andria* I.1.128–129):

> . . . . we went, we reached the tomb,
> [The body] was placed in the fire.

This works best, of course, when we want to bring many things together in a great heap, passing quickly over the individual items. This technique we call looseness.

5. And we should not ignore antithesis, since it adds no little strength, no little dignity to style. Take as an example these lines of Naso (Ovid, *Metamorphoses* I.19–20):

> The cold strove against the warm, the damp against the dry,
> The soft against the hard, the weightless against the leaden.

But this is enough about these things.

VI

1. The metaphor is a trope which frequently appears in writing, and which contributes a certain apparent dignity. For the method of speaking in metaphors has this characteristic: it turns one's attention from the particular qualities of the object [being described]; somehow, by this distraction of attention, it makes the object seem something different; by making it seem different, it clothes it, so to speak, in a fresh new wedding garment; by so clothing it, it sells us on the idea that there is some new nobility bestowed. And what else can I call it but "selling us," when a man takes a story that is petty in its content and heightens it by his

treatment so as to convince us that it is all new, all delightful? If a meal were served up in this way, it would disgust us, would nauseate us, would be thrown out. One will succeed in producing a delicious banquet by offering a greater selection of dishes and thus increasing the variety of the supper. Take care that in your eagerness to please with some novel delight, you do not start serving "poppycock."[16] Be careful, I say, that when you invite someone to enjoy himself you don't afflict him with boredom to the point of vomiting. But that is enough said about that subject. However, let me append an example of a metaphor: "On the feet of reason you move forward; you walk the path of truth, the highway of justice; you never wander from the way of integrity." Likewise we speak of horses "having wings" or we say (Isidore, *Etmyologies* I.37.2–3):

The pine tree plows the sea, the high keel digs its furrow.

In the same way we speak of "the flower of youth," of billows and ships "soaring high." So you should recognize from these four examples the kinds of metaphor.

2. Here we should add to metaphor a kind of figure which we may call enlightenment; indeed it truly is a beam of light, because it pierces as with a bright ray whatever elements of the metaphor are obscure, it seeks them out, it illumines them. You will see how powerful it is if you will examine with your searchlight of explanation not the metaphor itself but instead how far removed it is from the essence of the object it describes and from popular usage. You might carry out this kind of investigation by using the interrogative word "what?" or the universal conjunction "whatever," or "since" or "because" or other words of this kind. It sometimes happens that the question does not apply, but ordinarily most of the time [the metaphor] can be examined in the manner indicated. Take an example. The filth and slime of sensuality befoul the life of a man; the mire of unspeakable lust is like grime. For what other name than mud and grime can I give to something that causes the soul to wallow like a pig in its own vices, to something

16. *papaver omasum.*

that interferes with the progress of the mind as though by putting some kind of yoke on it. It is very important also to note that one can establish the validity of a metaphor only in its own application of the comparison; the same sense will not apply if the terms are clumsily turned around. Notice that there is a valid comparison in saying, "You stink with the filth of your lust, you are wrapped in the darkness of your ignorance, you labor under the weight of your own sin." But if one were to interchange the terms to say, "You are wrapped or your labor is filthy" or "You stink or you labor in darkness," or "You stink or you are wrapped under the weight," this would be to speak total nonsense and deserve only ridicule. So stick with the valid comparison.

3. Now I must not overlook the use of double-talk (*circumscriptionem*), which has the power of applying the beautiful appearance of eloquence to the process of avoiding honest statements; it uses vague generalities to clothe lies so that they will appear to be something else. This technique appears, indeed, under many guises; frequently, the use of figures is designed to further it. Since there are so many other (flaws in style) let us pass over them in silence as vulgar. We will proceed instead to the proper function of the work.

4. Having considered the aforementioned points, build up your vigilance with great care, so that you may watch over, protect, defend your own property, both in thought and in word. If you fail in this, the goal and the method of your work will fall flat: failing this, I repeat, you will not seem to speak at all, barely even to mumble. It is the nature of words that we use them either by application or by agreement. We use them by application if the word itself seems to fit the use made of it, by agreement if the use seems to be independent of the application. It is judgment, after all, that determines the choice of words. When presenting opinions it is best to express the harsh with harshness, the gentle gently, the noble nobly, the simple simply, always considering the topic, the place, the time, the person, so that one does not, by the indiscriminate use of words, destroy the strength both of his words and his ideas. When we have tied up all these loose ends, then it remains for us to get down to business. I believe that the

one thing to be done in order to assure that appropriateness is not lacking is to see that the composition neither lacks any of the essentials nor bulges with superfluities. The former is the cause of ignorance, the latter of confusion. Let the vices be avoided completely; let neither vulgarity nor excessive novelty nor *acrylogia* nor cacophony force their way in, nor anything else that performs the same function. With as much vigilance as one exercises to stamp out, avoid and despise these vices, with so much prudence should he cultivate all the necessary refinements. So you should know how to treat your topic according to your intention; you should know, I mean, how to build a tight case with the elegance of your composition, how to beautify it with the originality of your words.

5. You know what emphasis can be. Its special property is that it magnifies the topic itself, it bedecks and enhances it; in other words, it has the special talent of adding a greater value to the treatment. Nor are there lacking examples to create the images of beauty, like "Even Homer himself could hardly have equaled your presentation of a speech as noble as it was beautiful to hear. Tullius [Cicero] has bestowed on you his command of words, Maro [Vergil] has poured out his learning upon you." Notice how this effect is gained by the use of the pronoun "himself" or [the adjective] "the great," or some such word, often by the unadorned use of the name of a person of great reputation. All this has been evident in the examples used above.

6. On the other hand, we should not ignore the opposite method, which uses words contemptuously so as to minimize, spurn, and crush an opponent's argument, which is of itself noble. This technique we call diminution (*attenuationem*) because of its effect. It is of special importance to use this when showing the difference between two contrary opinions; it can be used, that is, when one party extols something and the other, lacking the arguments to deny it, can at least deprecate it by diminution and minimizing. Thus Vergil says (*Bucolics*, Ecl. III.25–26):

Can you vanquish him in singing? Have you ever owned a wax-jointed
  pipe?

And Ulysses said to Ajax:[17]

You act only with weapons, driven by the force of your rage,
While I have always moved with caution, guided by a clever plan;
Compare and see which wins its goal, my cleverness or your carnage.

VII

1. We should not pass over in silence the three levels of style,
either, unless we want to be passed over in the eyes of history.
We recognize that a suitable simplicity of language gives real
beauty to simple themes, brilliant eloquence belongs to topics of
some importance, and majesty of speech is essential to overwhelming ideas. Let us take care to preserve this balance with
the greatest diligence, so that we apply ourselves not only to
attaining beauty and grace, but also so that we can acquire
delicacy, as much in words as in thought. We acquire delicacy
when we move the heart of the reader to the extent that the
theme merits. Usually one will succeed in thus moving the heart
when he suits both his words and his thoughts to the dignity of the
theme; therefore he must study the subject, the person, and the
purpose. The subject to determine whether it is trivial and
whether it is true, as well as whether it is sad or joyful; the person
so as to determine who is speaking, to whom, when, how, and
about what. One ought always to understand the nature, background, and life style of the person. Thus he will be able to vary
his approach according to the nature, making it different for an
old man and a young one, different for a child and for an
adolescent; he will determine the age levels, so that he can in-
corporate the qualities suitable to each. The child just learning
to walk likes to play games, he sticks close to his peers, he has
learned to fear anger; let him put aside his fear, let him not
abandon his age and gaiety. The growing lad, on the other hand,
now loves dogs and horses and racing; one must recognize that
he is ambitious, eager, passionate, generous with his goods,
flighty, lazy, impractical, a burden to his teachers. A man, how-

17. Since Alberic does not indicate the source of this quotation, it is
impossible to determine whether it is from some medieval version of the
Iliad or from a composition of Alberic's own.

ever, will govern his powers; loving his reputation, he will guard
it jealously; he will avoid frivolity; he will labor over what is
beneficial. Finally, one must deal with the aged man in the knowledge that he is grasping, miserly, timorous, cold, difficult, queru-
lous, self-centered, a faultfinder. So one must carefully adapt his
material to the age of the listener. Nor should one ignore the background, which makes itself apparent in many areas. One treats
the mistress of the house in one way, her maid in another; one
treats the small farmer differently from the small shopkeeper.
Nor does one describe things in the same way to a Greek, a
Frenchman, and an Italian; one expects the Greek to be light-
hearted, the Frenchman to be brave, the Italian to be crafty, and
deals with each according to his own nature. One does not consider a Theban and a Mycenean inwardly the same; the soldier,
the emperor, the beggar, and the philosopher do not all speak the
same language; the thieving pirate and the relentless soldier do
not agree. Besides this, one must also study who is speaking, what,
where, with what aids, when, why, and how; by scrutinizing all
these elements very carefully, he will be able to treat each one
according to its merits. I have now treated theme, person, and
purpose as they apply to the principles of letter writing; this I
believe is enough as regards *ethopoeia*.

2. No less attention should be given to seeing that the style is
touched up, as it were, by certain little flourishes. Whenever an
idea is presented in this way, when a suggestion of these touches
is applied, a writer can emphasize what is good, guide the wise
with his advice, strengthen those who are in any trouble, teach
calm restraint to those who are prospering, denounce the rash,
control the angry, encourage the strong, reprimand the hesitant;
he can love, seek after, and capture a moderate frugality, a welcome justice, and peace; he can despise, avoid, and reject the
pestilence of greed and lust, injustice, and the brutality of strife;
he can oppose the arrogant, he can console the wretched. Moreover, he can love, praise, and extol virtue, detest, spurn, and totally
disavow the vices. Lucan especially makes use of these flourishes,
as we can see from the following examples. Of Brutus he writes
thus (*Pharsalia* VII.588–594):

Oh, ornament of the empire, last hope of the Senate,
Latest offspring of a family glorious in history,
Rush not so rashly into the enemy's center lines—
Seek not to hasten the fates not due till Philippi
And to forestall your own Thessalia. Nor will your plan
'Gainst Caesar's life here count for aught; Not yet has he
Attained a tyrant's power.

Similarly, he exclaims (*Pharsalia* V.310–316):

Do you not feel shame, O Caesar, that you alone find joy
In a war which your own supporters have already condemned; Shall
    they
Sicken of gore ere you? Shall they disown the sword while you rush on
Without regard to right and wrong? Rest now and learn to endure a life
Without weaponry; let yourself call a halt to this evil.
Why press you so relentlessly these men who refuse to fight?
You are losing the civil war!

And again (*Pharsalia* IV.373–378; 380–381):

Greed, being profligate and wasteful,
Is never content with a small piece of something;
And hunger, in its most ambitious form, calls for food to be served
At a splendid table, from over land and sea.
Learn thou how little is necessary to maintain life,
How little nature requires. . . .
. . . Pure springs can sustain life;
Water and simple bread are all people need.

Vergil also writes thus (*Aeneid* III. 56–57):

Oh, inhuman desire for gold, to what do you not
Drive the hearts of men?

But let us take care that our examples do not become tedious;
let us, then, pass on to another topic. If you need any more examples of this, the works of the great authors are rich in them.

3. It often happens also that a written work involves persuasion
or dissuasion, or praise or blame. And if you want to apply the
beauty of style to these, if you seek to enhance them either by
witty thoughts or clever words, you must on no account ignore or
overlook what follows. When you seek to win someone over by

persuasion, you must establish and demonstrate the dignity of whatever it is that you are calling for. Indeed the very mention of nobility to one who yearns for it will of itself increase that yearning. And if you can remember to show utility as well, you will add fuel to the fire. For when longing is based upon dignity, then usefulness will fan the flame. And the persuasion will lack no strength at all if these two arguments are accompanied by a third—the argument of possibility.

Dissuasion is the opposite of persuasion, and is attained by the opposite kind of technique. I will render opposition to something as firm as a rock if I can show that it is ignoble, useless, and impossible to accomplish. Let us look at some examples. Vergil writes (*Aeneid* II.289):

> Alas, child of the goddess, take flight . . .

This is the goal of persuasion. The first reason is that it is useful:

> . . . and save yourself, he said, from these flames.

He adds to this the nobility (*Aeneid* II.293–294):

> Troy entrusts to you her shrines and her gods;
> Make them your companions in the flight, find a home for them.

And finally the argument of feasibility (*Aeneid* IV.295):

> [A home] which you shall build in strength after crossing the sea.

Likewise, examine this (*Aeneid* IV.305–306):

> Did you expect to hide so monstrous a crime
> And to depart my realms, oh traitor, by stealth?

This is an argument of dishonor. It is followed by one of uselessness (*Aeneid* IV.307–308):

> Does not our love nor the favors I have bestowed on you
> Nor will the imminent death of Dido hold you back?

And, finally, one of infeasibility (*Aeneid* IV.309–310):

> Do not in the dead of winter prepare your fleet;
> Set not out across the seas amid northern blasts!

Later on, he writes (*Aeneid* IV. 381):

> Go, seek Italy among the winds, find a kingdom across the sea.

This, of course, gives an impression of nobility in that one grants something because one is forced to: but even in the concession there is an argument against it on the grounds that it is useless. It should be noted, moreover, that dissuasion is usually argued on the grounds of ignobility or uselessness, and seldom on the grounds of infeasibility.

4. Praise and vituperation comes next. This should be properly clothed if it is to be listened to attentively. One can apply praise in any of three ways. It can be offered in terms of the past, in terms of the present, or in terms of the future. This will be clear from an example. Vergil writes (*Aeneid* I.605):

> What fortunate day brought you here?

This is in terms of the past. In terms of the present, he writes (*Aeneid* I.597):

You alone are compassionate toward the unspeakable sorrows of Troy.

And in terms of the future (*Aeneid* I.607–609):

> As long as rivers flow in their banks, as long as clouds
> Crown the mountains . . .
> So long shall your fame and honor and praise be known.

And since vituperation proceeds along the same lines, it is enough that I have demonstrated praise, in order that you know how the other fits in.

5. I would not want to overlook *collectio* (parallelism); although it is a figure rarely used, yet it adds no little brilliance to a work. Of course whatever is rare is usually precious as well; gold, precious cloths, gems—all these their rarity enhances, while stones which are common are despised. The foods that are seldom tasted please the palate greatly, while that which is served often becomes unappealing. *Collectio* is a technique for bringing together different and contrasting ideas. For example, "What you could do in the name of virtue you would not stop doing when it

became a crime; what you lack in calm rationality, you would make up for in rage, though he calls for nobility, dignity, and honor, he demonstrates wickedness, crime and degradation." So also Tullius says when speaking in behalf of Milo (*Pro Milone* 41): "Is it not true that he refused to act when he could have acted with the approval of all, but that he is now ready to do it when it is opposed to many? That when he might have slain him legally, openly, and opportunely, he did not do so; but now that it is illegal, inopportune, and at the risk of his own life, he has not hesitated?" This then is *collectio,* which occurs but rarely in writings but which brings added beauty, brilliance, and power to style.

6. Nor would I be silent regarding *prosopopoeia,* for it is not a technique to be ignored. It is a method of applying foreign characteristics to objects; that is, it ascribes to things qualities which nature does not bestow. It often happens, for instance, that a phrase about an inanimate object attributes one of the senses to it. Thus we say, "The mountain pricks up its ears," "the river pays attention," "the wolf shouts in reply," "the tiger is conciliated," "the answer presents itself." This is the usage which leads us to say, "If you would repeat a thing often enough to a stone, the stone would understand; let not the heart be harder or deafer to an appeal." In speaking concerning Catiline Tullius said (I *Catil.* 27): "If the fatherland, being dearer to me even than life should speak to me and say. . . ." There are some who maintain that this is the same thing as metaphor; in reality, though the two seem much alike, yet it is clear that they are different: the metaphor can be used in many ways, but this is extremely limited, in that it is an expression attributing senses to things which lack them.

7. Now, since I promised earlier that I would discuss brevity, now I will keep to that promise. Let us not be silent concerning the two opposites, richness of language and brevity. Brevity is to be cultivated, wisely used, most carefully nurtured; it is brevity which adds strength to thoughts and lends to them a kind of beauty; it captures the reader's attention, it assists him in understanding, completes his mastery. Verbosity, on the other hand,

degrades the style, diminishes the strength and beauty of the work, distracts the reader's attention and comprehension, generates boredom and a kind of intellectual indigestion. But enough has been said about this topic. Let briefness be your most important study in all things; ponder it, master it, practice it, use it. What do you gain by being drawn off with irrelevancies, making jokes, being reminded of inanities? You will only protect the health of a wounded man if you cut away all the corruption of his wounds. But be particularly careful lest in cutting out the diseased part with your knife you probe too deeply into the vital organs; watch out that in the process of chopping off the foolish and inane irrelevancies you do not carelessly remove something that is essential. Even brevity demands that one say enough; if you go beyond that, brevity ceases, since it cannot begin to exist if the essentials are cut away. Both your language and your ideas must be so directed that you do not escape the wolf only to fall into the jaws of the lion; that is, while you devote such care to being brief and thus avoid one sin, do not fall into the vice of obscurity. For if you lack art, you may become silly; but if you deprive your theme of what is necessary to understanding it, how can you be of any more value to me than Apollo when he hides his face? Therefore obscurity must be avoided; no less, however, should suffocating prolixity also be. Often indeed we are caught up in a sort of trance; we are carried away by a sort of spectacle of eloquence; the result is that we bring in so many unrelated words and thoughts that we can hardly grasp the central idea beneath all the excesses. This is why it sometimes happens that the very thing you are trying to clarify gets lost in the shadows cast by your forest of words; what you could say plainly in a few words you instead render unclear because of too many. Brevity is to be treasured, then, primarily as a means for avoiding obscurity; the essentials are to be cared for, but in such a way that indiscriminate garrulousness is avoided. Here is what I mean by garrulousness: "I consider myself worthy of the affection of all the fatherland; with great joy I note that I am considered in excellence of character a proper heir and worthy successor to the estates of my ancestors, both on my father's side and on my mother's, and am worthy of the blessing of the gods and of fortune." Do you see how I have confused my point with foolish verbiage? I scarcely know what I have said. However, so as to limit our discussion of brevity, we must eschew garrulousness, repetition, involved sentences. Concerning eloquence, then, I am prepared to make even this point: if one does not pay attention to brevity, then he is not eloquent. For if he wanders about in digressions, if he gets lost in making jokes, if he occupies himself with remembering inanities, I would say that he is not eloquent but verbose, nay, worse, that he is wasting time. Let him confine himself to the essential elements, let him labor over them, let him stick with them; then he need not fear, his work will not lack for an adequate presentation, it will have a pleasing variety, it will clarify what has been obscure.

8. And what shall I say about *effexegesis* [*epexegesis*], comparison or simile? The brilliance of these techniques certainly lends variety to a work and illumines it; the one explains what was formerly difficult, the other demonstrates a thing by bringing together objects which resemble it. Lucan writes (*Pharsalia* I.8):

What madness, oh my fellow citizens, what wild orgy of blood. . . .

And he also writes (*Pharsalia* I.151; 155–157):

Driven forth from the clouds by the storm, the lightning
Rages in its sanctuary. . . .
. . . Rising and falling in mighty waves
It spreads destruction and summons its flames together.

It must be noted, moreover, that not all the points in a comparison always agree with all the points of the object [being considered]. Since examples of all this could, however, stretch far and wide, let these few words suffice. But let us add this about *epexegesis:* use it only where some points need to be clarified which do not allow for the use of direct explanation but which demand words of equal strength in presentation. All explanation has this effect, that it makes the explained thing stand out more clearly; and that is enough about this.

9. It is also necessary not to be careless as you study, investi-

gate, and ponder the power of connectives. It is well known that you may use some that are transitional, some adversative, some probative, and some expository; without proper balance the structure of the entire work disintegrates. Just as the various organs make up one body, so these serve to bind and hold in place the different sections of the composition, like stones in a wall. But this sort of discussion seems to be childish; since it can quickly become tiresome, it is better to offer a few general observations. What can I say about the clear arrangement of words? Indeed if the arrangement is carefully put together, with attention to sound and with skill, it strengthens the ideas, it polishes the entire work, it aids in emphasis and in committing to memory phrases which flow easily, it caresses the ear, it pleases the mind; on the other hand, if it is awkwardly put together, harsh sounding and, I might say, like the squawking of a gander, then it offends the ear, it displeases the mind. Both (the ear and the mind) avoid affectation as a kind of boredom. Is it not true that if the strings of the lute are properly tuned, you will play it at length, being completely engrossed, and that you will take pride as well as pleasure in your melodies? Now, granted that this is the very law of human nature, yet in dealing with any things that are supposed to fit together, a man reacts the same way, seeks what is pleasing, treasures it. Therefore the compositions of the intellect should be very carefully arranged; for this reason, let us give a brief instruction about it. First, see that the phrases themselves fit together, that they do not howl dissonantly, that they do not hiss, that they can be spoken easily, that they say amen to one another. Do not bring in strange or unfamiliar or barbarous words, but cultivate sweet-sounding and familiar Latin expressions. By the use of combinations that fit together, one can build his work into a fortress and add a valuable beauty to his words; by proper arrangement he can give new and effective value to words which have become as it were despicable through excessive use. To accomplish this, avoid an avalanche of vowels, especially those which clash badly with one another. Be extremely careful how you fit consonants to vowels, and be very careful how you fit consonants to other consonants. Also beware lest those sounds

frequently come together which form cacophonous unions, that
r, s, x do not battle inelegantly among themselves, although in
some circumstances their juxtaposition might be barely tolerable;
on the other hand, r, s or x with x, or x with s is always totally
intolerable. Notice these examples: *Rector Xerxes, rex Xerxes
bonus.* Also m though it is less discordant, does not fit with vowels.
No composition will fail to be noteworthy if its parts are in any
way at all harmonious with one another. Nor do I say that the
harmony you need is that which occurs in the middle of phrases or
in the syllables at the ends of words, or in one syllable only, or in
the rhythm (like *agimus, assumus, aspicimus*); rather, what I say
is that it is needed "whenever my theme is displeasing to you";
but this will not happen all the time.

VIII

1. Let us not delay any longer, then, but move rather to the
conclusion of this work; let us touch upon the remaining figures.
On no account should the author be ignorant of *conversio*, which
is also called *apostrophe.* This occurs when one changes the first
person into the second, or transforms the third person to the
second, which is more common and a more elegant approach.
Vergil writes (*Aeneid* IV.596–597):

Are you unhappy, Dido? Do your wicked deeds at last strike home?
You deserve it, you who gave away your rights. . . .

And Sallust writes (*De Conj. Catil.* 52.29):

> By watching, by acting, everything turns out well; but when you
> would betray yourself through your own ignorance and cow-
> ardice, then you implore the gods to no avail; they are angry and
> hostile.

This is also a trope, which can be effectively used to say something
as though it were not being said. Sallust also writes (*De Conj.
Catil.* 13.1):

> How can I say those things which no one would believe who had
> not seen them with his own eyes, that the mountains were over-
> thrown by a troop of ordinary men and the seas left in turmoil?

2. Who is not familiar with exaggeration? The effect of it is to repeat almost the same thing unchanged, yet to add greater weight to the way it was first said. Cicero said (*In Catil.* II.1.1): "He departed, he fled, he vanished."

3. We should not overlook the use of varying methods of comparison. At one time you do a thing directly, at another you change to a question; in one situation you express yourself in short syllables; in another carefully constructed verses. The mind of the reader is given life by such changes of style, while things which are always the same become a burden to the mind. Nor is this the only kind of variety you should cultivate; praise and blame should both be present in your work, you can exclaim in wonder, be struck dumb, be saddened, be happy, make your oration serve the purpose of arousing, calming, consoling or reprimanding. You may love one thing and hate another. Thus you beautify your composition with pleasing diversity and keep the mind of your reader fresh with your variety.

4. There is also a trope called *executio*, which enables a person to develop a method of speech in accord with his method of life. It imitates moods, it resembles nature; whatever is appropriate to the topic, whatever should be said at such a moment it works out and produces.

5. There is another mode of speaking as well, called *postpositio* by some, *postsuasio* by others. It is the character of this trope to speak of things that have been done as though they had not been done, and to use them in an admonition like an apostrophe in order to bring out the point desired. Vergil uses this example (*Bucolics,* Ecl. IV.60–62):

> Begin, oh little boy, to smile and know your mother:
> The weary months have brought to that mother great suffering;
> Begin, oh little boy. . . .

Such a style is both popular and honorable.

6. Neither more nor less effective in a composition is *correctio*. This type of figure either allows one to rise to a higher plane or it disdains one expression and replaces it with another. Here is a clear example: "I have poured out on you the love of a friend, say

rather of a son." Terence uses the method thus (*Andria* I.1.29–30):

> . . . Consider it said;
> I suppose you want these things arranged properly.
> Simo. No, that's not it.

Here we have two different ways of using *correctio*.

7. We should not be unmindful of *moderatio* either. This is a technique which pours out, as it were, new light on what was written; it does not spare the object, but seems to soften the attack on a thing by suggesting other words as somehow more suitable. Here let us append an example from Horace (*Ars Poetica* 270–272):

> Yet our ancestors were wont to hear Plautus and his rhymes,
> And to praise them, to enjoy his wit; this admiration was tolerant
> (I shall not say foolish) to an extreme.

8. This is sometimes done through the use of "as if" or "somehow"; at times one may add, "I wouldn't say"; or one may use "more accurately, I should have said" or "let me put it this way." This related technique can be added to those mentioned above; when added, it will please the reader more than the others; pleasing him, it will move him and serve its purpose; serving its purpose it will enhance and sell the work. Rarity will further strengthen it. It sometimes happens also that "in such a way" or "as" is omitted preceding a verb with the conjunction "if" or one changed into a participle and left understood. For example: "How wonderful it would be if you loved virtue as completely as you understand it; if you loved and pursued it."[18] This can be done easily with most participles.

9. These are the figures, the most useful tropes for composition. If one knows them, he may consider himself in the company of writers; if he does not know them, let him not usurp the title of author. Amen.

---

18. *Quid sit virtus, si scires amares virtutem; si amares et sequeris.*

16. GUIBERT DE NOGENT

A Book about the Way a
Sermon Ought to be Given[1]

Translated by Joseph M. Miller

As the twelfth century began, Guibert, a Benedictine monk at St. Geremar Abbey, later to become Abbot of St. Mary of Nogent, composed his *Commentary on the Book of Genesis*.[2] Of itself, neither the commentary nor the fact of its composition was remarkable; both fell well within a pattern of scriptural commentary dating back to Jerome and Augustine, and including works by nearly every important writer of the middle ages.

Guibert provided a major innovation in at least one way, however. Although earlier authors like Pope Gregory I, Rabanus Maurus, and Bruno the Carthusian, to name but a few, had all recognized at least implicitly that their works would be of most value to preachers, yet Guibert was the first to add a discussion of how to preach to his offering; he prefaced his work with a book about how to give a sermon, the *Liber quo ordine sermo fieri debeat*. Admittedly, negative assertions are not easily proved; nevertheless a serious examination of J.–P. Migne's collections of medieval documents indicates that none of the writers from the period between the death of Augustine (430) and the First Crusade (1095) had attempted any organized manual for preachers; rather they had confined themselves to exhortations concerning the need for the preacher to live a virtuous life and to know the Bible.

Guibert went beyond this limited though laudable approach. In the *Liber quo ordine* he demonstrated a knowledge of solid principles for building ethos and for proper use of pathos; he made incisive observations on invention, organization, style and delivery; he showed himself,

1. *Liber quo ordine sermo fieri debeat*, PL 156.11–21. The translation first appeared in *Today's Speech* 17: 4 (Nov., 1969), and is reprinted with permission.
2. *Ad Commentarios ad Genesim*, PL 156.11 *et seq.*

whether by instinct or by training, a master of Aristotelian and Ciceronian rhetoric.

It is extremely dangerous for a man who has the obligation of preaching ever to stop studying. For just as it is damnable to set an example of vice, so it is almost equally worthy of damnation to refuse to aid sinners through preaching.

Individuals have different ideas about preaching, however. Some refuse to do it out of pride, some out of laziness, and some out of envy. Some, I say, despise it because of pride: they see that many preachers display themselves arrogantly and for the sake of vanity, and they wish to avoid the epithet "sermonizers," which describes so contemptible a breed, a class which Gregory Nazianzen called "ventriloquists, because they speak for the belly's sake (*pro suo ventre loquuntur*)."[3] They despise all preachers as of this unspeakable type.

If a comparison between the two is justified, however, the man who preaches out of a desire for praise does the more good and harms only himself. He at least proclaims to others the teachings they need; the other vilely conceals matter he knows to be useful, and so neither benefits others nor does anything to help himself.

Again there are some who refuse to preach out of jealousy. They take this stand for one of two reasons. Either they fear their neighbor's virtues and are afraid to acknowledge him as superior in life, and so they pretend to lack even that knowledge of scripture they have; or else they fear to discuss spiritual subjects with eager and intelligent listeners, lest those listeners may come to equal or even surpass them in their own sphere of learning.

There is also a third kind of envy. A man resents others who insist on good preaching, but burns to outstrip them. For this reason he deals with the more difficult passages of Scripture, expounds matters of little value, and strives to enunciate grave platitudes in carefully polished phrases, not in order to help his hearers live better, but to feed his own ego by demonstrating that

---

3. *Apologia,* Oratio prima. This citation is Guibert's, as are all others, unless the contrary is stated.

he knows more. Yet, even though he dispenses good tidings for a bad reason, even though he feeds his own damnation by his search for applause, yet at least by his action Christ is proclaimed, and that is a source of joy.[4] No one who deals sensibly with the matters of faith is totally rejected; even the preacher who seeks for glory is useful in many ways.

Finally, some men are simply too lazy to speak well. But this is no surprise; if they refuse to put their hands to any acts of virtue, it follows that they are too slothful to put their tongues to any virtuous speech. Where, I wonder, would a man who does nothing praiseworthy ever find the ability to think of holiness in his inner self? On the other hand, there are those who live virtuously and continently but have no pastoral responsibilities in the Church; they think that because of this they do not owe to their brethren the word of holy preaching. This is, of course, ridiculous; if one is mute under the yoke of his own vocation, he is like the ass; yet, according to St. Peter,[5] God willed to restrain the foolishness of the prophet through an ass. But it is much more suitable to use human beings to teach and enforce discipline upon their fellows.

Let us speak, therefore, if we have acquired any knowledge of the sacred pages, as inspired by God, that is, as recognizing that God is the foundation of all that we say. After all, if there is any obligation incumbent upon the instructor of souls, it is that he ought to speak only of God. If he must speak of anything else, then let him treat it as it relates to God and flows from Him as from a special fountain. How great a sacrilege does a man commit when he presumes to seek his own glory in his treatment of things that should tend only to the glory of God. If thievery is the most nefarious action in human relations, what a crime must it not be to steal from God in order to increase ourselves!

Let us, therefore, take great care lest we be counted among either of these two vicious and contemptible classes, those orders, if I may call them so, who exist in the Church not as brethren of

4. Philippians 1:18.
5. II Peter 2:16. The reference to Balaam occurs in Numbers 22.

ours, but as tolerated visitors: the one class of those who do evil, the other class of those who are unwilling to do good. Let us view them as the two sons of Juda, Her and Onan. The former did evil in the sight of the Lord and was struck down by Him; he represents the life of sinners who are punished by God for their sins. The latter refused to raise up children to his brother's name and was justly cut down by the Divine wrath; he represents those who balk at fathering the children of virtue to the glory of Christ, who refuse to plant the seed of the word of God in the hearts of the faithful. They are no less deserving of damnation than those who actually do evil.[6]

Now if the man who does not ward off injury from his neighbor when he has the power to do so is, as St. Ambrose has said,[7] equally guilty with the man who causes the injury, why should we not say that the man who refuses to take measures against sin is equally guilty with the man who commits the sin? According to the Apostle, not only are those who act worthy of death, but also those who consent to the act.[8]

So even if a man is not a bishop or an abbot, if he does not exercise official authority over others, still he acts for the One whose name he bears, as St. Augustine said.[9] He is a Christian; if he wishes to live as a Christian, then let him glorify the name of Christ both in himself and in others.

In Deuteronomy we read: "No Ammonite or Moabite shall enter the assembly of the Lord; even to the tenth generation, none belonging to them shall enter the assembly of the Lord forever."[10] And the reason for this law is added: the Moabites, because they did not supply the Israelites with bread and water during their flight from Egypt; the Ammonites, because they hired the sorcerer Balaam to curse them.[11]

6. Guibert does not indicate the source of this reference, but the story of Her and Onan appears in Genesis 38:1–11.
7. *De officio*, 1.36.
8. Romans 1:32.
9. Guibert does not indicate the source of this epigram.
10. Deuteronomy 23:3.
11. Though the text in Deuteronomy offers the two reasons which Guibert mentions, it does not state that one applied to the Moabites and the other to the Ammonites. Indeed, the actual narration of the incident differs substan-

What do the Moabites and Ammonites represent if not the very same kinds of people as those we have been mentioning: the ones who refuse to do what is good and the ones who do what is evil? Where the story says that the former did not meet the Israelites with bread and water, it is stating that they sinned by failure to act; where it says that they sinned by hiring Balaam, it condemns them for the evil thing they actually did. And the punishment, that they shall not enter into the assembly of the Lord, means that they shall never be part of the Church, the body of Christ, not merely if they occupied themselves with the doing of evil, but even if they failed to bestir themselves zealously in feeding others with spiritual food and drink.

Let them be removed, then, as (I will not say dead members) useless or diseased teeth are removed. Even if they reach the tenth generation, that is, if they promise to have faith in the Trinity by accepting Baptism and if they receive the seven gifts of the Holy Spirit from the hand of a bishop,[12] still it is evident that, because of the iniquity of their hearts, they can never be part of the body of the Lord. The number ten comes from adding three to seven, and therefore represents the Trinity plus the sevenfold gifts of the Holy Spirit.[13] So even though they receive the sacraments of the Church in company with the true believers, yet they remain outside the body of the faithful, like dead members. Even as they [the Moabites] would not harm the Israelites except by bringing in Balaam to curse them for a price, so they [the modern

---

tially from this interpretation. It was the Moabites who hired the diviner Balaam to curse the Jews, and the Amorites (not Ammonites) who refused food and water to the wanderers. We need not be surprised at this inaccuracy as to detail, however. Much medieval use of scripture was based on memory rather than on documented reference; as a result, minor inaccuracies frequently creep in.

12. This is a reference to the Sacrament of Confirmation, usually considered the Sacrament which confers the Holy Spirit. It is administered by a bishop, and the ritual includes both the imposition of hands upon the recipient and a symbolic slap on the cheek, delivered by the bishop.

13. As strange as this computation appears, it is no more farfetched than much numerical symbolism used by Augustine, Jerome, and other great theologians. E. R. Curtius, *European Literature and the Latin Middle Ages*, tr. Willard R. Trask (Pantheon, 1953), pp. 501–509, offers an excellent discussion of numerical composition in the Middle Ages.

sinners] will not now harm their brethren except by first calling
in the devil to assist them. Then, in conjunction with him, they
are willing to launch their attacks against true Christians.

It is clear that, according to the Covenant, whatever spiritual
acts are performed in the Church are common to both the just and
the unjust. When Baptism, the Eucharist, and the Conferring of
the Spirit are administered by sinful priests, they are of no less
value to the recipients than when they are administered by the
saintly. Though it is true that, as it is written, "the Holy Spirit
flees from deceit," yet we must remember that the text in question
includes also "the Spirit of discipline."[14] The Holy Spirit flees
from the unjust to the extent that He does not bring salvation to
those who live unworthily; but he is present to them inasmuch as
through them, despite their own guilt, he dispenses his bountiful
gifts of grace to others. A channel receives water, but only for the
purpose of carrying it to others, without any benefit for itself; in
the same way these sinful men have grace for others, but none for
themselves. They lack the spirit of discipline because "They are
not in trouble as other men are; they are not stricken like other
men."[15] Therefore, as the Apostle says, "If you are left without
discipline in which all have participated, you are illegitimate children and not sons."[16]

It is that Spirit who, because He is Himself good, teaches us
goodness; that is, He confirms us in a pious and whole-hearted
devotion and thus teaches us discipline. In this way we do not feel
harassed when God examines us; the judgment He speaks upon
us is rather a gentle reprimand which will prevent us from being
damned along with the rest of the world. Through this reprimand,
we acquire much knowledge and discretion, so that we may know
that eternal glory follows temporal suffering and that temporary
discomfort is but the preparation for everlasting happiness. Herod
and Antiochus lacked the Spirit of discipline; though He tried to

14. *Spiritus sanctus et disciplinae. . .* , Wisdom 1:5.
15. Psalm 72:5. This is Guibert's citation, based on the Vulgate numbering
of the Psalms. Current numbering, based on the Septuagint, would identify
the source as Psalm 73:5.
16. Hebrews 12:8.

touch them with a spiritual sense of resignation in the midst of their sufferings, though He tried to make them learn something (for the word "discipline" is a cognate of *discere*, "to learn," yet because of their obstinacy, He condemned them to a double penance, here and hereafter.

I have, perhaps, exaggerated somewhat in order to show that the difference between the good and the wicked lies exclusively in the attitude of the mind. The proper attitude is nothing more than good will, devout love, and a clear conscience, the most precious of all qualities, as Christian authors have always taught us.[17] In this attitude we are distinguished from sinners if we so wish; by it we are preserved from their fate. This is the wedding garment without which one is excluded from the company at the sacred table.

As to the rest, all those other qualities which appear outwardly, as the virtuous, so also the sinful give and receive the same; they administer and receive the same sacraments, they perform the same miracles.[18] Let us then be members of the holy Church, not dead, but performing properly our functions in the body of the Lord, so that, as we celebrate the external rites of the holy mysteries in the manner of the just, we may also be like them inwardly, in the devotion and expression of all piety. Let the book from which flows the text of our speaking[19] be a pure conscience; in that way, while our tongue announces joy to others, the memory of our own sins will not destroy us within and dissipate, with hidden guilt, the force of our speaking. Let a prayer always precede the sermon, so that the soul may burn fervently with divine love; then let it proclaim what it has learned from God so as to inflame the hearts of all hearers with the same interior fire which consumes it. For a tepid sermon, delivered half-heartedly,

17. St. Ambrose, *In Psalmis*, 28.1; *De officiis*, 2.1.

18. Guibert here uses the word miracle to describe the acts of spiritual healing and power which every priest performs in administering the Sacraments and in saying Mass.

19. In this case Guibert uses the word *orationis,* which ordinarily means "prayer" rather than "oratory" or "speaking" in Christian documents; the context, however, seems to indicate that he is referring here to the entire sermon, which always included a prayer.

cannot please even the preacher; wonder of wonders, then, if it should please anyone else. And how can a mangled or stammered phrase serve to inspire others, when we know perfectly well that speech of that kind does not usually soothe the minds of listeners, but rather oppresses them with boredom and seriously irritates and angers them. For this reason, when we recognize that our intellectual acumen is not at its best and that what we ought to be saying simply does not come and that the workings of the mind are under a heavy cloud, then, as I see it, we know that no real usefulness can result from a sermon drawn out to great length in these circumstances.

After all, if a sermon ought not to be given at excessive length even when the words come easily and the fluency is pleasing to the heart, how much less when the memory fails, the delivery is halting, and the mind is sluggish. As St. Ambrose said,[20] a tedious sermon arouses anger; and when the same things are repeated over and over, or when unrelated topics are dragged in during the sermon, it usually happens that the hearers lose everything from the sermon equally, because of their boredom, the beginning, the conclusion, and everything in between. Where a few ideas might have been presented effectively, a plethora of ideas presented at too great length leads to apathy and even, I fear, to hostility.

We know that when food is taken in moderation it serves to nourish the body, but when taken in excess it works to the detriment of the body and even provokes vomiting. Or, again, a man who uses his seed properly and chastely in the marital act generates offspring, while he who masturbates accomplishes nothing good and only befouls his body. So a preacher who abuses words interferes with what is already planted in the hearts of his hearers, what he should be helping to grow. For this reason, if the preacher has great fervor of spirit and has mastered all his material, then he can add the possibility of eloquence and style to the essentials, his own virtues. Let him think of those who must listen in silence to pompous inanities, and he will realize that it is much better for

20. *De officiis*, 1.22.

them to hear a few things well-presented than a great many things from which they will retain almost nothing. Then he will not delay making an end to one sermon so that, when he preaches another his audience will be eager rather than resentful.

There is something else he should consider, too. Though he preaches simple and uncomplicated matter to the unlettered, at the same time he should try to reach a higher plane with the educated; let him offer to them what they are capable of understanding. When he expounds such things by explaining them in detail, he will make clear and lucid for the peasants and common people ideas which at first seem difficult and confusing even to the very learned. For just as a diet of milk is familiar and even necessary to small children, so much so that infants cannot live without it, and not to children only, but also to men of mature age, who dip their crusts of bread in it, so also the preacher who offers simple doctrine to the people and at the same time adds something more substantial whereon the more educated can exercise their intellects, by so doing is able both to feed with his words the dull and sluggish of mind and also to inject weightier ideas as well by adding something more solid to the porridge, thus delighting the educated audience as well. For example, the authors of the Gospels, in their narratives, frequently add certain phrases from the Old Testament, using them to make their hearers more attentive thus, when they announced some new doctrine, they reassured their hearers by relating it to the familiar phrasing their ears were accustomed to. Those who wish to explain Scripture now should seize upon this and always seek to imitate it. We learn simple stories to please some, and we bring into the sermon the histories of old and we embellish our words like a painter using many different colors on the same canvas.

Let us also note what treatment is especially suitable to the preacher. There are four ways of interpreting Scripture; on them, as though on so many scrolls, each sacred page is rolled. The first is history, which speaks of actual events as they occurred; the second is allegory, in which one thing stands for something else; the third is tropology, or moral instruction, which treats of the ordering and arranging of one's life; and the last is ascetics, or spiritual enlightenment, through which we who are about to treat of lofty and heavenly topics are led to a higher way of life. For example, the word Jerusalem: historically, it represents a specific city; in allegory it represents the holy Church; tropologically, or morally, it is the soul of every faithful man who longs for the vision of eternal peace; and anagogically it refers to the life of the heavenly citizens, who already see the God of Gods, revealed in all His glory in Sion. Granted that all four of these methods of interpretation are valid and can be used, either together or singly, yet the most appropriate and prudent for use in matters referring to the lives of men seems to be the moral approach.

Although it is true that the allegorical method of interpretation is widely used in prophetic and apostolic works, still it seems to do little more than strengthen our faith. Even though we read the various revelations of God as He spoke in many ways through the prophets, we already know that in the Christian dispensation we have the sacraments which were only prefigured there. By the grace of God, faith already dwells in the hearts of men; even if it is proper for us to teach prophecy, therefore, and to repeat it often to our hearers, it is no less fitting—indeed, it is more so—for us to say those things which they can apply in their daily lives. We speak more easily and confidently about the nature of virtue than about the mysteries of faith, concerning some of which, we must admit, mild disputations are still taking place. Among the less intelligent, error can result from preaching which is too esoteric; but in moral instruction, we can especially learn the utility of discretion.

Therefore, although the allegorical interpretation can be very agreeable to many when it is brought into the sermon now and then; and although it will strengthen our faith and our understanding of the Sacred Scriptures when it is used as it should be used, with moderation, yet all our efforts and all our words ought to deal first with the interior life of men, that is, with the thoughts which are common to all. In such a case, treatment of this type of subject matter will be absolutely clear to everyone, especially

since each will retain within himself, as if written in book, something which he has drawn from the tongue of the preacher to help
in temptation.

The admonition of the preacher should deal as much with the
control and avoiding of vice as with the development and protection of virtue. As a teacher let him show earnestly and clearly
which sins are "natural" and which are "contrary to nature," which
sins are the consequences of others, and how pernicious they all
are in themselves and in what they bring about. Let him show the
fruit of sin in every glaring detail. When the secrets of the Scriptures are interpreted for the unlettered and uneducated, they
quickly forget; they are accustomed to dealing with physical
objects, so it is of no great wonder that they do not possess the
same power of understanding the spiritual, which they cannot see,
as they possess for the material substances which they can see and
touch. Some of them are almost animals and scarcely comprehend
anything, unless it is material and evident even to beasts; they are
completely ignorant of the vices of their bodies and souls, unless
someone explains this to them. Once that is done, however, they
will always, we pray, understand and recollect what they have
heard.

I have said clearly and I have said often that sometimes as
much is accomplished with a discussion of the nature of the vices
as with a discussion of the nature of the virtues. For if I do not
recognize what a vice is, how can I love the purity of a virtue?
And how can I avoid sin unless I am seeking an object which is
good, healthy, and untainted, one which I can pursue and enjoy in
the very act of fleeing evil? There are nutritious green herbs and
there is hemlock; the herbs are of much value, the hemlock is
poisonous. If someone likes to eat green vegetables, but knows
not the difference beween the herbs and the hemlock and believes
that hemlock is as edible as other herbs, of what use to him will
all his eating of healthful herbs prove to have been on that day
when, through his own ignorance, he eats hemlock, falls into a
coma, and finally dies?

The roots, therefore, of every sin ought to be carefully examined,
so when the nature of sin is clearly recognized, its opposite, the

nature of virtue, will be known with equal clarity, as grain is clearly distinguished from chaff. And the more zealously the life which is virtue is pursued, the more carefully the death which is sin will be avoided. It seems to me that no preaching is more efficacious than that which would help man to know himself, that which brings out into the open all that is deep within him, in his innermost heart, that which will shame him, finally, by forcing him to stand clearly revealed before his own gaze.

But perhaps someone may ask how he can be sure of what to treat regarding the interior life of men. I answer that he should master the *Moralia* of St. Gregory and the book called *De institutis et collationibus Patrum* by the famous Cassianus, who is also called John;[21] both of these works will prove extremely fruitful to sincere readers, as will the writings of the other holy authors who have treated this subject. But I think that the most valuable help to the knowledge and understanding of vice for those who know themselves and are unceasingly battling their own weaknesses will be that they are anxiously guarding themselves against their own instability and lack of purpose regarding both acts and thoughts. If they strive faithfully in this, there is no better source from which they can hope to learn about the conditions in which man lives. One who tries to gain mastery of this subject from reading alone, no matter how many volumes he studies, only forgets the more quickly; he never relates what he has read or heard to his own experience. Moreover, nothing is more useful to the human mind than experience: the spirit is always aware of its own struggles and sometimes rejoices in the triumph of its own victory. Also, when the posture of the spirit undergoes a change, when it grows weak in its opposition to the temptations both of the mind and of the flesh, when a man who formerly rejoiced that his soul was adamant against evil suddenly finds himself drained of resistance and willing to tolerate sin, when one's soul vacillates and wavers between hope and fear, then he arises joyfully when God gives him the opportunity and he returns from the treacher-

21. The two ascetical works which Guibert here mentions offer some index to the type of spirituality he considered basic; Both Pope St. Gregory I and Cassian were Benedictine monks, as was Guibert.

ous swamp where he has wandered blindly, or even drunkenly, and reaches the solid ground of rational behavior. Thus he has gone full circle.

When we have been thus trapped either in the mire of temptation or in the quicksand of weariness, God gives us the opportunity of rising again from the struggle in one of two ways. Either He suggests a spirit of penance to our reason and makes us aware of the wretchedness our own wilfulness has brought us to, or He offers us the grace of hearing someone else praise Him, or He forces us to offer consoling words of exhortation to another. On these occasions we must look at ourselves, where we have fallen, and so we are brought to true sorrow. Certainly when we are aroused from languor of soul by the eloquence of another's words or by reading a spiritual book or by any of the other completely distinct forces, we are recalled to a life of virtue.

It must, therefore, be our confession to the Lord, especially those who are "all at sea,"[22] that is, who are beaten down by the storm of temptation, but are still protected in their ships, that is, who still follow the compass of devout intentions, that even if we veer off our course we will not sink while "doing business on the great waters," that is, among the shipwrecks and storms which result from the battle between our bodily and our spiritual parts. In this situation men accomplish good work, because they neither abandon their zeal on account of distaste nor fall into a pit of despair because they are weighted down by too many difficulties. Rather, under the guidance of reason, they cast themselves upon God, who is all-powerful; "they see the works of the Lord, His wondrous works in the deep": in other words, despite the dejection of their spirit, despite the confusion of their wanderings, despite their fear of sinning, they become aware of God's power. Those who are greatly tempted and more greatly rescued owe the greatest thanks to Him.

So, when men who have escaped such dangers contemplate within themselves the state of virtue in which they are placed,

22. This direct quotation and the detailed development of the metaphor of a ship at sea are both drawn from Psalm 107:23–30 (cited by Guibert as Psalm 106:23–30).

the certainty they felt that they could preserve unspotted faith without great fear and trembling, the foolishness with which they congratulated themselves on their own virtue and ability to persevere therein, and their ultimate fall into either temptation or sloth and indifference, they can learn much. First they gave into their passions, then they overcame them; that is they avoided the furnace of their own desires. The man who experiences this can profit much from the conflicts within him which effectively instruct the intelligent soul without benefit of books or studying.

Through these points and others of like nature, anyone having the office of teacher can, if he wishes, be prepared in every detail, first by knowing himself, and, second, through the lessons his experience of interior struggles has taught him; this training will be far richer than anything I could express. In this way the events of his life, both good and bad, are indelibly imprinted on his memory; because of them he is able to act wisely for his own salvation and that of others. Any man, even one without experience, one who has never been part of a battle, can talk at great length about war, just because he has seen warriors or heard stories of war; but what a difference there is between this and the man who can reminisce about war, who has fought or been besieged, who has gone to war and suffered!

It is the same in spiritual matters when we hear people speak with overpowering eloquence about what they have read in books or heard from others; how greatly they differ from the man who speaks with real authority of his own spiritual struggles, whose experience is like a mark to underline what he says, whose personal knowledge is the witness to the truth of what his mouth speaks. Certainly it will benefit educated listeners much more also if the speaker uses his eloquence in dealing with matters they themselves have experienced; but if the treatment is inaccurate, they will allow themselves to become bored or even contemptuous. That is why, when we deliver an admonition to the educated and uneducated seated side by side, we must offer to each group something that is not overly familiar, but is, nonetheless, easily understood; this is how we are able to avoid the tedium of saying only what they already know quite well. So it follows that in expound-

ing the lessons of the holy Gospel we must do something more
than mouth traditional platitudes; we bring in the moral application, bringing in new stones, as it were, for the reconstruction of
an old wall.

Of course there are certain chapters of the Gospels, treated only
in the allegorical manner by the Fathers of the Church, which
were designed for the instruction of both Jews and Gentiles.
Nevertheless, if an alert and serious student of the Scriptures
wishes to examine them according to the other methods of interpretation, such approaches will never, or hardly ever, be out of
the question. On the contrary, when the spirit and the will of the
reader would follow a new road, then the chariot, which is the
holy Scripture, will carry him there. Nevertheless, though this
kind of approach is quite proper for those who have a strong
foundation in Holy Writ, it should not be undertaken by anyone
who has not mastered to the full by long usage the proper way
to collate the different meanings of allegories which use one and
the same subject to express many different ideas.

It should not, I repeat, be undertaken by anyone who is not
thoroughly grounded in scholarship and completely instructed in
how to recognize many different ideas represented by the same
symbols or words. For instance, words like "rock," "foundation,"
"water," "sky," "plant," "tree," "sun," and "moon," as well as in-
numerable others, represent many different ideas in the Bible;
therefore this must be carefully noted by one who wishes to delve
into the hidden meanings, since any of these words may occur in
any of the accepted scriptural uses. Thus, "gold" could signify
divinity, "gold" could signify wisdom, "gold" could signify nobility
of life; the speaker, then, should be sure to use whichever meaning
seems applicable in the text he is treating. Then, as his confidence
grows little by little each day, he first begins to see how easy it is
for him to recognize the various kinds of symbolism in the Holy
Scripture; next he proceeds to the more difficult tasks which he
would never have dared to attempt on his own, moved by the
prodding of his desire for better things, and he is greatly com-
forted in his effort to penetrate these secrets by the sudden appearance of a mass of evidence from the sacred writings. All this

can be done in one of two ways: either by example or by the use
of reason. As I have already shown, he can show examples from
other scriptural texts; and if no such examples are available, he
uses his reason: through consideration of the nature of whatever
symbol he is treating he can find the appropriate allegorical or
moral meaning. For example, if the text speaks of precious stones,
of birds, of beasts, or of anything to be taken figuratively, there is
always a connection to be drawn based on the natural qualities;
and even if this is not clearly stated anywhere in the Scriptures,
still an examination of the nature of the thing will certainly
reveal it.

Gregory of Nazianzen, an amazingly learned man, testifies in
one of his books that it was his habit to improve his mind by
studying carefully everything he saw, for the purpose of finding
an allegorical application. So if anyone at all wants to cultivate
the habit of sharpening his intellect in this way, not only regarding
the divine books, but even regarding everything that comes to his
attention, he will find enough metaphorical material to furnish
him an ample supply of examples and useful symbolism; there is
an extremely rich vein of such material even in subjects which
frequent use has caused us to dismiss as commonplace. These are
considered all the more useful in the benefits they bring to people
and all the more pleasant as well, to the extent that they are not
treated in ways already overly familiar to the hearers.

A great deal more might be said about the use of common
sense in dealing with this kind of interpretation; but I fear that
if I begin to go into detail, I may exceed the space allotted me,
and I doubt that even then could I explain it as lucidly as I should
like.

My next point is that a preacher is especially likely to help his
listeners if he speaks from the heart and without any desire for
praise. It will be clear in such a case that he is seeking only the
instruction and edification of those who listen to spiritual matters,
and that he is not calling their attention to his overwhelming
eloquence for the sake of his own fame nor using beautiful figures
merely for the sake of novelty. For the listener will consider nothing more offensive than that a preacher leave the impression that

he is disputing with his audience either for the sake of gain or in order to display his own talent.

A preacher who is recognized as doing this angers his hearers, he does not edify them; the more he attempts to bedeck his thoughts in outlandish style, the more, alas, he arouses the hearts of his audience to contempt even for the things he may say wisely, and the more he makes people despise him. The very things which he proclaims with arrogance ought to be offered humbly, as divine precepts for the soul.

I have spoken, to the best of my ability, about how you ought to preach, most dear friend; now let me try to suggest a little something about where you can, with God's assistance, find material to speak about.

To every man who is enveloped in a mass of vices it is most useful to describe the pains of hell—how horrible they are and how their unending terrors are beyond description. Make clear that just as no happiness is lacking to those who are established in the kingdom of Heaven, so, on the other hand, nothing which could intensify the tortures is lacking to the man condemned to everlasting torment. Let them know when they are suffering with no relief, or with only brief respite, that the thing which will punish their souls beyond comprehension is this: the fact that they will have no hope of escaping their tortures, not even after a million years, but will suffer unceasing death for all time. For hope, even though it is false, sometimes refreshes the spirits of those suffering adversity, but in hell there will be no hope, either true or false, by which they can be consoled. But for the bestial man, for the man who lives like an animal, for the man whose senses are concerned only with what he can see with his bodily eyes, blinded as he is to the things of God by his desire for sensual pleasure, since nothing you can say about the next life will avail to change him, and even if he could be brought to a brief halt, he would still not understand what you are saying, dismiss this approach from your mind.

What you must say to him is to stress the torments he suffers now in the way of anxiety and fear between the time when he sins and the time when he is punished for sin; then remind him of the fact that he can expect nothing except toil and unspeakable pain. For instance, if someone is a confirmed thief, driven by greed for some kind of valuable goods, I do not think that he will give up stealing out of fear of the dark, which I should certainly tremble at, and not even because he fears the loss of his limbs or the hanging which he knows he must endure if he is caught; but he will be afraid, he will tremble from head to foot, if he is threatened with the loss of what he has stolen. Convinced that this will follow, he will be converted.

I would like to speak of unchastity now, but I can best make my point with the words of the noble Boethius: "What is there left to say concerning those pleasures whose desire is filled with shame, and whose gratification is its own punishment?"[23] One beset with this outrageous lust is torn apart: he burns with the knowledge that his vile desire will lead to a viler result;[24] and while he fears that his acts may become known, he is consumed with horrible and intolerable anguish. While his impatient ardor strives to express itself, he assents, he refuses, he seeks eagerly for a solution to the conflict within himself. He calls himself the most wretched of men, so that he despises himself and loathes his own life, and when he has satiated his lust, what tortures, what miseries, what belated repentance overwhelms this pitiful man!

Regarding this, I may say without hesitation that if the sinner would have as much true sorrow and genuine remorse after committing the sin as he has after he experiences the result of lust or any other sin, then before he indulges in the act, while he is in the act of planning it, he would recall the whole course of his agony. He would think, even as he schemed about how to gratify his desire, of the lasting grief which will blanket him from the moment of satisfaction until the time when the habitual desire

---

23. *De consolatione philosophiae*, 3.7. Though Guibert uses the word incestus to identify the vice he intends to treat, the text in question and the subsequent treatment seem to indicate that the preferable translation of the word in this context would be "unchastity," a translation indicated as acceptable even in classical Latin.

24. The play on words which Guibert uses in this sentence is completely lost in translation: *Aestuat cogitans qualiter pravum affectum ad nequiorem ducat effectum.*

begins again; he would think of the disgust he will feel for himself, and would offer his contribution to God, completely and
wholeheartedly, as the proper fruit of his act. But truly is it
written that "the children of this world are wiser in their own
generation than are the children of light,"[25] and they are more
alert also. It was said to the Apostles, "Do you not see Judas, that
he does not sleep?"[26] This does not mean that the wakefulness of
Judas is more virtuous than the sleep of the Apostles, but that his
alertness in evil ought also to characterize the devotion of the
Apostles to good. And Paul, "speaking in human terms because
of the weakness of the flesh," urges, "Just as you yielded your
members to impurity and greater and greater iniquity, so now
yield your members to righteousness for sanctification."[27]

He knew that the drive and cleverness in a human being determined to do evil would, if directed with similar intensity to virtue,
be worthy of the highest praise. Therefore we ought to bring up
again the terrible tortures and punishments which render these
pleasures so wretched; we ought to recall to mind the foul reputation which by itself contaminates the virture of the unhappy victim
with open or secret accusations. Then, if our listeners do not feel
moved to fear the future punishments which are not immediately
visible or at hand, they will at least fear being so violently hated
as the result of so small a pleasure. They will realize that they can
gain nothing for themselves but a ruined and destroyed reputation
for virture. I return to the already mentioned Boethius, who says
that this pleasure will be very much like that of a bee; it will be
like honey in the mouth, that is in the first suggestion of delight,
but will carry a sting in its tail, since, after the first taste of foul
pleasure, it dies in the savagery of its attack.

St. Gregory has said[28] that nothing is a greater blessing than an
unperturbed spirit. Someone else, on the other hand, has said that
a heart burdened with sin is continually agitated because of its

25. Luke 16:8.
26. This is apparently a reference to the episode in the Garden of
Gethsemani; Peter, James, and John slept while Judas was preparing to
betray Jesus. However, the words quoted appear in none of the Gospels.
27. Romans 6:19.
28. *Moralia in Job*, 12.21.

own urging, since it is consumed unceasingly by internal fires, both in the act of doing evil and in the resultant fear of the evil already done. If, therefore, a man is fearful of eternal damnation, let him be wary of shamelessness in the present; let him take counsel in his heart so as to learn to resist his vile leanings; let him inquire anxiously to discover the difference between the flesh and the spirit (or, more accurately, what the flesh is and what the spirit is). For it is useless to train a soldier in the use of weapons unless he has a strong desire to drive back the enemy. And what is the use of knowing the virtues opposed to the lusts of the flesh, if a lethargic and apathetic spirit refuses to gird itself for battle?

Let us, therefore, take our examples from the events of true history; while we study its deepest meaning, we can at the same time, avail ourselves of new tools for effective teaching. And no one should think that we are suggesting any new methods in this matter; remember what the poet said: "It is proper and will always be proper to imprint our own identity upon whatever comes to hand." Therefore it is much more proper for one who is well versed in the inspired writings, provided that he respects matters of faith and observes the traditional interpretation, to seek out further riches through the various senses of the Sacred Scriptures. Therefore, let us preach.

HERE ENDS THE PREFATORY ESSAY.[29]

29. The remainder of the work begins immediately under the caption: INCIPIT MORALIUM GENESEOS. It consists of the presentation of numerous possible moral lessons to be drawn from the Book of Genesis.

17. HILDEBERT OF LAVARDIN

Second Sermon for Pentecost[1]

Translated by Joseph M. Miller

Hildebert of Lavardin (1056–1133), also known as Hildebert of Le Mans and Hildebert of Tours, was head of the Cathedral School at Lavardin until his election as Bishop of Le Mans in 1096. His ecclesiastical career there and at Tours, where he became archbishop in 1125, was stormy, marked by violent quarrels with two kings, William II of England in 1099–1100, and Louis VI of France during his primacy in Tours. Hildebert's reputation lies not on his disastrous political activity, but on his scholarship. His Latin style was a model of excellence, and his letters were examples in the increasingly popular study of epistolary prose for the next century. His sermons demonstrate an awareness of rhetorical principles.

The sermon for Pentecost here offered is of value both because it demonstrates Hildebert's style and because it indicates the sort of connection one might draw between a liturgical text and a practical application. In this case, the Feast of Pentecost, connected in Scripture with the gift of tongues and with the tongues of fire, leads to a sermon on preaching. In Migne (*PL* 171.592, n.4) the text carries the annotation, "This sermon seems to have been delivered by Hildebert as bishop to his associate priests or curates, perhaps when they were gathered for a synod, such as was frequently convoked by every bishop in those days. The entire content is addressed to priests and deals with pastoral offices."

When the day of Pentecost had come, they were all together in one place. And suddenly a sound came from heaven like the rush of a mighty wind, and it filled all the house where they were sitting. And there appeared to them tongues as of fire, distributed

---

1. Hildebert of Lavardin. *Sermo 52: In die Pentecostes sermo secundus,* *PL* 171.592–595.

and resting on each one of them. And they were all filled with the Holy Spirit (Acts 2:1–2).

It is most fitting, my dearest brothers, that you have come together in the house of God on these days,[2] since the holy disciples came together in Jerusalem on these days in the same kind of house; there they received the Holy Spirit with His manifold graces, so applicable to our own office. Let us see, then, what was given them, that we may learn what may be given us.

To the apostles the Lord gave the power to drive out devils and to cure sickness; He even gave them the power to forgive sins, when He breathed on them and said, "Receive the Holy Spirit. Whose sins you shall forgive, they are forgiven; and whose sins you shall retain, they are retained" (John 20:22). But since they were to go forth to all nations, and were to preach despite many persecutions, in accord with the command, "Going into the whole world, preach the Gospel to every creature" (Mark 16:15), they were first to be instructed and strengthened, then the tongues of all nations were bestowed upon them. They were to be instructed so they could know what they were to preach, and they were to be strengthened so they would dare to preach it. Then the gift of tongues was made so they might be able to address all people in their own languages. For three things are necessary in preaching to the whole world: knowledge, courage, and the gift of speech. If they had possessed knowledge but were afraid, they would have failed. If they had knowledge and boldness, but lacked the ability to speak, still they would have failed.

That is why the Holy Spirit came to them under the guise of tongues of fire. Fire has both light and heat: light represents the illumination of teaching; heat, the zeal of courage. The form under which the fire seemed to come upon them represents the essence of speech, which is tongues. In this enlightenment, it was given to them to know the Gospel perfectly, which they had not been able to understand perfectly before the coming of the Spirit, as the Lord had once said to them (John 16:12), "I have many

2. The use of the phrase "these days" seems to imply that the sermon was part of a synod lasting several days during the season of Pentecost.

things yet to say to you, but you are not now able to bear them."
And elsewhere (John 14:26) He said, "The Paraclete, the Holy
Spirit, whom the Father will send in my name, He will teach you
all things." And so the new law was formed and imprinted on the
minds of the apostles at the coming of the Holy Spirit. They were
stirred to boldness, so that even Peter, who had once trembled
at the voice of a maid,[3] did not, after receiving the Holy Spirit,
even at the voice of Nero, since "By the word of the Lord the
heavens were made, and all their host by the breath of His mouth"
(Psalm 31:6).[4]

We should note my dear brothers, that the Spirit came with a
great noise; this signifies that He was preparing them for the
sound of preaching. Further, we should note that they were
gathered in an upper room. Now it is the prerogative of teachers
and judges to be seated, and they were to be teachers and judges
of the Church. The fact that the room was elevated indicates the
loftiness of their duties and their gifts. That they were gathered
together demonstrates the unity of the Church.[5]

You have heard my dear brothers, what gifts were bestowed
on the apostles in those days, and why they were bestowed on
them. Now the same gifts are showered on us who are, though
unworthy, their successors,[6] for our own good. But since these
gifts were prefigured to a great extent in the Old Testament, let
us turn first to the Old Testament, so that we may compare the

3. An apparent reference to Peter's denial of Christ during the passion
(Matt.26:71). The subsequent reference to Nero relates to Peter's martyrdom
in Rome in A.D. 65.

4. The textual reference is inaccurate; the actual reference in the Vulgate
is Psalm 34:6.

5. The extreme brevity of this series of applications of scriptural detail
indicates that it may have been merely an outline for a more fully developed
explanation. Hildebert used this method of composition at times; cf. the note
appended to *Sermo 28: In Quadragesima sermo nonus:* "This sermon is perhaps one of those in which, judging from the method of citing Scripture and
the few explanations, it is clear that he was composing an outline of un-
assimilated material suitable for preaching rather than the sermon itself as
actually delivered (*PL* 171.471, n.41).

6. The editor adds this note (*PL* 171.593, n.5): "This proves that the
author was a bishop." However, the point about being successors to the
apostles seems to refer more to the priests who were being addressed than to
Hildebert the speaker, so that the editor's assumption would fall.

two covenants and better know what they are to mean for us. We may read in Exodus that on the fiftieth day after the sacrifice of the lamb in Egypt and the departure from Egypt, the law was given on Mount Sinai in this way: the Lord came down upon Sinai in fire which smoked, and thunder and the sounds of trumpets were heard, and lightning flashed, and clouds covered the mountain; the people were forbidden to approach the mountain, lest they see the Lord and lest they cross the limits which Moses set up. Then Moses and Aaron went up to the mountain and were given the precepts of the law by the Lord.

Now notice how the Old and New Testaments complement each other. After the sacrifice of the lamb, after the departure of the children of Israel from Egypt, on the fiftieth day the law was given. Likewise, after the passion and death of Christ, after the liberation of the children of God from Hell, on the fiftieth day there was given to the apostles a perfect understanding of the new law. As the Lord came in fire, so also the Spirit appeared to the apostles under the guise of fire; as there was a great noise in the former case, there was also a noise in the latter. The trumpet signifies preacher and the thunder, a warning;[7] the lightning represents the glory of miracles, and the clouds, the obscurity of the law. The apostles also preached truth and warned of the punishment of everlasting death. Each law was given in a high place: one on a mountain, the other in an upper room. As Moses and Aaron were on the mountain and the people below, kept back from the mountain, so the teacher in the Church draws near to lofty mysteries, but the people are unable to penetrate what is of a higher plane. Even if, through our own fault, we do not understand all these things, my dear brothers, drawn as they are from both Old and New Testaments, yet they ought to mean something in our ministry. We are priests gathered in an upper room,[8] placed on a mountain in that we have been raised to a high office, so that,

---

7. The reading in the body of the text (*PL* 171.594) uses the word *communicationem* (communication) rather than *comminationem* (warning). However a note suggests the alternate reading, which I have adopted here as more suitable to the context.

8. Ed. note (*PL* 171.594, n.26): He speaks as bishop to his fellow priests and associate pastors.

as watchmen of the flock of God, we may protect them against the craftiness of a wily enemy. We sit in the upper room of God's house because we are teachers and judges in God's house.

We ought then to teach those who are subject to us; but he who is to teach must have knowledge of what he teaches. It is necessary for him to be enlightened by the flame of learning if he is to assume the high duty of teaching. It is very rash to accept the priestly office if one has not the gift of knowledge. Only they should sit in the upper room as apostles who have not rejected wisdom's light. And if we are judges, we must judge justly and fearlessly. Justly, lest we oppress the poor, fearlessly lest we submit to earthly power. Those who sit in the upper room must receive zeal and courage against opponents, obedient to Him who said (Matt. 10:28), "Fear not those who kill the body." Thus therefore the fire of the Holy Spirit will be in us, so that we may be found filled with the light of knowledge and the earnestness of zeal. Moses was filled with zeal for justice when he stood against the people of God who had sinned. We read in Exodus that when he had remained many days on the mountain, accepting the commandments of the law and beholding the figure of God, the people, after many days, sinned and worshipped a golden calf. Then the Lord spoke to Moses saying, "Go down; my people have sinned and worshipped a golden calf."[9] And Moses went down and destroyed the golden calf and ground it into dust which he sprinkled into water and gave to the Israelites to drink; then, standing up, he said, "Whoever is on the Lord's side, let him join me." And the sons of Levi were faithful to him. Then he said, "Let each man gird his sword about him. Then go through the center of the camp, and let each man kill his brother and his friend and his neighbor." And they did so.

Moses is to be imitated in this, my dearest brothers: if the people of the Lord sin, let the priests gird on the swords of correction. First, let each priest put on the strongest possible sword, by disavowing the unlawful attractions of personal gain; then let

---

9. The quotations are not taken directly from Exodus 32, but are paraphrases.

him go through the middle of the camp. There let him who judges in this way destroy the camp, being in no way distracted by personal affection. With his sword let him spare neither brother nor friend. The priest ought to break into pieces the body of the idol, grind it into dust and sprinkle it in the water, and give it to the children of Israel to drink. The body of the idol is that of the devil or of the impious man. It is to be broken from pride and crushed into the dust of humility by the preacher's words. Then it is to be sprinkled in the water of baptism and incorporated into the body of the faithful by confirmation.

Now you have heard how you can have the fire of the Holy Spirit; we must see with what gift of tongues it is to be expressed. When we preach, there is not just one kind of preaching to be used; when we correct, we ought not to correct always in one way. What is preached to some people must be simple in style; to others it may be in the middle style.[10] Likewise, some arguments are to be sharper; in others sharpness should be mitigated by gentleness. These are, so to speak, the various tongues. He has the gift of tongues who knows how to use all the ways of speaking. So you will be worthy to sit in the upper chamber of God, my dearest brothers, if you have in your heart knowledge and zeal, and in your mouth the discretion of moderation. He who wishes to rule the people of God without knowledge is like the blind leading the blind. Think, my brothers, what a burden you have undertaken and what care you ought to exercise in it. Two talents are entrusted to you, the one of intelligence, the other of action. Keep what you have and multiply what you keep. It is not enough to keep what has been entrusted to you; you must also strive to increase it. But God, who has made us stewards of His treasure, will guard it in us and will multiply what He guards, so that He will reward our labors in His everlasting kingdom. Who lives and reigns forever and ever. Amen.

10. It is interesting that Hildebert carefully mentions *simplicia* et *mediocria,* but omits Cicero's (and Augustine's) most elevated style, which would here have been expressed *grandia.*

18. RUPERT OF DEUTZ

A Dispute between a Monk and a Cleric about Whether a Monk Should Be Allowed to Preach[1]

Translated by Joseph M. Miller

Rupert of Deutz (*c*.1075–1135), abbot of the Benedictine monastery of St. Herbert in Deutz, Germany, was born near Liège, and was first a monk in that area. Because of his reputation for holiness and learning, he was elected Abbot at St. Herbert, a post he filled until his death. He was quite conservative in his staunch adherence to traditional Benedictine monastic customs, as well as in his mystical orientation, thus prefiguring Bernard of Clairvaux in both these characteristics. His conservatism also extended, as did Bernard's, to a strong distrust of the application of scholastic logical methods to matters of theology. He was renowned both as a scriptural exegete and as a graceful Latin stylist.

In the brief dialogue translated here, the graceful style with which Rupert treated more profound subjects becomes much more colloquial, in keeping with the subject: an argument about whether monks should be allowed to preach.

Monk: You are acting unfairly when you oppose me to my face and deny me the right to speak. It means I don't dare to open my mouth in the middle of the Church[2] and proclaim the word of God. Now, tell me, by what authority do you have the right to seal my lips?

Cleric: I'll tell you, and I'll prove that I'm not acting unfairly as far as your rights are concerned. First, you call yourself

---

1. Rupertus Tuitiensis, *Altercatio Monachi et Clerici*, PL 170.537–540.
2. This phrase, "to open one's mouth in the middle of the Church," is a liturgical text, used in the Mass in honor of a Doctor of the Church.

a monk, so you're admitting that you are already dead. After all, a monk is nothing if he isn't dead to the world; and how can he be dead if his voice is still heard on the outside? So a man isn't a monk if he is still alive to the world; by the very noise he makes when he preaches, he admits it.

Monk: So you think you've caught me! Well, now, I'll just throw your own dart right back at you. I say you are dead too. The Apostle [St. Paul] was talking to you as much as to me when he wrote, "For you have died, and your life is hidden with Christ in God."³ Or do you think he was writing only to monks? The Colossians and all the others to whom he was writing, were they all monks? And was he speaking only of the death symbolized by religious profession,⁴ or of the death that Baptism demands? In the Epistle to the Romans he said, "Do you not know that all of us who have been baptized into Christ Jesus were baptized into His death? We were buried, therefore, with Him into death through Baptism."⁵ So either you must keep silent about the word of life because you too are dead, or you must let me join you, the dead joining the dead, in bringing that kind of death to those who still live in the world.

Cleric: I won't. I'll never allow this. The Canon Law of the Church forbids it and all the best authors reject it. For Pope Pius said that "a monk may not preach, no matter how learned he is,"⁶ and Jerome taught that "a monk does not have the office of teaching, but that of weeping.⁷

Monk: Oh, you silly cleric! You read the Scriptures with your mouth open and your eyes closed. If those words of Jerome were to be taken as you think, he would himself

3. Colossians 3:3.
4. Religious profession frequently includes a ceremony in which the candidate is covered with a black pall, representing death to the world.
5. Romans 6:3–4.
6. This quotation would have to be from Pope Pius I, although I have been unable to trace it.
7. "Ad Riparium Presbyterum," in *Decr. Grat.* Pars Secunda, C.16,1.4.

have been a contradiction to them. You can see that Pius countered his own opinion that a monk may not preach, no matter how learned he is, when the Apostolic See admitted Gregory, an outstanding example of a monk, as well as a great many others of that class, to work of apostolic dignity.[8] And Jerome, who spoke of a monk's duty, was himself a monk at the time he said this about teaching by monks. He had spent his entire life not just in teaching but also in writing out his teachings for others to devour; he is ranked now among the greatest of teachers. Didn't you know that Jerome, whose words you quote as the basis for your whole argument, was a monk? No wonder you blather (*blateras*) so stupidly about monks, you're so completely ignorant about the sacred writings. You stand stupefied when you hear that Jerome and Gregory and all the other stars of the heavenly court were monks.

Cleric: Then doesn't that mean that every one of them was a contradiction when he did the very thing he said should be completely foreign to the monastic state? You say I read Scripture with my eyes closed; you tell me, then, what else can you see in such clear statements? How can you dare to challenge my interpretation? Or do you presume to as much authority for your opinion as for the Scriptures themselves?

Monk: All right, I'll tell you, if you'll answer a few little questions for me first.

Cleric: Ask anything you like.

Monk: You are such a staunch defender of the clerical state, and so violent a detractor of the monastic; you take such pride in the clericate and view yourself as so raised up and exalted above monks by that vocation—do you know even this, why you are called a cleric and what the clericate is?

8. Rupert is not claiming that Pope Pius I (*c.*140–*c.*154) admitted Pope Gregory I (590–604) to the priesthood, but that whatever any Pope does is the work of the same authority. Thus "Pius" simply means "a Pope."

Cleric: Do you mean the defintion? Are you asking the etymology?

Monk: No, it's easy to answer that. A cleric is called that because he is chosen by lot.[9] I'm asking more. What I want to know is, what is the significance of applying that term to the state we're talking about, the clericate? Well, what are you waiting for? Either answer me, I warn you, or be quiet and listen.

Cleric: I'm listening.

Monk: The clericate is not the knowledge of letters or the tonsure or even the cassock you wear; no, it is service at the altar. And here is how the word developed: in the Old Testament, when the Lord decided to divide the land in shares among the tribes of Israel (Psalm 77),[10] the tribe of Levi received as its portion the prerogative of serving in the sanctuary. They had no other portion than the Lord himself, that is, the altar of the Lord; in this way those who served at the altar ate by the fruits of the altar. Thus those whose portion is the altar are the clerics, and the clericate means nothing but "the duty of the altar."

Cleric: I see that.

Monk: Now you must admit that you are called a cleric and that you are one for just one reason—you are ordained to serve at the altar.

Cleric: I agree.

Monk: But I am also ordained for the very same purpose. As a matter of fact, I have been ordained a priest, in accordance with one of the privileges of my Rule. Perhaps while you are only reading the Gospel, I am saying Mass.[11]

Cleric: I can't deny that.

---

9. The Greek word *klēros* means "lot"; *klērikos* is the adjective, meaning "chosen by lot." For the remainder of this section of the dialogue, Rupert uses the Latin word *sors*, which has several meanings. According to the context, I translate it as "lot," "chance," "share," and "portion."

10. "He apportioned them for a pcssession and settled the tribes of Israel in their tents." Psalm 78:55.

11. The implication of this sentence is that the "Cleric" of the dialogue is not a priest.

Monk: Then I am a cleric.

Cleric: Ah ha! Then you aren't a monk![12]

Monk: On the contrary. You think of the two as opposites, as though it is impossible to be both. But your eyes are sleeping: they don't see monks clearly. It is true that monks and clerics are different and that it is possible to be one without being the other. Thus you—or any man—can be a cleric without being a monk; and in the same way any man can join a monastery without becoming a cleric. But when I maintain that you and the monk are equal, I have behind me the authority of Canon Law, which prescribes the identical punishment for a monk without orders who falls into sin and for the cleric who has the rank of Levite.[13] But for me, I enjoy both the dignity of monastic profession and the honor of functioning with priestly and levitic rank; I definitely do not think of you as my equal. There is an old saying: "Mary was a virgin and so was John. But the dignity was greater for Mary, because John was only a virgin, but Mary was both virgin and mother." So the same difference exists between you and me, for you are only a cleric while I am both monk and cleric. As I said earlier, the two are different without being mutually exclusive, for sometimes both states appear in the same person. So you know now that it happens that I who am a monk am also a cleric, because I have been ordained to function at the altar.

Cleric: I can't argue with that.

Monk: Yet you still argue that you have the right to preach because you are a cleric.

Cleric: And that's the way it is.

Monk: Then you can't deny that I have exactly the same right to preach without denying it to yourself.

---

12. This is the only gloss in the *P.L.* 170 text of the dialogue. This line begins either *"Echo, tu . . ."* or *"Ergo, tu. . . ."*

13. Apparently Rupert uses the word Levite to mean Deacon, since he has earlier referred to "reading the Gospel," which is a privilege reserved for Deacons.

Cleric: I'd like to allow it, but I'm convinced that it's forbidden; and unless I find something to invalidate that opinion, I can't do anything to change.

Monk: All right, then, let's examine your original thesis.

Cleric: What thesis?

Monk: The one on which you based your whole argument.

Cleric: And what is that?

Monk: I'm going to show you that the learned doctor Jerome, himself a monk, was not contradicting himself when he said that a monk does not have the duty of teaching, but of weeping.

Cleric: Go ahead. Argue as you will.

Monk: First, you should realize that he wrote this in answer to the blasphemies of Vigilantius.[14] He was defending those who leave the world and give all their possessions to the poor and embrace a life of solitude. Of them he had said earlier: "Monks should not be kept from study by the poisonous tongues and the savage attacks that you are launching. If all became recluses and retired to hermitages, who would instruct in the churches, who would bring light to men in the world?" Then a little later he said, "The monk does not have the duty of teaching, but of weeping." This he said, however, only in regard to the life the monk has chosen. On the other hand he wrote to Nepotianus about the life of monks and clerics—that those who are monks are the same as those who are clerics.[15]

Cleric: Now, wait. You are interpreting that in your own twisted way.

Monk: I'm twisted?

Cleric: Well, it certainly doesn't mean that.

Monk: Then what does it mean? Do you think he was proposing a rule for monks in one place and a rule for clerics in another? Open your eyes when you read and you'll see what I mean. Nepotianus, to or for whom he was writing,

14. *Liber contra Vigilantium*, 15, PL 23.353–368. All the texts quoted here are in cols. 366–367.
15. Epistle LII, PL 22.527–540.

was at one and the same time both a monk and a cleric. A little later on, Jerome said to him: "I know that you have learned from your blessed uncle Heliodorus, who is now a bishop of Christ, and that you are continuing to learn daily what your duties are, and that you have the standard of his way of life as the inspiration for your own virtues. But now take this piece of advice that I'm giving you and join it to the counsel you have received from him; in that way, while he instructs you in how to be a monk, I'll teach you how to be a perfect cleric." With that beginning, he tried to inculcate into Nepotianus a sense of how a man should act if he wears either dignity of office, the clerical or the monastic. For example, he speaks later on of certain acts that are clearly the responsibility of the cleric—such as visiting a widow or counselling a virgin. And besides, the letter itself is called, "About the life of clerics and monks." Concerning that aspect, he says in the same letter: "The priesthood is honored by the one presented for it, and the one presented is honored by the priesthood."[16] And these words ["A monk does not have the duty of teaching, but of weeping"] from his epistle to one who is only a monk and who would despise the very idea are the same as he wrote to Heliodorus.

Cleric: Where did you pick up that idea?

Monk: From the very words of the epistle. Jerome argues, for instance, about whether Nepotianus should go out among the people because of love for his parents or because of his hope for an inheritance; in regard to that, he says: "What business have you in the center of a crowd, you who are a solitary?" And then he adds: "The pious urgings of your brothers call you to the clerical state.[17] I rejoice

16. This adage simply means that when a monk becomes a priest, it raises the standard of the priesthood while it bestows additional honor on the monk himself.

17. This refers to the custom among early monks of choosing one of themselves to be ordained for the service of the others.

for your elevation: I shudder at your fall."[18] And if he says somewhere, "I am not permitted to take precedence over a priest,"[19] he is not writing in his own person, for he is himself a priest; rather he is writing from the viewpoint of his correspondent who is a monk only and, for that reason, does not rank as an equal with one of those who "consecrate the body of Christ with their sacred lips," thus acting as successors to the Apostles. Likewise, in his epistle to Paulinus, he indicates that Paulinus himself is only a monk and therefore has no business going into cities: Jerome says to him: "If you want to have the power of the priesthood, if the obligations and rewards of the episcopate draw you, then live in the cities and towns and make the salvation of others the goal of your life."[20] So it does not seem that Jerome was contradicting himself, since he attributed the authority of teaching not just to you but to all who "bring honor to the priesthood by being proposed and to themselves by being priests." And the Apostolic See did not act contrary to that opinion either by admitting monks to the obligation of the apostolic ministry while forbidding monks to preach. So, please, before you open your mouth to speak, try opening your eyes to read.

Cleric: Aren't you getting a little angry?

Monk: Say rather I am eaten up with zeal for the house of the Lord.[21] You are the one who is angry because you have lost an argument; since you have no arguments, you rush forth to care for your wounds. But, I beseech you, wait just a minute. There is still one more thing I'd like for you to think about.

Cleric: What's that?

18. Jerome rejoices that Nepotianus is now a priest, but fears lest this cause him to lose his love of solitude.
19. I have not been able to locate this sentence in the Epistle to Nepotianus.
20. Epistle LVIII, PL 23.582.
21. Psalm 69:9.

Monk: Why do you think the Holy See and Jerome, in his opinion
that we have been discussing, close off preaching to all
those monks who lack clerical status?

Cleric: Go ahead. Talk all you want, since you have already
started on these amazing and quite odd lines.

Monk: Amazing, yes—and also important. But if these things
seem wonderful or important to someone, then he is not
great or wonderful; according to the Scriptures, he is
unsatisfactory as a witness in his own behalf.

Cleric: Please tell me what you mean by that.

Monk: The Apostle, speaking of preachers, wrote: "How can
they preach if they are not sent?"[22] Simply, that means
that the preacher ought not assume the right to preach
on his own authority. But, as Christ said, "As the Father
sent me, I also send you."[23] The Father sent Christ, Christ
sent the apostles, the apostles send the archbishops, the
archbishops send the bishops, and the bishops send the
priests, all at the time of ordination. But the monk is
immune from this mission if he is not ordained to sacred
orders. So, how could he be a preacher?

22. Rupert identifies this text as Romans 6; however, the actual verse is
Romans 10:15.

23. John 20:21.

19. ANONYMOUS OF BOLOGNA

The Principles of Letter Writing[1]

Commentary

As was evident in the *Flowers of Rhetoric* of Alberic of Monte Cassino, the art of letter writing became the outstanding beneficiary of classical rhetorical theories during the later Middle Ages and early Renaissance. What began as an essential communication development in a rapidly expanding world quickly became the preeminent tool of persuasion in a politically sophisticated society. Where Alberic had used terms drawn from oral discourse to describe many of his points, an indication of the rhetorical origins of his theory, the anonymous author of the *Rationes dictandi* (c.1135) took for granted that his readers were interested in letter writing for its own sake, not as an extension of rhetoric; he offered neither explanation nor justification for his "Principles," but took for granted their acceptability.

The tract consists of thirteen sections, the longest of which treats the Salutation of the recipient. This involves a complex discussion of social levels and the language appropriate to each. Of the other sections, one is as short as one sentence, others run to several hundred words: they deal with the parts of a letter and its grammatical elements.

Nothing is known of the author. He was probably a lay teacher in Bologna. The translation by James J. Murphy is available for comparison with Alberic's earlier work.

---

1. Latin text in *Briefsteller und Formelbucher des eilsten bis vierzehnten Jahrhunderts*, ed. Ludwig Rockinger (München, 1863; reprinted New York, 1961), I.9–28. The translation and commentary from which this abstract is drawn was prepared by James J. Murphy in *Three Medieval Rhetorical Arts* (Berkeley: University of California Press, 1971), pp. 1–25.

20. HONORIUS OF AUTUN

Concerning the Exile of the Soul and its Fatherland; also called, About the Arts[1]

Translated by Joseph M. Miller

Honorius (d.1136) was a scholarly priest of Autun, in the province of Burgundy. He wrote many didactic works on scripture, theology, liturgy, ecclesiastical life, and philosophy. His most important contribution to rhetoric was his handbook for preachers, one of the first such handbooks to appear in the Middle Ages, the *Speculum Ecclesiae* (*PL* 172.807–1108). The tract *De animae exsilio et patria* is also of pedagogical interest, since it deals with the liberal arts as guideposts to men seeking to return to their homeland, heaven. An interesting sidelight is the fact that Honorius clearly identifies not seven but ten *artes liberales*.

Prologue

To Thomas, chosen for the apostolic dignity and remarkable for his many gifts of wisdom,[2] Honorius offers this attempt to seek in the glory of the Father Him whom the doubting Thomas deserved to touch with earthly hands. Because you see with your watchful eye so many persons seeking their homeland, and, of course, straying from the way because they are ignorant of the right road, you have urged, most learned of men, that I point out the direction for them as though I were skilled in this matter, and that

1. Honorius Augustodunensis, *De animae exsilio et patria: alias, de artibus,* *PL* 172.
2. The Thomas to whom Honorius dedicates the work was probably the bishop of the province in which Honorius served.

I indicate with my pen the places leading to it. In this way, perhaps, they may be kept from wandering off the highway to be
held back by false paths and kept even longer from their home,
as were the Israelites who went forth from Egypt, seeking their
homeland in heart as well as in body, and wandered for a long
time in the desert, so that they very nearly did not reach the
promised land. Now, therefore, despite the fact that my unstable
pride may keep me from following dutifully on the path, I shall
try to follow your commands with alacrity. Those who are sincere
I shall lead through uncharted wilderness to the homeland they
know of; those who are vicious and unworthy of that haven I
shall leave in the darkness of their sins, bruised and dying at
heart. But you, as you burn with zeal, inspire the sluggish and
arouse the negligent; stir up the reluctant; draw those who are
willing but weak along the delightful road to a jubilant homeland.
Ward off the sons and servants of sin who are striving to follow
and take back from the dogs what is holy—snatch your pearls
away from the swine.

**Chapter I. The exile of man is ignorance; his native land
is wisdom and he reaches it through the liberal arts,
each of which is like a city on the road.**

As Babylon was the place of exile to the people of God while
Jerusalem was their homeland, so ignorance is the exile of a
spiritual man while wisdom is his homeland. Those who rest in
ignorance are really living in a dark swampland, which is why
they are called "sons of darkness" (I Thessalonians 5:5). Those,
however, who live in wisdom are dwellers, as it were, in a bright
meadow and are, therefore, called "sons of light" (*ibid.*). The
way home from exile, therefore, is knowledge: knowledge of
physical matters which becomes true wisdom when it relates to
divine things. This road cannot be traversed by the labors of the
body, but only by the affections of the spirit. The route goes
through the ten arts and the books dealing with them, like a highway through ten cities and the villages subject to them. This
number, ten, is filled with spiritual implications. The divine law,

after all, is contained in ten commandments, and all secular knowledge can be broken into ten categories. The entire Church is compared to ten virgins, and ten contains all the numbers which can be used in multiplying. Even in the vineyard, the amount promised to the laborers was a denarius.

Chapter II. Of the first city, grammar.

The first city on the highway to the fatherland is grammar. The gate by which it is entered is the voice with its four ranges, through which there is a highway made of the three kinds of letters: vowels, semivowels, and mutes, all of which lead to the dwelling places of ideas. Moreover the syllables of speech, whether produced correctly or distorted, are like the doorways into those houses. The city is broken down into eight areas, eight being the number of the beatitudes and of the parts of speech. Among these, the noun and the verb rule like two consuls; the pronoun is the proconsul and the adverb serves as prefect of the city. The other parts of speech are also dignitaries, to whom gender, case, time, and species are slaves, like a conquered people. Here in the city, Donatus[3] and Priscian[4] teach travelers a new way of speaking and show them the clear directions which will lead them toward home. The villages subject to this city are the works of the poets, which may be broken down into four categories: tragedies, comedies, satires, and lyrics. Tragedies treat of war, as did Lucan.[5] Comedies deal with love and marriage, as did Terence.[6] Satires, which offer criticism, are like the works of

3. Aelius Donatus was a mid-fourth-century Latin grammarian, author of a popular textbook on style.

4. Priscian (*fl.c.*490–510) was an important figure in the history of both grammatical and rhetorical studies. He composed the Praeexercitamina, actually a translation of Hermogenes' *Progymnasmata,* which became indispensable as a handbook on elegance of style during the later Middle Ages.

5. Marcus Annaeus Lucanus (A.D. 39–65) was a nephew of Seneca and the author of *Pharsalia,* an epic dealing with the civil war between Julius Caesar and Pompey.

6. Publius Terentius Afer (*c.*190–*c.*159 B.C.) was born in Carthage and came to Rome as a slave to a Senator. Six of his broad comedies survive; all are adaptations of Greek originals.

Persius.[7] Lyrics are odes like those of Horace, in praise of the gods or of kings, meant to be sung in a hymnlike fashion.[8]

Chapter III. Of rhetoric, the second city.

The second city through which the road toward home passes is rhetoric. The gate of the city is civil responsibility, and the highway is the three ways of exercising that responsibility: demonstrative oratory, deliberative, and judicial. On the first approach we see the rulers of the Church, who proclaim the laws of God and the Church; on the other two we find earthly kings and judges issuing their decrees. The former consider the common good, the latter deal with the laws of equity between men. Cicero instructs those journeying to this city to speak eloquently; he regulates their lives by four virtues, which are prudence, courage, justice, and moderation. The citizens who live here are histories, romances, and books written to deal in an oratorical or ethical way with their subjects. Through these the mind is directed along the road to its homeland.

Chapter IV. Dialectic, the third city.

The third city which must be visited en route to the homeland is dialectic; its great fortifications are questions. Visitors enter its territory through five gates: genus, species, difference, substance, and accidents. These investigations are also called introductions, since they "introduce"[9] those returning home. The wall of this city is substance; the nine towers which girdle it are the accidents. Within it there are two warriors who destroy their opponents with unchallengeable reason; they fortify travelers with glorious weapons, the categorical and the hypothetical syllogism. Aristotle invites them in with his *Topica*, he instructs them in techniques of argument, and he leads them through the encircling deserts to the

---

7. Aulius Persius Flaccus (A.D. 34–62) was a Roman satirical poet, author of six short satires which were very popular during the Middle Ages.

8. Quintus Horatius Flaccus (65–8 B.C.) was one of the greatest of all lyric poets, author of *Ars poetica*.

9. Honorius uses a play on the word *introducere* which is composed of *intra* (inside) and *ducere* (to lead).

broad plain of syllogisms. In this city passersby are taught how to resist heretics and other enemies with the weapons of intellect; these weapons assist them as Amalec once assisted the people of God, while they proceed on their way.

Chapter V. The fourth city, arithmetic.

The fourth city on the road to the homeland is arithmetic. In it, as Boethius[10] teaches, even and odd numbers work together in many ways. It converts a problem to simple numbers through multiple numbers. With the fingers, the abacus multiplies by moving objects and subtracts by removing them; it breaks down a unit made up of minute particles into a thousand segments. In this systematic process it calls odd and even numbers into battle, it explains the appearance of certain numbers in games of dice and reveals the probabilities of chance when the dice are thrown. In this city the traveler learns that God arranges all things according to measure and number and weight.

Chapter VI. The fifth city for those progressing toward wisdom is music.

The fifth city is music. Through it we reach the choirs of heaven. In this city, according to the teaching of Boethius, there is a choir which praises God, first in deep manly voices, then in the sweet soprano tones of youth. The organ is played by blowing into pipes, the harp by stroking with the fingers, and the cymbals by being struck until they echo; also seven unrelated vocal ranges melt into beautiful harmonies. The three ways of playing instruments, by breath, by touch and by blows, bring the dignity of rhythm to the seven vocal tones, thus making a single composition; at the same time the use of intervals and of a balance between sounds produces an attractive melody. In this city travelers are taught to participate in the heavenly concert by blending into it their own habits.

10. Boethius (Anicius Manlius Severinus), c.480–524, a brilliant scholar whose works were much admired throughout the Middle Ages.

Chapter VII. The sixth city, geometry.[11]

The sixth city through which the fatherland is reached is geometry. In it Aratus[12] draws a map of the world, on which he shows the location of Asia, Africa, and Europe; he identifies all the mountains, cities, and rivers of the world, through which the traveler must pass.

Chapter VIII. Concerning astronomy, the seventh city.

The seventh city which leads to the dwellings of the homeland is astronomy. In this city Hyginus[13] uses the astrolabe to investigate the changes of the moon, its course, the rising and setting of the sun, and the functions of the planets; he has built a planetarium in which he depicts the signs of the zodiac and the other heavenly monsters which appear in the distant stars. In this city also, Julius[14] explains the computation by which he calculates the years back through a long series of kings. Here the heavenly bodies dance gracefully in their pattern, thus moving travelers to praise the Lord of all.

Chapter IX. Physics, the eighth city.[15]

The eighth city through which we journey toward our goal is physics. Here Hippocrates[16] teaches travelers the nature and power of herbs, trees, stones, and animals; he leads them through the healing of bodies to the healing of their souls.

---

11. As this paragraph shows clearly, Honorius uses the word geometry to mean "the measuring of the earth," an exact literal etymology of its Greek origin.
12. Aratus of Soli (c.315–245 B.C.) was a Greek poet who wrote a great deal of didactic poetry as well as the *Phenomena,* a treatise on nature.
13. Gaius Julius Hyginus (*fl.c.*30 B.C.) was a freedman of Augustus who wrote *Poeticon Astronomicon Libri IV.*
14. Julius Caesar reformed the calendar in 46 B.C., using the records of the early kings of Rome.
15. Honorius uses the term "physics" as a combination of natural science and medicine.
16. Hippocrates (c.460–c.370 B.C.) was a Greek natural philosopher, the father of medicine, and author of numerous works on natural science.

Chapter X. Concerning the mechanical arts, the ninth city.[17]

The ninth city on the road to our native land is mechanics. It teaches travelers how to work with metals, wood, and stones, and how to produce paintings, statues, and other works of beauty which proceed from the minds of men. Here Nimrod built his tower,[18] here Solomon constructed his temple (I Kings 6), here also Noe fashioned his ark as a fortress for the whole world (Genesis 6), and here we learn how to weave all sorts of garments.

Chapter XI. Economics, the tenth city.

The tenth city is economics, which leads us to the treasure houses of heaven. This city disposes of kingdoms and honors, it identifies dignities and nobility of rank. It teaches men who are traveling homeward where they rank according to their merits in relation to the angels.

Chapter XII. Having followed the liberal arts, we reach our homeland, true wisdom, which shines forth from the pages of Holy Scripture and reaches perfection in the vision of God.

After passing through all these arts, as through so many cities, we come at last to the Sacred Scriptures, our true fatherland, where wisdom rules in all its aspects. Indeed, Scripture has built for itself a house which it supports with the seven gifts of the Holy Spirit as its columns (Proverbs 9:1). It uses four kinds of interpretation to form its four walls: these are the historical, allegorical, tropological, anagogical.[19] The historical interpretation simply expounds the event as it is; thus, Jerusalem is a city of the

17. Honorius uses the word *mechanica* to describe the creative arts.
18. Although the book of Genesis tells the story of the Tower of Babel (Gen. 11) shortly after identifying Nimrod (Gen. 10:8), there is no other reason to connect the two.
19. The following explanation of the possible ways of interpreting Scripture is a perfect example of the medieval use of commonplaces. Not only do the ideas appear in nearly every discussion of scriptural interpretation from Augustine on, but the same words appear in many of these. For example, both Guibert de Nogent's *Liber que ordino sermo fieri debeat* (PL 156.25) and the Victorine *Sermones centum* (PL 179.999) use the explanation almost verbatim.

Jews in which the temple was located. An allegory is the application which uses one thing to represent another; for example, Jerusalem represents the Church, and we ourselves are symbolized by the temple of the Lord. Tropology is the moral interpretation; according to this, Jerusalem is any faithful soul, who has a pure heart as the temple in which the dweller is the Holy Spirit. The anagogical sense is a transcendental application, relating directly to God and to eternal life; thus, Jerusalem is the heavenly city in which the saints are united with the angels in experiencing the presence of God (Apoc. 21). In this house [Scripture] Wisdom prepares a banquet for those who come to her, and fills them with varying and delicious foods. At last she will lead them into the heavenly Jerusalem, where the King of Glory is visible in all his majesty, whose beauty even the sun and moon adore. Here the nine choirs of angels never cease to praise the King of Kings, upon whom they long to gaze without end. In this country, the patriarchs prefigure Christ in their persons, the prophets proclaim His coming through their writings, the apostles preach Him to the world through their virtues and their miracles, the martyrs offer their blood to Him, the virgins adore Him by offering their chastity. In this land also those who wish may climb the mountain of contemplation, there to behold Christ in snow-white garments, standing between Moses and Elias, radiant as the sun. Through the Sacred Scripture they come to know Him as judge of the living and the dead, coequal with the Father, and they recognize the glory of visible creation in which He is clothed.

Chapter XIII. God will be seen by His Saints, each according to his own merits.

Now, to meditate on such things is to contemplate heaven. When we have put off this flesh and see all these things face to face, it will mean that we are enjoying the rewards of heaven. There are many mansions there, that is, many ways of seeing God. In these mansions, the saints will see the God of gods in Sion (that is, in the beatific vision) as they go from virtue to virtue. For example, the good will see God as an extension of their own goodness; the just will see Him as the perfection of their justice;

the wise will see Him as embracing all wisdom; the peacemakers will see Him as absolute peace; and all others will see Him as infinite in their own virtues.

Chapter XIV. God can be comprehended perfectly by no one except Himself. The vision of God will delight the Blessed forever; the memory of the crimes they have committed will torture the wicked without ceasing.

According to a statement which surpasses all understanding, no one has ever seen God and no one ever will see Him. "No one has ever known the Father except the Son, nor has any one known the Son except the Father only" (Matt. 11).[20] Yet whenever the ancients received a revelation of God, they referred to it as to God Himself; thus Jacob said, "I have seen God face to face" (Genesis 32). Likewise it was said of Moses, "Moses talked with God, face to face, as with a friend" (Exodus 33). And the prophet wrote, "I saw the Lord sitting upon a throne, high and lifted up" (Isaiah 6). Also the clean of heart will see God in Sion, that is, in the beatific vision, when He will appear to each in a different way and will manifest Himself to those who love Him. Each one will see God according to the ideal he has sought within himself and in all other creatures when God is all in all. Those who attain this kingdom will see the King of Glory in all His majesty, and He will be their joy and the light of their eyes. On the other hand, those who have found delight in transitory pleasures will remain in exile; they will go down into darkness and will flee from the light forever, as though their eyes were wounded by it. Instead they will endure many different visions of vice, which will run about before their eyes like savage beasts. These they will strive constantly to escape, though they prove unable to do so; rather new visions will continually thrust themselves in among the old, and they will sink deeper in their horrible chasm of misery and despair. Therefore train yourself in these matters, and teach others what they must do. Thus you will escape these visions and attain to the ones we discussed before. Amen.

20. The slight inaccuracy in this quotation illustrates the medieval habit of quoting Scripture from memory, sometimes at the cost of exactness.

21. HUGH OF ST. VICTOR

Didascalicon[1]

Commentary

Although Hugh of St. Victor (1097–1141) composed no specifically
rhetorical treatise, his *Didascalicon* (*The Matter of Teaching*) is an
important work for the student of rhetorical theory; because Hugh was
concerned with how men arrived at wisdom, he perforce included his
discussion of rhetoric in the context of man's use of logic. He argued
that logic, the last of the theoretical arts was divided into a linguistic
and a rational science. Rational logic included argumentative logic,
which he further divided into linguistic and rational science. Hugh
accepted as fact that men wrote and spoke before grammar was perfected; they distinguished the true from the false before there was
dialectic; and they discoursed on civil laws before there was rhetoric.
Still, after men discovered and perfected the arts, their usage also
became more perfect. For the men of Hugh's generation, the arts were
closely related (as was clear in the *De animae exsilio* of Honorius), yet
each art had its own characteristics.

In the *Didascalicon*, IV.1, Hugh notes that "wisdom is a kind of
moderator over all human actions . . . the actions of the rational soul
are not swept away by blind impulse but are always preceded by Wisdom as their guide," and he defines philosophy as the discipline which
investigates comprehensively the ideas of all things, human and divine.
In *Didasc.*, II.1, he refers to philosophy as "the art of arts and the
discipline of disciplines," because all other arts and disciplines are
oriented toward it. He divides philosophy into theoretical, or specula-
tive, wisdom (including theology, mathematics, and physics); practical
wisdom (solitary, private, and public knowledge); mechanical wisdom
(fabric making, armament, commerce, agriculture, medicine, hunting,
theatrics); and logical wisdom (grammar and argument); argument he

1. Hugh of St. Victor, *The Didascalicon of Hugh of St. Victor: A Medieval
Guide to the Arts,* translated from the Latin by Jerome Taylor (New York:
Columbia University Press, 1961).

207

then divides into demonstration, probable argument, and sophistic, and probable argument he subdivides into dialectic and rhetoric.

In Hugh's appendix to the *Didascalicon,* intended for eventual incorporation into the text, he stresses that while logic was the last art to be discovered, it should be learned first by the true seeker of wisdom. To overcome life's three chief evils, ignorance, vice, and life's weakness, the eloquence born of devotion to logic is, according to Hugh, man's chief asset. Having learned grammar and argument as key aspects of logical wisdom, the seeker must learn ethics, so that the eye of his heart may be cleansed by the study of virtue, and may subsequently see clearly for the investigation of truth in the theoretical and mechanical arts. Without eloquence and ethics, Hugh asserts, any other knowledge is useless.

22. WIBALDUS OF STAVELOT

Letter to Manegold (EXCERPT)[1]

Translated by Gerard Ellspermann, O.S.B.

Wibaldus (1098–1158), an outstanding scholar and humanist, served at various times as abbot at Monte Cassino, Corvey, and Stavelot. Because of his political acumen, he exercised great influence over decisions of the emperor, Conrad III (1138–1152).

In a letter written to Wibaldus during 1149, one of his admiring protégés, Manegold, Master of the School at Patherburn, praised the abbot for his learning and his ability to arouse enthusiasm for learning in others (*PL* 149.1248–1249). In response to this, Wibaldus composed a brief outline of his philosophy of education, emphasizing his attitude toward the liberal arts. The following paragraphs from that letter, though not exclusively concerned with rhetoric, include in their somewhat random comments a number of statements which shed much light on twelfth-century German attitudes toward rhetoric as the art of oral discourse.

The translation has been prepared especially for *Readings in Medieval Rhetoric* by Gerard Ellspermann, O.S.B., Ph.D., Prior of St. Meinrad Archabbey and Professor of Classics and Homiletics at St. Meinrad Seminary.

This rather long digression[2] has been for this sole purpose, that you may know that unless God is known, unless He is loved, it is of little or no avail to be able to write correctly, to read aloud clearly, to speak distinctly, to know all the categories and fonts of argumentation, to persuade by speech, to understand the power and nature of numbers, to perceive the difference between

1. *Wibaldi abbatis ad Mangoldum scholae magistrum* (Epist. 147), *PL* 149.1249–1257. The excerpt appears in cols. 1253–1256.
2. In the first part of the letter, Wibaldus has discussed the importance of study and application of the liberal arts to the Christian life.

harmony and intervals, to excel in the use of the abacus, the
sundial, and the astrolabe, to pass judgment on the shapes and
areas of figures.[3] But if we have learned to know Him, if in loving
Him we have followed Him, and if in following Him we have
come to Him, then we shall know all things with Him who knows
all. Though unlearned and unlettered, one can gather his material
intelligently, sift it discretely, and discuss it fully. This is the
correct way to learn—the way that leads to being, for every living
creature fears not to be.

I encourage you, then, I exhort you, to read and not be negligent; i.e., read books, but don't neglect your conduct. "A good
understanding belongs to all who do it: the servant who knows the
will of God and fails to do it will be whipped with many blows,
and the mighty will be mightily punished."[4]

Subtleties and sophistic conclusions (which are called Guali-
dian, after a certain Gualo) you should neither use proudly nor
entirely contemn. Examples of such are:

> What you have not lost, you have;
> But you have not lost horns;
> Therefore you have horns.

or:

> *Mus* (mouse) is a syllable;
> But a syllable does not nibble cheese;
> Therefore *mus* (a mouse) does not nibble cheese.

Our lord and king, Conrad, used to marvel at the remarks which
were spoken artfully by lettered men, and he was wont to say
that it was not possible to prove that man was an ass. Once, when
we had been jovial at a meal, and a good crowd of learned men
were with us, I said to him that in the course of nature that this
was not possible; but if one makes an unlimited concession, a lie
springing from the truth may be embraced as a false conclusion.

---

3. Although this is a very loose translation of the Latin *complexiones et
graduum connexiones judicare,* it seems the only one justified by the context,
which is a listing of the talents connected with each of the other six liberal
arts; a reference to geometry is essential at this point.

4. This quotation from the Bible is an adaptation of phrases from three
unrelated texts: Psalm 110:11 (RSV), Luke 12:47, and Wisdom 6:7.

But when he did not comprehend, I made a sally with a ridiculous sophism:

"Do you have one eye?" I asked.

When he answered that he had, I countered, "Do you then have two eyes?"

And when he again assented without reservation, I said, "One and two are three. Therefore you have three eyes."

Captivated by this sophistry, he swore that he had only two eyes; still, enlightened by these and many other examples, he continued to hold that an educated man enjoyed a pleasant life.

But, on the other hand, if it is true that we can't possibly answer all these, what danger, I ask, hangs over us? When the chance has been missed to consider correctly justice, compassion, temperance, the two types of chastity (both the one that refers to keeping away from another's body and the one that refers to one's own), then a real loss results, not just because the public carrying out of a dispute has been made to appeal to popular taste, but because the real conduct of life has suffered a loss. Finally, I must say that when you allot to me some eloquence, your judgment has been deceived by your love.

It requires no little time, no small effort, no mean dedication, to know the strength and nature of rational souls, to arouse the sluggish, to hold back the hasty, and expertly to bend the strong of mind. For granted that one's nature is agreeable, open, receptive to whatever forms are suggested, yet even if the teacher serves them up diligently and fully, when the lesson is not augmented by frequent use (as has long been the case in monastic cloisters), light becomes suffocated by darkness, fire is no longer maintained in the embers, but becomes extinguished. The orator must both be attacked and attack, that he may know how to protect himself and his own with the shield and how to strike with the sword.

Read Quintilian's book on the foundation of oratory.[5] He began

----

5. Wibaldus does not capitalize the title of the work, but uses the phrase *de institutione oratoria* as a descriptive identification. It must be remembered that the great re-discovery of Quintilian's work did not take place until three centuries later (see 36: *Two Letters* of Poggio, below).

to form the infant immediately after birth, and to mold him in the shape of a perfect orator. This study and power is far removed from our own age. All legal activity is either ecclesiastical or secular. Now in the court of law, laymen who are illiterate, though sometimes gifted with great natural ability, expound the law. Among the German people, the practice of declaiming is quite rare, for their speakers make their points quickly and, so to speak, by means of illustrations rather than by explanations.

The other kind of law, called canonical, is administered by the most learned men of letters, in whose mouths is the law of the Lord. From this law they hear the words, "Judge not, that you be not judged" (Matt. 7:1), and so learn that among Christians a man is not truly wretched when he suffers injury, but when he causes it. In the edict of the supreme lawgiver they read, "Let your speech be 'Yes, yes,' 'No, no'; what goes beyond that is from the evil one" (Matt. 5:37). One speaker in that highest court says, "Turn away the reproach that I dread" (Psalm 119:39 (RSV). But if nothing is recognized as subject to proof or disproof from suspicion, conjecture, or circumstance, then there is left only the unvarnished presentation of the case. Have you done that? Either I have or I have not.

Brilliant men among the pagans have established in their rules that the accuser (censor) should speak in one way, the advocate in another. The advocate is allowed to use false maxims, lies, deceits, quibblings, just so long as they appear true; they are allowed to insinuate with any kind of subtlety, if their purpose is to influence men's minds. Moreover, advocates think it is wrong to leave any tool unused to challenge and assault an unfavorable case. However it is not proper for a holy man, one blessed with faith and a deep seriousness, to present to the ears of Christians anything which does not seem to be true either to himself or to all men. The man who speaks elegantly in a canonical case seems to be more interested in his own glory than in presenting what is necessary for the case itself. The strictest Areopagites of Greece and judges of Athens allowed one to use neither introductions nor epilogues, but only narration, simple and with a minimum of elaboration. Thus they almost shook the foundations of rhetoric.

Yet at times there are in the Church certain eventful moments when the artistry of eloquence is employed without blame, and especially (we can say this) in the office of preaching. In my judgment, at least, at the head of those so gifted stands a man of our times, the exceedingly illustrious abbot, Bernard of Clairvaux. With good reason I would call him an orator, since rhetoricians describe an orator as "a good man skilled in speaking." For that good man, worn out by the roughness of the desert, its fasts and mustiness, and reduced to a thinness consonant with a spiritual image, first persuaded others as soon as he was seen, even before he was heard. He was blessed by God with an excellent disposition, with the best learning, with outstanding energy, with a great deal of experience, precise habits of speech and bodily movement, perfectly accommodated to every type of speaking. It does not come as a surprise, then, that he, by the powerful influence of his great talents, stirs up those who are asleep, yes, I could even say the dead. By virtue of God's help and backing he changes men, and those who had been in the service of the chariots of Pharaoh he now subdues to the yoke of God. Indeed you would have termed him eloquent who did not tear down with his actions what he preached with his mouth, who is not inwardly a Nero and outwardly a Cato.

If you see the examples of another, you are taught; if you listen to another, you are instructed; if you follow another, you are brought to perfection. And so, if you are moved by the fame coming from eloquence, pick out someone to emulate, and let your spirit be gently touched by his eloquence. It is the unanimous opinion of the best speakers that there is a greater possibility of speaking more elegantly and fluently by imitating the eloquent than by following the rules of rhetoric.

But up to this point, how knowledgeable you are about these matters in which I am ignorant! Influenced by the testimony of your friendship and not of truth, you have praised my manner of life. But if you had been brought into the dwelling place of my heart (which is small and inscrutable) and if, in the course of my mind's judgment when reason sits on the judgment seat, you would listen to the most serious clamorings and bitter questionings of my thoughts tumbling out in accusation, one against the other, where neither tonsure nor monk's garb nor sickly pallor nor leanness can cast their vote, there you would be looking at a terrifying human being, more ugly than any ogre. At that scene, the plaintiff earnestly submits convincing and truth-laden arguments; there too the defendant is conspicuous by his absence or else acknowledges his guilt. And be careful not to say that moral character comes from nature, because "every good gift and every perfect gift is from above, coming down from the Father of lights" (James 1:17).

For, though I was conceived in the summer and born in the spring (which times are considered in the opinions of your natural philosophers the best combination of circumstances), yet by the grace of God I am what I am and daily with His help, I strive to become better. It is not then the circumstances of my birth or of my descent from my particular parents that make me live as I do, but it is the effect of divine grace which runs before me and helps me. And to this grace, which calls, yes, draws me, I can't afford as an ungrateful creature, to kick against the goad and resist. To be sure, I do have brothers in behalf of whom God has not deigned to show forth the great power of His goodness. You praise my household highly. Indeed it is much better than I deserve, but still it is not as well ordered as I would wish.

In the remainder of the letter, Wibaldus discusses problems he is encountering in his monastery, and adds an interesting interpretation of the spelling of his name.

23. JOHN OF SALISBURY

Metalogicon[1]

Commentary

John of Salisbury (1115–1180), one of the most learned men of his time, composed the *Metalogicon*, which offered an analysis of Aristotle's treatise on logic. Though himself a Scholastic, John was concerned about the lack of practical utility in such subjects as logic, dialectic, and rhetoric, as these appeared in the works both of the ancients and of his own contemporaries. Recalling his own days as a student, under learned but vain masters like Alberic of Rheims, who was full of questions about every subject, and Robert of Melun, who was full of answers for every question, John concluded that he had learned far more from scholars like Richard the Bishop, Peter Helias, and Master Adam of Littlebridge, who taught him both the theoretical bases and the practical uses of dialectic and rhetoric.

John's attacks against the empty Scholastic disputations of his day did not present a direct challenge to traditional Aristotelian and Scholastic logic and rhetoric; but they were in the English tradition which had first raised its head in Bede's stylistic emphasis: they foreshadowed the revolt which led Peter Ramus to say in the mid-1500's that all Aristotle had written was false and to divide dialectic from rhetoric, and they pointed the way for the Port Royalist rejection of Scholastic deductive logic in favor of inductive reasoning. While John of Salisbury, like Hugh of St. Victor, did not offer a comprehensive treatise on rhetoric, his *Metalogicon*, like Hugh's *Didascalicon*, concerns itself with the entire educational system of the later Middle Ages. In it John struggles to make relevant on a practical as well as a theoretical level the educational principles which had come to his generation from the ancients, so that his students would have material of value to pass on.

John resembles Hugh of St. Victor in the way he envisions eloquence to be the ability and facility to express one's mental perceptions ver-

1. John of Salisbury. *The Metalogicon*, trans. by Daniel McGarry (Berkeley: University of California Press, 1955; reprinted, 1971).

bally. He holds that nothing is quite so useful, nothing is to be preferred to this precious gift of nature and grace. Quoting Horace, John lists in order the things to be desired: "Virtue and wisdom, which perhaps, as Victorinus believes, differ in name rather than in substance, rank first among the desiderata, but eloquence comes second. Third is health, and after this, in fourth place, the good will of one's associates and an abundance of goods, to provide the material instruments of action."[2] Eloquence adorns men of all ages, but it particularly serves the young, the prosperous and wealthy, and the most powerful and successful. John disputes the Cornifician claim that a person must be naturally eloquent, eschewing all dependence on effort and instruction, by citing examples of well-known persons who achieved eloquence by study and care. Further, against the same Cornificians, who hold that all arts which promise eloquence are useless, and who would, therefore, do away with logic, John responds that in destroying logic as the cornerstone of eloquence, they thereby block the way to philosophical studies, and exclude both sense and success from all understanding.

John defines logic in its broadest sense as "the science of verbal expression and (argumentative) reasoning." He argues, "If, as has frequently been observed (and as no one denies), the use of speech is so essential, the more concisely it (the use of speech) is taught, the more useful and certainly the more reliable will be the teaching."[3] Agreeing with Aristotle and numerous others who have held that argumentative reasoning does not profess to bring about the impossible (on which there is no need to attempt persuasion), John offers a concise and direct method of doing what is possible.

John's arguments for dialectic, grammar, and rhetoric as the trivium, making up, in conjunction with the quadrivium, what are called the liberal arts, are still cogent in the twentieth-century liberal arts context. He calls them arts either because they delimit by rules and precepts, or from the Greek *ares,* because they are virtues which strengthen the mind to apprehend the ways of wisdom, or from the Greek *arso,* because they represent the reason which the arts nourish and cause to grow. He calls such arts as grammar, dialectic, and rhetoric "liberal" either because the ancients took care to have their children (*liberi*)

---

2. *Metalogicon,* p.27.
3. *Metalogicon,* p.32.

instructed in them, or because their object is to effect man's liberation, so that, free from cares, he may devote himself to wisdom as his first goal. While John agrees with Cicero that eloquence without wisdom is futile, he insists that eloquence becomes positively harmful when it is divorced from wisdom, because the utility of eloquence is in direct proportion to the measure of a man's wisdom.

24. PHILIP OF HARVENG

On the Training of
the Clergy, VI.20[1]

Translated by Joseph M. Miller

Philip of Harveng (d.1187), second abbot of the Premonstratensian monastery of Bona Spes, left an indication of how far an understanding of eloquence had entered into the training of preachers in *De silentio clericorum* (*On the Silence of the Clergy*), sixth and last tract of his series of instructions, *De institutione clericorum* (*On the Training of Clergy*). Despite the title, the tract is as concerned with the proper use of speech as it is with the control of the tongue. Though it includes an inspirational discussion of what preaching ought to be, somewhat reminiscent of Guibert de Nogent's *Liber quo ordine*, by no stretch of the imagination could the work be considered a handbook on preaching or even a directive as to technique or content; still it makes a clear point: Philip describes and demands an eloquence far beyond the traditional sermon. He seems to consider real eloquence an important aspect of good preaching—a great advance over the position taken barely a century earlier by Peter Damian: "Nor does almighty God need our grammar to draw men . . . since he sent not philosophers and orators, but simple men and fishermen."[2]

After discussing in VI.19 the coming of the Holy Spirit upon the Apostles, and noting their subsequent fearlessness in preaching the Gospel, Philip makes an application to the clergy of his own day.

1. Philippus de Harveng, *De institutione clericorum*, PL 203.665–1206. This excerpt (VI.20) is 203.976–977.
2. Peter Damian, *De·sancta simplicitate*, praef., PL 145.697.

Chapter 20

Then the command was given them that they should not wear shoes when they went forth to preach, but should go barefoot (*nudis pedibus gradiantur*) (Matt. 10:10; Mark 1:6), having only sandals to protect their feet from the earth, so that they would not be harmed by thorns or thistles or the fangs of snakes. Thus the soles of their feet would be protected, but the upper parts would be exposed. This would insure that their preaching would neither be mired in the filth of the earth nor hide beneath the equally foul shade of silence. For when preaching accommodates itself to earthly considerations, when it must avoid the thorns of avarice or the stings of vainglory, when its hasty and imprudent feet do not evade the poisonous bite of falsehood, when it does not consider this type of danger a serious problem to itself, then the foot of the preacher does not wear a sandal, but is planted directly on the muddy ground. On the other hand, when the preacher keeps silence because he fears the tongues of detractors or because he trembles before the threats of persecutors, either from anger or from fear, if he remains quiet when he ought to speak, his foot is not exposed, but is covered by a sort of bandage; then a vile cancer grows in the guise of the word.

When Moses was called to become the leader of the children of Israel, out of Egypt, he was taught what sort of preaching he ought to use by the symbolic command of the Lord, "Put off your shoes from your feet" (Exodus 3:5). This meant, "Let your preaching be declared openly to all, not shaded by a veil of rancor or fear." So also, when the Apostles were commanded to go forth barefoot to preach, this meant that fear of no one, the insults of no one, should be able to obscure their preaching; rather their voices should be like a light shining on a mountaintop before all men, for the glory of God rather than their own. This also seems to make clear what is meant by a prophetic utterance, when the preacher is ordered to lift up his voice and not whisper because of detestable fear or conceal his meaning by excessive ornament: "Cry out," says the Lord to Isaiah, "and do not cease; raise your voice like a trumpet, you who speak to Jerusalem, raise it and do not fear. Say to the cities of Judah, Behold your God" (Isaiah 58:1; 40:11). The Lord wants him who preaches not merely to cry out, but also not to stop crying out; He wants the voice to be neither soft nor gentle, but He commands the preacher to lift it up like a trumpet, which bravely and effectively summons all hearers to battle.

The trumpet has been used in battle for a long time; its music tells how the battle is going. When its sound is heard, the army will be more eager; when it is not heard, the men will grow lethargic. The trumpet then is an especially apt symbol for a preacher, who exhorts the minds of his hearers to do battle against unseen foes; his exhortation is not useless or vain if he strives to raise his voice, if he makes his point with suitable force. "Lift up your voice in courage," we read, "lift it up and do not be afraid." Proper courage does raise its voice, just as true holiness strengthens the conscience; therefore the preacher neither fears to be beat down by the blows of his adversaries nor seeks to be rewarded by the favors of his admirers. One who is forearmed against either eventuality by proper courage will proceed unflinchingly to speak freely; whatever lies in his way he will overcome and brush aside, and no importunity will cause him to seal his lips when he should speak.

When he remembers to lift up his voice without fear, moreover, he adds the rest of the instruction: "Say to the cities of Judah, Behold your God." He tells the cities what is right, so that no one can effectively contradict him, and he ignores all fear of oppressive opposition, demonstrating that he desires the peace and safety of the cities with genuine affection. The cities of Judah represent the souls of the faithful who confess in word and deed their Creator. To them the preacher is commanded to give the wheat of God's word according to the measure in which he has received it, so that he can return them to the Lord with interest; accordingly, when he has said, "Lord, your coin has earned ten coins," then he will hear, "You will have power over ten cities."[3]

3. Luke 19:16–17. An interesting example of medieval application of Scripture.

And if he says, Lord your coin has earned five coins," he will be told, "You will have power over five cities." To as many cities as he receives power over, to that many cities he imparts the word of saving truth, around that many cities will he construct the wall and fortification of his preaching; that is, he will win that many souls to God through the word entrusted to him. He strives always to be at hand to those whom he is instructing, and it is not unjust to say that he is constantly at their side, since the giver of all blessings attributes to him as their teacher or guide whatever good results his learned and obedient teaching has brought about in them.

As a teacher or guide he is commanded not merely to speak, but to cry out and lift up his voice like a trumpet. This indicates that the intellect and reason which has been divinely infused into the spiritual soul may, when the faculty of speech is joined to it in a sort of marriage bond, become fruitful. For when reason remains bound in silence and does not join itself as a spouse to the power of speech, it is like a virgin who remains barren because she closes herself into a hidden chamber and refuses to take to herself a husband. It is not sufficient for one to have the power of reason unless he joins it to the power of speech, so that there may occur the conjugal act which will generate spiritual benefit as its offspring.

25. ALAN OF THE ISLES

Anticlaudianus, III.2-3; VII.6.270-295[1]

Translated by Joseph M. Miller and Thomas Extejt

Although little is actually known of the life of Alanus de Insulis (also known as Alain de Lille) beyond the generally accepted tradition that he was born in Lille around 1128 and died at Cîteaux about 1203,[2] his work certainly justifies the evaluation of Ernst Curtius, who calls him "one of the most important figures of the twelfth century, a poet with prodigious powers of expression, a theologian who tapped new springs in his study."[3] For his manifold accomplishments in the role of philosopher-theologian-educator-poet, he won from scholars of later ages the accolade *Doctor universalis*, which he shared with the teacher of Thomas Aquinas, Albert the Great.

Alan's importance to rhetoric lies particularly in two works: the *Anticlaudianus* and the *Summa de arte praedicatoria*, from which the next two selections are taken. In the former, an allegory of nine books, somewhat reminiscent of Martianus Capella, Alan demonstrates his vision of the liberal arts, including rhetoric. Although his poetry is far superior to the tortuous poetry-prose combination of Martianus, the work is, as a whole, in the tradition of that early piece of fantasy; it foreshadows the stylistic movement by portraying Lady Rhetoric as a woman whose purpose is to add ornamentation to an otherwise already complete production.

At the beginning of the *Anticlaudianus*,[4] Nature indicates that she is

1. Alain de Lille, *Anticlaudianus* (Paris: Librairie Philosophique; R. Bossuat, 1955), pp.93–97 and 165.
2. William H. Cornog, *The Anticlaudian of Alain de Lille* (Philadelphia: University of Pennsylvania Press, 1935), p.9.
3. Curtius, *Europaische Literatur und lateinisches Mittelalter* (Bern: A. Francke AG, 1948), p.125.
4. The title indicates that Alan is taking a position opposed to that of the fifth-century poet, Claudian, author of *In Rufinum*. Claudian portrayed

disappointed in man, who is supposed to represent the perfection of her craftsmanship. To compensate for his shortcomings, she resolves to fashion a new man in whom all her gifts will be centered. She calls in the Virtues, fourteen in number, to assist her; they decide to send two of their number, Prudence and Reason, to God to obtain the needed human soul. Seven lovely maidens, the seven liberal arts, undertake to construct a chariot to carry the two emissaries before the heavenly throne. Grammar brings the raw material and shapes the framework of the vehicle; Dialectic fashions the axletree. At this point, Book III, chapters 2 and 3, Rhetoric enters and decorates the vehicle.

The following translation was prepared for *Readings in Medieval Rhetoric* by Thomas Extejt, a theologian at St. Meinrad Seminary, and Joseph M. Miller. The translators have used prose, since an attempt to use English verse would have interfered with the continuity of the thought.[5]

III.2–3

The third maiden is in no way inferior as to beauty and grace, nor is she at all less skillful. She does not deface the chariot by her handiwork; rather works out an overall plan and carefully puts it into effect; her hand carries out what her vision directs. She applies the final touches, completing the work of her sisters; when they have performed their task, she perfects it with her ornaments. She raises to the highest level what was made more simply, bringing to the ultimate beauty that which was originally destined to serve a meaner purpose. No wonder that she perfects with her adornment what was already constructed, decking the chariot with more splendid colors; she is so favored with beauty of form and face, her gracefulness so outstrips the painter's art, that she embraces in her own breast all his beauty. Her hair, as beautiful to look upon as pure gold, is elegantly dressed, falling gently about her neck; her face glows with warmth, and the

---

his hero, Rufinus, as a paragon of depravity, embodying all vices; Alan, on the other hand, is trying to describe a man representative of perfection. Andrew J. Creighton, *Anticlaudian* (Washington, D. C.: Catholic University, 1941), p.2.

5. For a summary of the entire work, see Creighton, *Anticlaudian*, pp.2–3.

matching fire of her eyes heightens the gentle blush upon her
cheek. At times an unfamiliar pallor passes over her face, as if
striving to drive away her natural beauty. At one moment a flood
of tears covers her countenance, at the next she is wreathed in
smiles, all her tears wiped away. Now she wears a severe frown,
majestic in her sternness; the lightning of her glance flashes
toward the heavens first, then drops to scan the earth beneath her
feet, and finally moves from side to side, seeking out those things
which are hidden in shadow.

In her right hand she bears a trumpet, and in her left a bugle
on which to sound a battle call. She wears a robe of the greatest
beauty, whose brilliant colors shimmer in ever-changing beauty.
Here the beauty of the ornaments of rhetoric becomes even more
beautiful because of the power of the artist, so that the painting
enhances the beauty of the model painted. Here one can read, as
in a book, what is the end and origin, the form and function, the
cause, the structure and the properties peculiar to the art of
Rhetoric; what her powers are and how she pursues her goal;
how she thunders with threats, then gleams with the lightning
flashes of brilliant language, then rains entreaties, and finally
inundates the ear with blandishments; what kind of case moves
her, what her aims are, on what basis she judges or affirms as
right or asserts as honorable; what the divisions of her art are and
how they are related; how the art begins by discovering arguments, then arranges them, writes them out, commits them to
memory, and finally proclaims them, so that the entire argument
fits together point by point; what and how many are the parts of
which a properly prepared oration consists and in what order
they come; how the introduction moves the mind, appeals to the
ear, excites the audience, prepares the judge for the decision, how
it renders the hearer more attentive and amenable, how it wins
sympathy and makes the audience more receptive to the argument; how the narration in a few words sets the scene, explains
the truth, and exposes falsehood masquerading as truth; how the
partition neatly summarizes all that is to follow, organizing scattered arguments and bringing together all different ideas; how
the assertion upholds our side of the case, designates the argu-

ments to be used, examines them, presents them, ties them together into a single unit, and brings them to conclusion; how the
refutation deals with the arguments of the opposition, attacking,
weakening, shaking, piercing, and destroying them; how the conclusion ties everything together into one package, bringing the
oration to a satisfactory end by drawing in the reins of discourse.

[Here also one can read] what facts, what kind of facts, and
what name is appropriate to every question after the scaffolding
of logic has been erected; what kind of litigation arises from the
fact, what question of law; what and how many are the kinds of
cases; which are simple, which interrelated, and which relative
to some external factor; why one argument strengthens an indict-
ment, one changes it substantially, one refutes it, and one compares it to something else so that it seems unimportant when
weighed in a scale of values; how a single argument can draw
strength from both sides when two laws seem to contradict one
another, or when there is a strong opinion opposed to the express
law, or when the phrasing of the law allows for two different
interpretations, or when the act is defined in such a way that the
definition of the term remains as ambiguous as the term itself, or
when the law changes according to place or person or time so as
to change the very question and raise serious doubts, or when a
case comes up to which no law applies and which must build its
arguments on precedent.

[One can also see] how arguments properly fitted to the persons
involved gain the strength of weaponry, while name, character,
prestige and fortune which pretends to be something else, clothing, mannerisms, pretended wisdom, studies, examples, oratory
and activity only provide a false appearance of strength; what
events surround the deed, what issue of fact seems to dominate it,
what accidents are added to it or usually follow upon it, as the
case itself demands. Whatever relates to the fact, whatever
changes the complexion of the deed, whatever place or time,
occasion, cause, or circumstance exists, a particular part of the
painted garment bears the image; and finally, another part deals
with the forms of the rhetorical devices. Here Marcus alone
adopts rhetoric to himself, or rather gives birth to it, so that the

art which Tullius has begotten can justly be called the daughter
of Cicero; the art which thus takes its origin from him can truly
be named Tullian. Here also Ennodius, with his nosegay of
rhetorical flowers surpasses poetry, and completely erases all the
blemishes of language. Quintilian is here, clothing the vague
shadows of cases under a kind of appearance of truth; he frames
new controversies, and considers how to enter into a lawsuit
without himself becoming part of the litigation. Symmachus,
sparing in words but prolific in thought, generous in idea but
terse in speech, impressive in mind rather than in mouth, more
blessed in fruit than in foliage, joins his greatness of sense with
brevity of discourse. Here the stately speech of Sidonius shines
forth, glistening like many stars, gleaming with expressions like
so many scintillating jewels, his variety as beautiful as the colors
of the peacock. Now he sings of the tender muse as with a gentle
flute, though his style seems neither flat nor bloodless and mourn-
ful; then he adopts a middle style, neither plodding through the
mire nor soaring to lofty heights; now he thunders forth his ideas
in towering language; finally, swollen with his emotion, he bursts
forth with overblown pomposity.

Brilliant in her own beauty, the virgin does not hold back her
art; rather she lavishes herself in beautifying her handiwork. The
shaft of the carriage blazes with gems; here and there she inlays
it with silver. The substance of the wood itself, though not of
noble dignity, she elevates by means of outward embellishment
in order to compensate for its meaner estate. A splendor which is
added on hides the original material and all its flaws; and the
wood itself rejoices in its old age, erasing the memory of its common origin. And the gems which encrust the shaft of the carriage
are like stars of such brightness that their light outshines the sun
and the day itself is dull in comparison; the natural daylight then
bows down in wonder before the artificially endowed light of the
wood.

So also the virgin entwines blossoms about the axle, making
the cold iron seem warm with its new beauty. Although iron
usually lies rigid and unfeeling, emitting an aura of hoarfrost and
midwinter, this iron knows no frost and has abandoned its natural

coldness; it puts on joyousness and gaity as its lot, and it brings to mind a meadow abloom with flowers. And while the virgin, generous with her gift of beauty gladdens the shaft with gems and the axle with flowers, encasing them in the very finest of ornament, the trumpet of war gives way to the reed pen, the bugle yields to the sculptor's chisel, and the newer pair take over the functions of the former pair.

VII.6.270–295

In Book VII, after Nature has begun the creation of the ideal man, each of the Arts bestows upon the new creation its own special gifts. In the following lines, the gifts of Rhetoric are depicted.

The beauties of Rhetoric are also present and her colorful flowers of speech which add brilliance to her starlike words, so that her speech dons a mantle of grace and every phrase shines with its own light. In her bounty, Rhetoric scatters a power of language, a beauty, a majestic sweep of words; she touches the tongue of the youth, giving to his words the seal of her colorful variety; she teaches him to speak succinctly and to clothe profound meaning in simple expressions, to enclose a great deal of thought in a few words, not to ramble in unregulated discussion; she aids him that his words may be brief, his thought rich, his discourse both elegant in form and eloquent in a fruitful harvest of wisdom. On the other hand, when his speech chances to flow too freely in a flood of loquacity, then she takes care that more meaning flows forth as well, an abundance of fruit from a forest of leaves, so that the richness of the grain makes up for the excessive chaff, the content for the verbosity.

26. ALAN OF THE ISLES

A *Compendium* on the Art of Preaching, Preface and Selected Chapters[1]

Translated by Joseph M. Miller

Probably no work of the entire medieval period contributed more to the recognition of the rhetorical aspects of preaching than the *Summa de arte praedicatoria*. Although it is true that Alan warns his readers against obsession with style and delivery, the two elements which he has already characterized in the *Anticlaudianus* as comprising almost the whole body of Rhetoric, yet his instructions here apply the classical rhetorical principles to the preaching art. Indeed, had Augustine been the author of this *Compendium on the Art of Preaching*, he would probably have entitled it *A Compendium on the Art of Rhetoric for the Use of Preachers*.

The work consists of a preface and forty-eight chapters; most of this material is an application of principles to specific preaching situations. The preface, chapters 1, 38, 39, and 41, however, are of interest to the rhetorician. The preface indicates the importance Alan gives to good preaching; chapter 1 begins to lay out the principles of preaching; then, after chapters 2–37 apply the principles of invention and disposition to specific themes, chapters 38 and 39 continue with a survey of the principles. In the middle of chapter 39, Alan begins to suggest themes that might be developed for particular audiences (certainly an application of *pathos*), and in chapters 40 to 47, he composes a series of complete sermons for identifiable congregations, concluding with a humorous discourse directed "To Sleepyheads (*Ad somnolentes*)." Chapter 41 is addressed to orators (*Ad oratores*), and is included here for that reason.

---

1. *Summa Magistri Alani Doctoris Universalis de arte praedicatoria*, PL 210.109–198. The chapters selected for inclusion here are: Preface and Cap. 1, *PL* 210.111–114; Cap. 38–39, *PL* 210.182–186; Cap. 41, *PL* 210.188–189.

Author's Preface.

Jacob saw a ladder rising from the earth and touching heaven, and angels ascending and descending (Genesis 28). The ladder represents the progress of the Catholic man who moves from the simple rudiments of faith to the perfection of the whole man. The first rung of this ladder is confession; the second is prayer; the third is the act of gratitude; the fourth is the study of the Scriptures; the fifth is the solution of difficulties in the interpretation of Scripture by asking the help of others; the sixth is the presenting of the Scriptures to others; and the seventh is preaching.

The man who is truly sorry for sin ought first to plant his foot firmly on the bottom rung of the ladder by confessing his sins; next he must climb to the second rung by praying that God will give him grace. His third step is to give thanks for the grace he has received. The ascent to the fourth rung comes when he studies the Scriptures to find out how to protect this grace, since the Sacred Scriptures teach how Grace which has been bestowed can be preserved in the soul; the fifth stage follows when a doubt arises and the reader asks guidance from his superior. He attains the sixth rung when he is able, as a reader, to offer the Holy Writ to others. And he has reached the seventh and topmost rung when he can clearly preach to others what he has learned from his study of the Scriptures.

Because it is necessary to move through all the other stages first, different authors have composed a number of treatises on how and when to climb those rungs; but as to peaching, few have said much about what it ought to be, whose task it is, for whose benefit it should be done, about what topics, and how and when and where. For this reason, I have deemed this project worthwhile, the composition of a sort of tract about these things for the benefit of those around me. First, then, we must determine what preaching is and what kind of form the composition of the words should take, and how significant the ideas should be, and how many kinds of sermon there are; next, we will decide whose task preaching is; third, to whom sermons should be delivered; fourth, why; and fifth, where.

**Chapter One. About Preaching. What it is and
what it ought to be like, etc.**

Preaching[2] *is an open and public instruction regarding behavior
and belief proposed for the formation of men, rooted in reason
and growing from the spring of the sacred text.* Preaching must
be *open* because it must be done in the open. This is why Christ
said, "What I say to you in a whisper, you must proclaim from
the housetop" (Matthew 10).[3] If preaching were hidden, it
would be suspect and seem to smack of heretical doctrine; in their
harangues the heretics preach in secret so as to deceive others the
more easily. And preaching must be public, because it is not done
for the benefit of one, but of many; if it were offered to one person
only, it would not be preaching but teaching. The difference
between preaching and teaching and prophesying and speechmaking is this: preaching is an instruction for many, given openly
to teach them about their way of life; teaching is offered to one
person or to a group for the purpose of adding to their knowledge;
prophecy is an admonition which deals with pointing out what is
likely to happen in the future; oratory is a civil discourse designed to further the political welfare of the community. By its
very definition, preaching, which is "an instruction regarding
behavior and belief," includes two theological concepts: the intellectual, insofar as it pursues knowledge in matters spiritual, and
the moral, which proposes the formation of a way of life. Preaching deals, then, sometimes with divine wisdom, sometimes with
human habits; this is the real meaning of the angels ascending and
descending the ladder. Those angels are preachers, who ascend
the ladder when they preach of heavenly matters and descend
when they concern themselves with the affairs of ordinary men.

What follows in the definition is this: "proposed for the formation of men." This identifies the final cause or ultimate goal of
preaching. And since preaching ought to be planted in reason and
to draw its strength from texts, we logically add the words, "rooted

2. Italics in text, *PL* 210.111.
3. Actually this is a paraphrase of two commands by Jesus in Matthew
10:27.

in reason and growing from the spring of the sacred text." This makes clear that preaching should not depend upon buffoonery or silliness or the kind of rhythmic melodies and echoing beats that are more suited to delighting the ears than to instructing the heart. This kind of preaching is more fit for the theatre or for the pantomime, and ought, for that reason, to be totally despised. Of such preaching the prophet said, "You stewards mix water with wine" (Isaiah 1). In this kind of preaching, water is mixed with the wine: childish and clownish words and even perversions of taste are offered to souls. Preaching ought not to glitter with the trappings of beautiful words, making use of purple prose; on the other hand, it should not be listless, and filled with expressions that lack blood. Rather, "Blessed are they that keep to the mean."[4] Since anything which is too vividly painted seems to be over-rehearsed, with a view to pleasing an audience rather than helping one's neighbors, it is not likely to move the hearts of the listeners. Those who preach like this can be likened to the Pharisees, who make their fringes long and their phylacteries broad (Matthew 23).

Although such preaching is to be considered suspect, yet it ought to be tolerated, not dismissed completely, in keeping with the words of St. Paul: "In every way, Christ is proclaimed; in this I rejoice and shall continue to rejoice" (Philippians 1). Let nothing, however, be improperly injected into the glory of Christ, for Christ is just as much angered by praise not based on truth as by a denial of the glory that is so based. This is the form the preaching of heretics takes, who first propose truths and subsequently interpolate falsehoods; of them it was written, "Even the jackals give the breast and suckle their young" (Lamentations 4).[5] These jackals have the appearance of young girls, but the feet of horses. The feet of horses are not marked by cloven hooves; they touch the ground firmly. By the jackals, therefore, we signify those

4. This is not a quotation from Scripture. Rather, Alan uses the form of the Beatitudes (Matthew 5:1–10) to clothe what seems to be an original apothegm.
5. The subsequent description of "jackals" as having the appearance of young girls with the feet of horses does not make sense. Alan, however, may have been interpreting the text in some unknown way.

heretics who display a virginal beauty at first, but subsequently
reveal the sting of the scorpion. First they preach the truth, then
later they speak falsely. They have horses' feet because their
heart's affection is not distributed between love of God and love
of neighbor, but is completely fixed on worldly delights. Preaching
of this kind is to be completely rejected as vile and detestable.
Good preaching on the other hand should have its weight in its
content, so that by virtue of the thoughts it contains it may appeal
to the ears of the listeners, awaken their hearts, arouse true
sorrow, pour forth wise teaching, thunder forth admonitions,
soothe with promises, and so completely serve the one purpose
of aiding other people.

There are some who view financial emoluments as the reason
for their preaching; as a result their preaching is indeed "rich."
They should rather be called merchants than preachers. Yet,
despite this, their preaching is to be heard and tolerated, in keeping with what is written: "Practice and observe whatever they
tell you, but not what they themselves do" (Matthew 23). There
are three kinds of preaching. The first is done by word of mouth,
as in the command of the Lord, "Go, preach the Gospel to every
creature, etc." (Mark 16); the second is done by writing, as when
Saint Paul said that he had preached to the Corinthians because
he had written them letters; and the third is done by example, as
it is written, "Every action of Christ is our instruction."[6] The
form preaching ought to take is this: let it be based on a text
from Scripture as its immediate foundation, especially on the
Gospels, the Psalms, the Epistles of Paul, and the Books of
Solomon. In them especially does the matter for moral instruction lie. From the other books of the Holy Scripture other texts
can be drawn if they are indeed necessary and useful to the
theme.

Next the preacher must earn the approval of his hearers for
himself by showing humility, and for the theme he is proposing
for their instruction by saying that he is presenting the word of

6. Alan does not indicate where this is written; perhaps it is another of
his original apothegms.

God to bear fruit in their minds, not to gain him any earthly reward, but to further and support their well-being. He must let them know that he is not moved by the foolish shouts of the crowd, not lulled by the pleasant breezes, not impelled by the applause of the theatre, but that he is speaking to inform their minds, and that they ought to pay attention not to the one who is speaking but to what he is saying. He should remind them that in a rosebush the sharpness of the thorns is not considered when compared to the fragrance of the rose, that honey can be sucked through a fragile reed, that flame can be struck from a rock. Next he ought to show how important it is for a person to hear the word of God in order to share in the effect.

He ought to promise that he will say only a few words, and that they will be of real importance; that he is drawn to his task only out of love for his congregation, and not because he thinks that he possesses greater wisdom or prudence or that he has greater virtue; that because some things are revealed to little ones rather than to the great, at such a time even the great must be silent; that sometimes too the great ones are unwilling to preach, and it is no wonder that the little ones babble on at these times, since if the learned are silent, the very stones will speak and cry out.

Next he ought to begin expounding the text he has chosen, developing his entire theme for the instruction of the congregation. Let him not propose too obscure or too difficult a text, for this might make his hearers less attentive. In explaining the text, let him not jump too quickly from point to point, lest the beginning be out of harmony with the middle or the middle out of harmony with the end. Let him also adduce other texts which will support his theme, especially those which will apply to it directly. On occasion he might even be able to interpolate the words of pagan authors, as Paul sometimes inserts into his Epistles the words of the ancient philosophers because they have a special aptness; besides, when they are cleverly introduced they add fresh vision to the oration.

Further, he ought to use words with strong emotional connotation, because they will soften the hearts of his congregation and prepare them to shed tears of repentance. Let this kind of speech

be brief, because too much wordiness leads to boredom; so, after
the preacher has caused spirits to be moved, tears to flow freely,
and countenances to be lowered, let him not draw out his emotional appeal for too long, but remember the words of Lucretius:
"Nothing dries up faster than a tear." Finally, then, he should use
familiar illustrations, for people remember things that are familiar
to them.

Chapter Thirty-Eight. Preaching is the sole prerogative of Prelates.

We have already seen what preaching is, what qualities it ought
to possess, and what topics it should deal with; it now falls to our
lot to point out whose function preaching ought to be. Preaching
is a function of prelates and should be propounded by them.[7]
Two things are demanded of them, therefore: learning and moral
living. Learning is important if they are to instruct others: a
proper way of life if they are to show others an example of virtuous living. To represent this, it is commanded that the crop of
the turtle dove offered in sacrifice be cast beside the altar
(Leviticus 1). The turtle dove represents the ingenuousness of the
preacher; by casting his head near the altar is indicated that the
preacher ought to perform in his actions what he urges with his
voice.

Likewise, the shepherd's crook atop the crosier curves backward
to indicate that what he preaches to others he should meditate on
in his own heart as part of his responsibility. To teach these
qualities, prudence and holiness of life, we read these words
about the steward: "Who then is the faithful and wise servant
whom his master has set over the household, etc.?" (Matthew
24). The preacher, then, ought to be faithful both in word and
in deed. Faithful in word insofar as he does not corrupt the truth

---

7. A close study of this chapter makes clear the implications of this statement: Alan is indeed assigning the function of preacher to bishops exclusively. This does not necessarily conflict, however, with the fact that priests
(and even deacons) preached regularly as part of their office at this time as
well as at all other times in the history of the Church. Rather it is emphasizing the distinction that bishops preach by virtue of their office, while all
others preach only with the permission of the bishop.

with lies; faithful in word because he does not sell his preaching for earthly recompense; faithful in word so that his words will not contradict his actions. Remember that it is written of false preachers: Our innkeepers mix water with their wine. They indeed mix water with their wine who preach falsehoods along with truth in the manner of the heretics; so also do those who sell their preaching for the approval of men in the manner of the hypocrites; so also do those who seek for a profit from their preaching in the manner of merchants; and so do those who contradict their words with their actions in the manner of false Christians.

The preacher also needs to be faithful in his actions, so that whatever he does he does with a good motive, making God the final end of his every action. He must be prudent in word and in deed. In word, so that he can recognize what ought to be preached and what ought not. In deed so that he will know to whom and when he should preach; for instance, he must know how to preach on more important themes on important occasions, on less important themes on less important occasions. He should judge to whom he ought to preach so that he will not present the Holy One of God as though he is casting crumbs to contemptible dogs or pearls at the feet of swine (Matthew 7). He should be prudent regarding when, so that he can proclaim the word when the time is right for preaching, and that he can remain silent when the time is inappropriate. As Solomon says, "There is a time for speaking and a time for keeping silent" (Ecclesiastes 3).

Preachers need knowledge so that they be experts in both Testaments, discriminating in their analysis of texts, fluent with words, reserved in all their movements, aloof to the world and dedicated to fulfilling their office. Malachy says of the prelate: "The lips of the priest guard knowledge and the people seek instruction from his mouth, for he is a messenger from the Lord of Hosts" (Malachi 2). And Sirach, the son of Jesus,[8] says: "If you have knowledge, answer your neighbor; if not, put your hand

---

8. This Jesus is an unknown Hebrew of about 200 B.C., not Jesus of Nazareth.

on your mouth; do not fall victim to undisciplined speech"
(Sirach 5). There is every reason to tremble at the dictum, "If a
blind man lead a blind man, both fall into the pit" (Matthew 15;
Luke 6). And the Apostle says, "If a man speaks in ignorance, he
will be ignored" (I Corinthians 14). And what will the master
say to the foolish virgins? "Amen, I say to you, I do not know
you" (Matthew 25). Besides, there is the statement, "Cursed is
the old man just beginning his education,"[9] which is just like "The
sinner one hundred years old will be cursed" (Isaiah 65). And
there is a deliberately cultivated kind of ignorance, when one
could know but refuses to learn; this is crass and supine and
vincible and therefore inexcusable.[10] Of this it has been written,
"He has refused to understand in order that he may do good"
(Psalm 34); also, "When a man enjoys honor, he does not understand; he resembles unthinking beasts, he is made like to them"
(Psalm 48). This ignorance characterizes those prelates who
choose disdainfully to coast along in their blindness; in their
pride, they persist in foolishness; they are priests and prophets
without reason, teachers of what cannot be, catalogues of things
that are not known.

O vile ignorance! O abominable stupidity! It imposes silence on
a prelate, it renders mute the watchdog, the shepherd; it is a frog
which, when placed in the dog's mouth, takes away his power to
bark. The prelates of our time occupy the chair of the master
before they have known the student's bench; they receive the
title of teacher before they have worn the gown of the pupil; they
would rather stand over than stand with; they prefer the riches
of unearned honors to the rewards of dedication. To a prelate of
this kind can be directed the admonition, "Physician, heal yourself" (Luke 4); orator, speak of yourself; you are the representative of Christ, imitate his works who "began to do and to teach"

---

9. Alan's *maledictus elementarius senex* is apparently an inaccurate quotation of Seneca's *Turpis et ridicula est elementarius senex, Epist. Moral,* 36.4.

10. The terms "crass ignorance," "supine ignorance," and "vincible ignorance" are technical terms in Theology. They identify various degrees of
guilt incurred by a person who deliberately avoids learning what he must
know. Based on the principle, "Ignorance of the law is no excuse," they
describe the amount of effort a person exerts in remaining ignorant.

(Acts 1). One who teaches without doing contradicts Christ. He imposes unbearable burdens on his subjects without lifting a finger to help carry the weight. Some hide in a napkin the very talent which divine wisdom has entrusted to them: namely, those who, because of carelessness, refuse to preach. Some hide it in a dungheap: namely, those who contradict their words by their behavior. Some hide it in mud: namely, those who, because of jealousy, hide the word of God.

Chapter Thirty-Nine. To whom preaching is to be done.

Having noted whose function preaching is and what qualities preachers ought to embody, it remains for us to indicate who ought to receive their preaching. Clearly, preaching ought to benefit the faithful, those who desire with great zeal to hear the word of God; of them, the Lord says: "Lift up your eyes and see the fields already white for the harvest" (John 4). The fields white for the harvest are the souls of men who are ready to receive the word of God. They are the good soil, ready to receive the seed and bring forth fruit. Preaching should be withheld from the unworthy and the hostile, however, because they spit on the word of God and so render themselves unfit. Thus the Apostles said to the Jews who despised their preaching: "Because you have rejected the word of God, you have proved yourselves unworthy of eternal life; behold, then, we offer it to the gentiles" (Acts 13). A man lessens the beauty of the mysteries when he opens those mysteries to the unworthy; the vessels of the Lord are not to be exposed to the view of the dwellers in Babylon. It is proper to speak in parables to the young, but to adults one should reveal the mysteries of the kingdom of God. Children are fed with gruel, adults sustain their strength with solids; this way the child is not killed by solids, and the adult does not vomit up porridge; everything is thus distributed properly as it is suited. It is the task of the preacher to apply the proper physic or medicine as needed. For just as medicine can produce different remedies for a variety of diseases, so the preacher should adapt his healing admonitions. For instance, if he is preaching to the lecherous, he should offer texts and construct his arguments to counteract lust; he should demonstrate that it is an abomination before God and men; he should show how the sinner stinks—his body stinks, he stinks before his neighbor, he stinks before God.

The preacher must first cut with a knife as he utters threats, then heal as he offers consolation; in this same way, let him attack the other sins, recognizing that his hearers are ensnared by many different vices. If he preaches to the poor, let him discuss poverty; let him show its blessings, taking his example from our master, Jesus Christ. . . . If he preaches to the wealthy, let him urge them to give alms, to despise their riches, to cultivate a love for spiritual wealth; let him warn them against allowing the increase of possessions to weigh upon their hearts; even though they have property, they should not cling passionately to it; to have is a matter of fortune, but to desire is a fault. . . . If he preaches to orators, let him warn them not to take up an unjust cause for the sake of reward and not to cripple a just cause out of personal rancor; to do this would be to sell one's tongue, to prostitute one's intelligence, to seek after falsehoods, to venerate deceit. . . .

Chapter Forty-One. To orators or advocates.

Scripture says to orators, "Do justice to the fatherless and the oppressed" (Psalm 10). And Isaias says, "Defend the downtrodden, plead for the widow" (Isaiah 1). The orator ought to be fortified with truth, moved by understanding, fervent in charity; he should despise greed and pursue justice; he should not allow falsehood to becloud his reason or a lack of discretion to drain off the truth from his speech or hatred to render him unreliable. He must never let greed weigh down his spirit nor injustice lead him astray; he ought never to chase after money with his tongue or after popularity with witticisms. Rather, let him establish a proper goal for his addresses, an honorable purpose to his speech. Let him not prostitute his tongue nor make use of deceitful language, nor sell the gift of God; let him not hire out for a fee a free blessing of God. What he has received as a free gift of grace, let him never put up for sale. Oh how detestable a form of simony it is to sell the heritage of a poor man, to rent out the resources of one who has no money.

Among the forms of charity, by no means the lowest place is assigned to him who offers support to a widow in her cause. One who uses his powers of intellect in this way protects her; thus he not only defends but even improves her lot. On the other hand, the orator ought never to allow the poverty or need of someone to drive him toward falsehood; neither should someone's good fortune lead him toward injustice.

Truth will always lend strength to an argument; in a speech, it adds might to the impotent. One who does not defend the right when he has the ability to do so is, for all purposes, giving his approval to injustice. To supply a defense for the downtrodden in a trial is the same as to visit the prisoner in his cell; it is the same as clothing the naked to bring the garment of defense to one who has been denuded of all protection in court; it is feeding the hungry, giving drink to the thirsty, offering medicine to the sick, providing shelter for the wanderer to undertake in court the defense of a man who has been stripped of all support. So the orator who offers counsel to a needy client in a just cause truly performs all the works of mercy. Orator, why do you fail to defend widows in their need?

27. THOMAS OF CÎTEAUX

Commentary on the
Song of Songs, III.31; X.141[1]

Translated by Joseph M. Miller

Thomas of Cîteaux, though not a key figure in medieval rhetorical history, was "a very learned man, especially as regards the Sacred Scriptures, which he used to keep always at hand and to meditate on constantly."[2] Over a five-year period (1175–80) he composed a commentary on the Canticle of Canticles, which he dedicated to Pontus, Bishop of Clairmont. Fifty years later another scholar, Cardinal John Algrin, edited it considerably and published it with his own notes added.[3] This version of the text, bearing the names of both men as co-authors, appears in *PL* 206.

The commentary is not explicitly concerned with preaching; it is rather an effort, as Thomas himself describes it, to imitate Origen, Bede, Gregory the Great, and Bernard of Clairvaux, among others, all of whom had composed mystical explanations of Solomon's allegorical epithalamium. Like his predecessors, Thomas carried his interpretation to hyper-Augustinian lengths, finding meanings far beyond the imagination of untrained and non-mystical readers. It is in one such flight of fancy that he finds a possible relevance for preachers, indicating that the sexual act of marriage can represent "the union between the trivium of expression and the quadrivium of ideas,"[4] through which it is possible that man can be taught to understand something about God.

The suitability of the work as an aid to preachers was obvious to some subsequent editor, since the title page of the 1655 edition includes a phrase praising the work as "a most useful thing for preach-

---

1. *Commentaria in Cantica Canticorum, PL* 206.
2. *Index Biographicus Auctorum, PL* 218.535.
3. "Outstanding and verbose (*insignis et prolix*)" are the words which Casimir Oudin uses to describe the original unedited original. *Commentarii de scriptoribus et scriptis ecclesiasticis*, II.1574 (Leipsig, 1722).
4. *Commentaria*, Praefatio, *PL* 206.17.

ers."[5] The two selections translated here are, however, the only references to preaching, except for the phrase about the marriage analogy already mentioned.

Commentaria, III.31; PL 206.167–168

The preacher[6] must have mastered the words with which to propose doctrine, for "for the lips of a priest should guard knowledge, and men should seek instruction from his mouth, for he is a messenger of the Lord of hosts" (Mal. 2:7). Otherwise they are the blind leading the blind; "and if a blind man leads a blind man, both will fall into a pit" (Matt. 15:14). And Isaiah says, "His watchmen are blind, they are all without knowledge; they are all dumb dogs, they cannot bark" (Isa. 15:10). Preachers must attract men with their words, inspire them with their way of life, invite them through their actions. Thus the Apostle commands, "Show yourself in all respects a model of good deeds, and in your teaching show integrity, gravity, and sound speech that cannot be censured" (Titus 2:7–8), emphasizing the teaching of doctrine, seriousness of demeanor, and integrity of action. Nor does he urge only seriousness of demeanor, but graciousness as well. Paul says, "He who contributes should do so in liberality; he who gives aid, with zeal; he who does acts of mercy, with cheerfulness" (Rom. 12:8). And to other disciples he writes, "I beg you to lead a life worthy of the calling to which you have been called, with all humility and meekness, with patience, forbearing to one another in love, eager to maintain the unity of the Spirit in the bond of peace" (Eph. 4:1–3). Of whatever character the leader is, the followers will be the same.

> Surely you do not expect a mother to teach her daughter
> Virtues or a way of life contrary to her own? Far more likely
> That the daughter of a wretched hag will be wretched also.
> (Juvenal, *Satire VI*)

"And when the living creatures went, the wheels went beside them; and when the living creatures rose from the earth, the

5. Oudin notes that he has seen this edition. *Commentarii de scriptoribus,* II.1574.
6. Thomas uses the word *doctor* (teacher), but the context clearly indicates that he means preachers.

wheels rose" (Ezek. 1:19). And regarding the preacher's actions: "Let your light shine before men so that they may see your good works and give glory to your Father who is in heaven" (Matt. 5:16). Also we are commanded, "Let your loins be girt and your lamps burning" (Luke 12:35). Otherwise preachers will be like those messengers David sent to Hanun. The latter drove them off after shaving off half the beard and half the hair of each, and after cutting off their garments half-length at the thighs, so that their buttocks were exposed (II Kings 10:1–5).[7] Preachers are indeed messengers sent by David, for they say to sinners what they are sent to say. From their heads beautiful hair hangs, representing the beauty of those virtuous habits which adorn their souls; they have a beard, representing manly strength, because they are brave and constant in the face of hostility; their garments are beautifully embroidered with the ornament of noble discourse. But Hanun (which can be interpreted "their woe") represents sinners whose woe preachers are sent to assuage. Often, though, the preachers are corrupted by the vices of their hearers, who cut off half their hair by demeaning the preachers to the level of their own lives; they shave off half their beards when they make the preachers weak and afraid; they cut off their garments when they degrade noble discourse to the level of idle chatter. Thus the buttocks are exposed, which means that as they lower the level of discourse, the sins of the preacher are seen. When we see this kind of teaching by the master, how we must pity those who are so cheated.

Commentaria, X.141; PL 206.680

The fourth chariot is preaching.[8] The first wheel is knowledge of Sacred Scripture, the second is skill in speaking, the third is

---

7. The book which Thomas calls II Kings is called II Samuel in traditional Protestant numbering. Thomas does not, by the way, quote the story verbatim, but uses phrases considerably more graphic than the original. In a concession to "good taste," this translation paraphrases Thomas' earthy expressions.

8. Immediately prior to this paragraph, Thomas has been identifying the possible ways in which men can approach God. To do this he has used the medieval commonplace of the chariot, comparing each method of approach to a chariot with four wheels (components of the act), and drawn by two horses (motivating forces).

the example of a holy life, and the fourth is delegation for the task by the proper authority. Concerning the first we read, "The lips of the priest should guard knowledge" (Mal. 10:7); concerning the second, we know that Moses complained, "I am not eloquent, either heretofore or since thou hast spoken to thy servant; but I am slow of speech and of tongue" (Exod. 4:10); concerning the third, St. Paul said, "Show thyself in all respects a model of good deeds" (Titus 2:7); and concerning the fourth, we read, "How can men preach if they are not sent?" (Rom. 10:15). There are two matched horses drawing this chariot, for preachers are moved both by compassion for their fellowmen and by a desire to promote the glory of God.

28. GEOFFREY OF VINSAUF

The New Poetics[1]

Commentary

As the title of his treatise indicates, Geoffrey of Vinsauf intended his treatise (written *c*.1210) to replace the "Old Poetics," the *Ars poetica* of Horace. Just as there had been a strong flavor of Ciceronian rhetoric in Horace's views on poetry, so Geoffrey's principles have much in common with the stylistic admonitions of Alberic of Monte Cassino; the emphasis was on the *colores* or figures traditionally associated with grammar and rhetoric, and on the orderly arrangement of ideas (*dispositio*) rather than with the more usual poetic considerations of rhythm and metre. Indeed, much of Geoffrey's material betrays a strong influence of the medieval rhetorical *vade mecum*, the *Ad Herennium*.

This link between rhetoric and poetic is not a new development, of course. In the Roman system of education, masters introduced their youthful protégés to grammar through the required study of both speeches and poems; they required exercises in the reworking and paraphrasing of models from both forms of literature; and they demanded extempore performances in both arts. Quintilian, for instance, lays down a dual purpose for the study of grammar: "the art of speaking correctly, and the interpretation of the poets" (*Inst. Orat.* I.4); later Aelius Donatus and Priscian, in their handbooks on grammar, treated rules of composition without distinguishing between rhetorical and poetic style. Thus the *New Poetics* is of value not because it changes the focus of rhetoric, but because it opens a long-standing relationship to a deeper cross-influence. The *Poetria nova* of Geoffrey of Vinsauf was the best known of all the medieval *artes poeticae*, and deserves attention from rhetoricians for that reason.

---

1. Latin text in *Les arts poetiques du XII*[e] *et du XIII*[e] *siècle*, ed. Edmond Faral (Paris, 1924); the English translation and commentary (from which this brief discussion is drawn) is Geoffrey of Vinsauf, *The New Poetics* (*Poetria nova*), trans. Jane Baltzell Kopp, in *Three Medieval Rhetorical Arts*, ed. James J. Murphy (Berkeley: University of California Press, 1971), pp.27–108.

29. HUMBERT OF ROMANS

Treatise on Preaching, II.8-9[1]

Translated by Dominican Students, Province of St. Joseph

Recognizing that St. Dominic first established his small band of mendicant friars for the purpose of preaching, and that Pope Innocent III (1198–1216) approved this emphasis by assigning to the new order the title Order of Preachers,[2] we should not be surprised that the earliest products of Dominican scholarship include an important textbook on preaching. The author of the *Treatise on Preaching* was Humbert of Romans, fifth Master General of the Dominicans (1254–1263).

Humbert's treatise, still studied by Dominicans of the twentieth century, deserves attention because it represents a remarkable attempt to apply the general principles previously enunciated by Guibert de Nogent and Philip of Harveng to a practical system of homiletic training. It consists of seven chapters, a total of forty-four numbered sections, dealing with such themes as "The Qualities of the Office of Preaching," "The Qualities Needed for the Preacher," "How He Should Enter His Task of Preaching," etc.

Book II: THE QUALITIES NECESSARY FOR PREACHING

Chapter 8. Knowledge Required by a Preacher

We must not overlook the high degree of learning that is necessary for preachers, who are commissioned to instruct others. St. Paul justly reproached certain ministers of the word for their deficiency in this respect. Here are some of his words: ". . . desiring to be teachers of the Law, when they understand neither

1. Humbert of Romans, *Treatise on Preaching*, trans. by Dominican Students of the Province of St. Joseph (London: Blackfriars, 1955), pp.38–44.
2. *Speculum Fratrum Praedicatorum* (Mechlin: Dessain, 1910), p.234.

what they say nor the things about which they make assertion"
(I Tim. 1:7).

This knowledge should be very extensive. First of all, it should
include a firm grasp of Holy Scripture, since in that there is substantially contained the doctrines that the preacher is bound to
preach. "From the midst of the rocks they shall give forth their
voices" (Ps. 103:12), wrote the Psalmist; or, to bring out the
point, they must draw from the Old and New Testaments as from
an inexhaustible quarry, which they evidently cannot do if they
do not have the requisite knowledge.

It is a fact worth noting that the Saviour, in choosing unlearned
men as preachers, endowed them Himself with a knowledge of
the Scriptures; hence, we see in their writings frequent references
to the texts of the Old Testament. And St. Jerome adds that learning, which ordinary men seek by study and daily meditation on
the Law of God, was granted directly by the Holy Ghost to these
chosen disciples. That is why it has been written: "And they shall
all be taught of God" (John 6:45).

After the study of the Holy Books, should follow the study of
creatures, for the Creator has placed in these many profound
lessons. St. Anthony, the hermit, observes that they are like a
book, containing many edifying thoughts for those who take the
trouble to read. The Redeemer often had recourse to this type
of knowledge in His discourses, as, for instance, when He said:
"Look at the birds of the air. . . . See how the lilies of the field
grow. . . ." (Matt. 6:26–28).

Next there should follow a knowledge of history for this science,
dealing with both the faithful and infidels, abounds in examples
which furnish the preacher with valuable lessons. Our Lord used
this branch of learning when, to confound the blindness of those
who despised His words, He said: "The queen of the South will
rise up in the judgment with the men of this generation and will
condemn them; for she came from the ends of the earth to hear
the wisdom of Solomon, and behold, a greater than Solomon is
here" (Luke 11:31). And, for the benefit of those who would not
do penance, He added: "The men of Nineve will rise up in the
judgment with this generation and will condemn it; for they

repented at the preaching of Jonas, and behold, a greater than Jonas is here" (Luke 11:32).

The preacher must also know the laws of the Church for many men are ignorant of them; and it is his duty to instruct these. It was with this intention that St. Paul ". . . travelled through Syria and Cilicia and strengthened the churches, and commanded them to keep the precepts of the Apostles and presbyters" (Acts 15:41).

It is equally necessary that the minister of the word be familiar with the mysteries of religion, upon which subject the Apostle noted: "And if I know all mysteries . . ." (I Cor. 13:2).[3] Religion is, indeed, full of mysterious figures and lessons, the recounting of which can be most edifying. Consequently, the preacher should be cognizant of them.

Then there will be applied to him the words: "And in the midst of the Church she shall open his mouth, and she shall fill him with the spirit of wisdom and understanding" (Ecclus. 15:5). The Spirit of understanding spoken of is exactly He Who aids us in penetrating the meaning hidden in words and figures, and "understanding" signifies "to read within" something.

On the other hand, the preacher should not neglect knowledge gained by experience, for those who have attained a wide experience in the care of souls are able to speak more competently about interesting subjects: "A man that hath much experience shall think of many things: and he shall show forth understanding" (Ecclus. 34:9).

In addition the preacher must be able to judge souls, which means that he should: firstly, know those to whom he should not preach the word of God, for it is not intended for dogs and swine; secondly, realize when it is convenient to preach and when to keep silence, as "there is a time for speaking, and a time for silence" (Eccles. 3:7); thirdly, preach according to the needs of his hearers,

---

3. In this passage St. Paul, in order to emphasize the supremacy of charity over all else, discusses the most excellent and the most heroic acts: "to distribute one's goods to the poor, to deliver one's body to the flames, to know all mysteries, to speak all the tongues of men and of angels"; and he declares that without charity all these wonderful things would be useless. He indirectly affirms by this the merit and worth of these acts, provided they are enlivened by charity.

as St. Gregory advises in his Pastoral, where he enumerates thirty-six varied subjects that a preacher may use; fourthly, guard against verbosity, loudness, unbecoming gestures, lack of order in the development of his thoughts, and other defects which are disastrous to preaching. Speaking of this subject, St. Gregory explains the words of Ezechiel: "The sole of their foot was like the sole of a calf" (Ezech. 1:7), by noting that the soles of the feet of a saintly preacher resemble those of the calf because of their form and that they symbolize (the sole of the foot being divided in two parts) the proper division of the subject under treatment. Finally, the preacher should be aware that the skill he possesses results from knowledge communicated by the Holy Ghost. This was the type of learning possessed by the Apostles, who grasped all things by the power of the Holy Ghost from Whom the inspiration for all their sermons came, as is observed in the Acts: "They began to speak foreign tongues, even as the Holy Spirit prompted them to speak" (Acts 2:4). Happy are those who are provided with this knowledge which makes up for the imperfections of all other kinds of learning!

Chapter 9. The Language of the Preacher

In reference to language, it is essential that the preacher have clear diction, lest a defect of speech make his words unintelligible. Thus Moses, having such a defect, excused himself from accepting the mission which God confided in him; and his brother, Aaron, who was eloquent, was entrusted instead with the task of carrying the word of God to the people. The account in Exodus is as follows: "Aaron the Levite is thy brother, I know that he is eloquent. . . . He shall speak in thy stead to the people and shall be thy mouth; but thou shall be to him in those things that pertain to God" (Exod. 4:14–16).

Furthermore, it is imperative that God's representative know the intricacies and the resources of language. If in the primitive Church God gave the gift of tongues to His ministers in order that they might speak to all men indiscriminately, would it not be improper for a preacher to be defective in speech, either because of a weak memory, or an ignorance of Latin, or an inability to express himself well in the vulgar tongue, or any other fault of this kind? The Apocalypse states: "And his voice was like the voice of many waters" (Apoc. 1:15). The preacher is actually the voice of Christ in this world and he ought to have in his words a fullness proportionate to the subjects that he will treat.

It is equally desirable that the preacher have a voice with a definite resonance, otherwise he will lose much of the fruit of his sermons, for the weakness of his voice will prevent his words from being clearly heard. Scripture even compares the voice of a preacher to the sound of trumpets, for it should be heard at a distance with force and clarity. And then it is that we can apply to the preacher the words of the Prophet Osee: "Let there be a trumpet in thy throat. . ." (Osee 8:1).

In regard to style, it should be so clear that the listener can easily understand, and not of the type that St. Augustine decries: "Those who cannot be understood without difficulty should never be commissioned to instruct the people; or at least only in rare instances and in cases of urgent necessity."[4] The Book of Proverbs has practically the same advice: ". . . the learning of the wise is easy" (Prov. 14:6).

The manner of delivery should be neither fast nor slow, for the one becomes burdensome and difficult to follow, the other occasions weariness. "A genuine philosopher," remarked Seneca, "should take as much care of his diction as of his life."[5] Nothing is in order where haste prevails, therefore the discourse should flow smoothly without tiring or overtaxing the listener. If this is demanded of a philosopher, who merely desires the esteem of men, how much more should it be of a preacher who labors for the salvation of souls!

Also, the delivery should be succinct, according to the advice of Horace: "Be brief in your speech so that the docile may understand and the faithful keep your words." That is why the Book of Canticles says: "Thy lips are as a scarlet ribbon" (Cant. 4:3)—a reference to preachers who, as the gloss holds, are the lips of the

---

4. St. Augustine, *De doctrina christi.*
5. Seneca, in *Epist.*

Church. And as a ribbon binds the hair of the head to prevent it from falling into disorder, so the lips of preachers should restrain the profusion of words.

A sermon should be simple, and devoid of all the empty ornaments of rhetoric, after the example of those Asiatic nations who went to battle armed only with a plowshare. "Guard against multiplying the solemn Divine words lest you thereby overburden your speech," is the advice of St. Augustine.[6] At the same time the Bishop of Hippo describes in detail the metre, the length of syllables, and the oratorical figures which may be properly used. There is nothing astonishing about the fact that a saintly Doctor concerned himself with such minor points, when we realize that the philosophers also considered them. Seneca, for example, declared: "Any discourse having Truth for its object should be simple and unaffected."[7] Leave the ingenious style to art; here it is a question of souls. A sick man does not look for eloquence in his doctor; and a doctor who gives his prescriptions in flowery language is like a ruler who cares more for elegance than practicality.

The preacher should, moreover, exercise prudence, varying his sermons according to the type of his hearer. Let your word, says St. Gregory,[8] be a sweet melody for the good, a rebuke for the wicked; let it encourage the timid and moderate the restless; let it arouse the slothful and stimulate the negligent; let it persuade the obstinate, calm the hotheaded, and finally, let it console those who are losing hope. This is exactly what the text of Isaias teaches, "The Lord hath given me a learned tongue" (Isa. 50:4).

But all of this will be of little use to the preacher if his speech is not pleasant, "for a man without grace is as a vain fable" (Ecclus. 20:21). He should have a graciousness and sweetness of speech like that which was written of the Master of all Preachers, "Grace is poured abroad on thy lips" (Ps. 44:3).

6. St. Augustine, *De doctrina christi.*
7. Seneca, in *Epist.* .
8. St. Gregory, in *Registr.*, lib. 7.

30. (PSEUDO) THOMAS AQUINAS

De Arte Praedicandi[1]

Commentary

Harry Caplan's English translation of the *De arte praedicandi*, which bears the name of Thomas Aquinas (1225–1274) as author, first appeared in *Studies in Rhetoric and Public Speaking in Honor of James Albert Winans*, edited by Alexander M. Drummond in 1925, and was subsequently reprinted in the 1962 edition of that volume, and finally in the collection of Caplan's studies, *Of Eloquence: Studies in Ancient and Mediaeval Rhetoric*, edited by Anne King and Helen North in 1970. Like the *Treatise on Preaching* by Humbert of Romans, it is of interest because it represents the considered attitudes of the Dominicans, an order specifically geared to the preaching ministry, and especially of the most famous Dominican scholar of all time, Thomas Aquinas.

Although the tract is consistent with the precepts which Thomas Aquinas offered regarding preaching, Caplan believes that Thomas was not himself the author; he feels that the tract is from the pen of a late medieval author who claimed a connection with the Thomistic school. Thomas' own precepts relate to the subject matter of sermons, the preacher's function, and his ethical qualities, in much the same way as the author of this tract; so valuable did Pope Leo XIII (1878–1903) consider Thomas' method of sermon preparation that he recommended it to all preachers. Thomas argues:

> The matter of preaching is twofold: what is useful for the present life, as concerns God, or our neighbors, or ourselves; and what we hope to have in the next life. . . . All preaching should be directed to two purposes: demonstrating God's greatness by preaching the faith; and showing forth His goodness by elucidating the truth. . . . A preacher must have three qualities: stability, to ward him

---

1. Harry Caplan, "A Late Mediaeval Tractate on Preaching," *Of Eloquence: Studies in Ancient and Mediaeval Rhetoric*, edited and with introduction by Anne King and Helen North (Ithaca: Cornell University Press, 1970), pp.48–76.

from error; clearness, to avoid obscurity in his teaching; utility, to seek God's glory rather than his own. . . . A preacher must have three powers: he must be endowed with a fullness of knowledge of things sacred, to prove to others; he must be able to prove what he says; he must fitly set forth to his audience the things he conceives. . . . Two things are necessary for preachers, that they may lead to Christ. The first is an orderly discourse; the second is the virtue of good works.[2]

Caplan indicates that this treatise and one attributed to Henry of Hesse, the *Tractatus de Arte Praedicandi*,[3] were the first homiletical texts to appear in Germany. This one is not dated, but probably was printed in the last decade of the fifteenth century; while it was most likely composed by a Dominican successor of the Thomistic tradition, no tract by Thomas resembling it is presently known. In the treatise itself, Caplan notes, the author frequently quotes from memory and imprecisely, to establish a comprehensive accumulation of authorities.

The author defines the art of preaching and the sermon; he identifies various kinds of preaching; he notes the four parts of a sermon; he warns the preacher of faults to be avoided; he lists the topics most suitable for discussion in a sermon; and he explains nine methods of amplification. After spending the bulk of the latter part of the tract in explaining each of these nine ways of amplifying thoughts, the author concludes by building a tree of preaching:

> As a real tree develops from root to trunk, and the trunk puts forth main branches, and the main branches multiply into other branches, so in preaching the theme develops into the protheme or prelocution as root into trunk. Then the prelocution or protheme grows into the principal divisions of the theme as the trunk into the main branches. And the principal branches should, beyond, multiply into secondary divisions, that is, subdivisions and subdistinctions, and finally expand as the example in the tree below shows.[4]

---

2. Caplan, "Late Mediaeval Tractate," 48.

3. Harry Caplan, " 'Henry of Hesse' *On the Art of Preaching*," *PMLA* 48 (1933), 340–361.

4. When Caplan first translated the treatise, he was unable to locate the tree to which the tract refers. Later he found it in the Bayer, Staatsbibl., Munich (Cod. Lat. Monac, 23865, fols. 19–20) manuscripts, and added it to the 1970 edition (p.76).

31. BRUNETTO LATINI

Li Livres dou Tresor, III.60-65[1]

Translated by James R. East

Brunetto Latini's *Tresor* (c.1260), like Bonaventure's *De reductione artium ad Theologiam* and Vincent of Beauvais' *Speculum historiale* (both dating from about the same time), had as its goal the establishment of a guide to moral living in terms of available knowledge. Unlike the other two works named, however, the *Tresor* devoted a large amount of space to rhetoric, both as oral discourse and as *dictamen*. Despite the emphasis he gave to Ciceronian principles, however, Brunetto has not enjoyed the attention his work would seem to deserve. He offers the standard definitions, showing a heavy reliance on Cicero, and combines the oral and written aspects of the art, giving extensive hints concerning the composition of letters; he also offers many practical suggestions for utilizing the arts of discourse in daily life, much as John of Salisbury had a century earlier.

Although the entire content of Book III, *The Book concerning good speaking,* deserves close attention as a summary of all that late medieval scholarship could supply concerning rhetoric and its ramifications, considerations of space prohibit reproduction of more than one lengthy excerpt. For this reason, we limit ourselves here to those sections of the work dealing with refutation (Book III, chapters 60–65).

LX. The Fifth Part of the Discourse, Which Is Refutation

After the doctrine concerning confirmation comes the fifth part of the discourse, which is refutation, of which Tully [Cicero] says that it is refutation when the speaker minimizes and weakens all or the greater part of the arguments of his adversary. You should know that refutation issues from the same source as confirmation,

1. James R. East, "Book Three of Brunetto Latini's *Tresor,*" Ph.D. thesis, Stanford University, 1960, pp.162–170.

for just as one thing can be confirmed through the properties of people and deeds, so can it be refuted, and therefore, you should follow the very principles which the present writer has established previously in the chapter on confirmation. And yet the present writer says such things about it in order to show better the significance and nature of confirmation, and thus everyone can understand more easily when each is put against the other.

All arguments are refuted in one of four ways. The first is if you wish to deny that point of your adversary which he wishes to prove. The second is if you admit the point but deny the conclusion. The third is if you state that his arguments are fallacious. The fourth is if against his argument you establish one as strong or stronger. Therefore the present writer wishes to show the principles which are necessary to each of these four kinds.

LXI. Refutation Which Denies Probable Argument

The first type of refutation is to deny what your adversary undertakes to prove by logical or probable arguments. And if what he says is a probable argument, you can deny it in four ways. The first is when he has established something probable, you say that it is not because his account is clearly false, in this way: your adversary says that there is no man who is not more desirous of money than of wisdom; it is certain that what he says is not true, since there are many who love wisdom more than chattels. Or if his account is such that the contrary is as believable as what he says, in this way: when your adversary says that there is no man who is more desirous of gentility than of money, certainly in the same way you can strongly establish the contrary, that there is no one who does not desire money more than gentility [sic]. Or if his account is incredible, in this way: a man who is strongly avaricious says that because of a small favor for one of his friends he gave up a great amount of profit. And for that which happens sometimes, your adversary says that it happens generally, or in the following way: he says that all poor people desire money more than gentility; it certainly happens that sometimes a poor man desires money more, but there are others who prefer gentility; just as in some deserted spots, murder is com-

mitted, but not in all. Or if his account is not credible, in the
following manner: your adversary says of what happens sometimes that it never happens at all, in this way: he says that no one
can fall in love with a woman through a single glance; however,
this is something that can happen, because one can fall in love
at first sight.

A second way of denying your adversary's account is when he
mentions the sign of something, and you refute it by the same
means by which he supports it. In dealing with all types of signs
it is necessary to show two things: the one, that the sign is true,
and the other, that it is a proper sign of the thing which he wishes
to prove, just as blood is a sign of combat, and coal is the sign of
fire. And then it is necessary to show that something has been
done which should not have been, or that it wasn't the fitting
thing, and that the one of whom the speaker talks has the habit of
doing the thing, because all of these parts belong to signs and
things similar. And, therefore, when you wish to refute the signs
of your adversary, you should watch what he says, because if he
says that something is a sign of a thing you should say that it is
not, in this way: he says that the bloody coat which you are wearing is a sign that you have been in a fight, and you say that it is
not; or you say that it is a misleading sign since the bloody coat
might be a sign that you have been bled by a physician. Or you
say that the sign is more to your favor than his; and if he says
that an untoward thing has been done, in this way: "You are red
in the face because you had blame in the misdeed," you say that
it is red not because of evil, rather because of a sense of honesty
and right. Or you say that the sign is completely false because if
he says that you had the bloody knife in your hand, you say that
it certainly was not bloody, but rusty. Or you say that it pertained
to another motive than your adversary says; for if he says something untoward was done, in this way: "You departed without
taking leave and this is a sign of thievery"; you say that it was not
done in evil, but it was done because you did not wish to awaken
the lord within.

A third way of denying your adversary's account occurs when
he makes a comparison in his account between two things, and

you say that the one thing is not similar to the other because they are of different kinds. For if he says, "Because you wish to have a better horse than your neighbor, you wish to have a better wife," and you deny his account because a woman is not the same as a horse. Or the comparison may concern different kinds of things: if he says that one should fear him like a lion, you deny his account, because man is of a different nature than the lion. Or the comparison may concern different strengths: because if he were to say that Pyrrhus should be condemned to death because of the woman Hirestis whom he ravished, just as Paris stole Helen, you deny his account, because the crime of Paris was greater than that of Pyrrhus. Or because they were not of the same magnitude: if he says, "This man should be condemned to death because he killed a man, just as the other man has killed two men," you deny his account, because the one has not done as much harm as the other man. Thus I speak in short of the diversity of time, place, concomitant things, and opinion, of all diversities which are in men and things. In each one, the good orator can reprove his adversary and refute his confirmation.

The fourth way of denying your adversary's account occurs when he mentions the decision of some wise men. He can confirm such arguments in four ways. The case can be confirmed by the praise of those who made the decision, as Julius Caesar said that the old wise men of Rome, because of their great wisdom, had pardoned the Carthaginians. Or he can prove it by the similarity of a decision to the thing of which he is speaking, as a praetor of Rome did when he said, "Just as our ancestors pardoned the Carthaginians, so should we pardon the Greeks." Moreover, one can also prove his case by saying that the decision that he refers to was confirmed by all men, or by all those who heard it and were able to confirm it, because that decision was greater and more weighty than the thing of which he speaks, as Cato did when he said that Manlius Torquatus condemned his son to die only because he fought against the French against his orders.

These are the four ways to confirm decision, and you should be prepared now to refute what he said by the contrary of his confirmations, if you can. That is to say, if he praises it, you censure it, and if he says the decisions were confirmed, you say they were not. Do just the same with all the reasons that he gives on the decision; namely, you give contrary reasons. Since the principles of speechmaking must be the same for one speaker as for another, the present writer says the speaker who mentions the decision should watch closely that the decision is not dissimilar to the matter under consideration, since his adversary could easily refute him. And one should also avoid relating a decision which offends some of the auditors, because they will rebel immediately, and say that it is against justice, and that the judge should be censured for it. One should also watch that when he mentions many good, commendable, and well-known decisions he does not mention a strange and unfamiliar one, since this is something which the adversary could easily contradict and refute another's account. Now you have heard how one can refute all probable arguments; it is necessary to consider refutation of logical arguments.

LXII. Refutation Which Denies Logical Arguments

If your adversary bases his account upon logical arguments, you should then consider if they are logical or if they only seem to be logical. If they are truly logical, you do not have the power to oppose them, but if they only seem to be logical and are not, then you can refute them by the same means which were set forth in the preceding chapter concerning logical arguments, that is, by means of dilemma, enumeration, or simple conclusion.

A dilemma occurs when the speaker arranges two, three, or more parts, of which if you confirm one, whichever it might be, you arrive at your conclusion certainly, if it is true. But if it is false, you can refute it in two ways, either by refuting all its parts, or by refuting one part or more. For example, your adversary wishes to conclude that you should not rebuke your friend, and according to this he arranges two parts, in this way: "He either respects or not; if he respects, you should not rebuke him because he is good, and if he does not respect, you should not rebuke him since he cares nothing for your principles." This argument is not perforce true, but only resembles it, and you should refute both parts at once, in this way: "On the contrary, I ought to rebuke him, for if he respects he will not condemn my advice, and if he does not respect, I should all the more rebuke him, because he is not at all wise." And if you wish to refute one of these parts and no more, you should say: "If he truly respects, I ought all the more rebuke him, because he will reform because of my advice, and will abandon his mistaken way."

Enumeration occurs when the speaker mentions many points in his account in order to prove one of them, as this discourse will set forth in the chapter on logical arguments. It is necessary then for you now to refute his enumeration, which can have three faults. The first is if he does not count that part which you wish to maintain. For example, your adversary says thus: "either you bought this horse or he was given to you, or he was bred on your estate, or he belongs to you through inheritance, or, if none of these are true, then you stole it; but I know certainly that you did not buy it, nor was it given to you, nor left to you by inheritance, nor bred on your estate; therefore, you stole it without a doubt." When he has concluded in such a way, you should mention at once the part which he omitted in his enumeration, and say that you won it at a tournament, and his argument is completely refuted if it is a truth which he did not relate. The second fault occurs when he includes a point which you can contradict, because if he says that the horse was not left to you by inheritance, and you can show that it was, it is certain that you have destroyed his argument. The third fault occurs when one of the points which he enumerates you can acknowledge and assert clearly without disgrace. For example, when your adversary says thus: "You remain here either for luxury, for ambush, or for the benefit of your friend," you can maintain certainly that you are here for the benefit of your friend.

A simple conclusion is used when the speaker concludes what he wishes to say on the strength of a point which he mentioned in the presence of his adversary. There are two ways, either proof through logic or by the semblance of logic. If he proves it by logic, you cannot contradict it; for if he says: "This woman is pregnant; therefore, she has lain with a man," or "If this man breathes, then he is still alive," it is certain you cannot contradict. But if it has only the semblance of logic, in this way: "If she is a mother, then she loves her son," you can certainly reprove it and show that it is not necessarily so, but can be quite the contrary.

LXIII. The Second Type of Refutation, Which Denies the Conclusion

The second kind of refutation occurs when one discerns that the adversary's resolution or undertaking is true, but one denies his conclusion because the conclusion follows from what you acknowledged, but is something different from what it must or can be. For example, the people of the city were marshalled up and it happened that when you were going, a sickness overcame you on your way there, which kept you from arriving at the rally, so that your adversary accuses you and concludes in this way: "If you had been at the rally, our constable would have seen you, but you were not seen there; therefore you did not choose to come." Now notice in this argument you agree clearly to the resolution of your adversary, that if you had been at the rally the constable would have seen you, and you agree to the undertaking, that he did not see you, but the conclusion, however, does not follow from this, because at the point where he says you did not choose to go, he does not speak the truth, because you certainly wished to go but could not. Because this example is so clear and apparent that it is an easy matter to recognize its fault, the present writer wishes to set forth another example which is more difficult to comprehend, in order to show the properties of good speaking. In case the fault is hard to understand, it can be proved as if it were true. This can be done in two ways, either because your adversary believes you agree for certain to a doubtful point, or because he believes you do not remember what you asserted and acknowledged.

If your adversary believes that you agree for certain to a doubtful point on which he bases his conclusion, then it is necessary for you to show at once the understanding you had when you agreed to the point, and indicate that he has turned his argument to another point. For example your adversary says thus: "You have need of money," and you certainly agree to his account, according to your understanding, which is that you wish to have a greater amount than you now have. But your adversary believes something else and says thus: "You have need of money because if you did not you would do business; therefore, you are poor." Notice that he concludes with some other sense, and for this reason, you can refute his argument in which he turned and changed what you meant. If he thinks you have forgotten what you have acknowledged and how, he will make a wrong conclusion against you, in this way: "If the estate of the dead man belongs to you, anyone must believe that you killed him." At this word, your adversary says many things and assigns many reasons for proving his case. When he has done this, he concludes his argument, saying: "Without a doubt the estate belongs to you; therefore, you killed the man." Notice that this conclusion does not necessarily follow from the fact that the estate belongs to you. It is necessary, therefore, for you to watch carefully the strength of his argument, and from where he draws it, and how.

LXIV. How One Should Refute the Argument Which Is Fallacious

The third type of refutation occurs when you say that the argument of your adversary is fallacious. This fallacy can be of two kinds, either because the defect is in the argument itself, or because the argument is not appropriate to what the speaker proposes. You should know that there is a defect in the argument when it is entirely false, general, universal, weak, farfetched, inappropriate, exchangeable, self-evident, unconfirmed, disgraceful, offensive, contradictory, inconsistent, or adverse. A false argument is one that has to do with lies. For example, "No one can be wise who scorns money, but Socrates scorned money; therefore he was not wise." A general argument is one which does not belong any more to you than to your adversary. If you say, "I shall briefly tell why I am right," your adversary can say the same as you. A universal argument is one that can be drawn upon a thing that is not really true, in this way: "Honorable judges, I should not have come before you if I did not think that right was on my side." The weak argument is one of two kinds. The one is spoken too late, as the peasant who says, "Had I believed that my oxen would be stolen, I would have locked the stable." The other kind is to conceal a disgraceful thing with a weak excuse, as the knight did who abandoned his king when the king was at the height of his power; and when the king was exiled, his knight met him one day and said, "Sir, you should have pardoned me for having abandoned you, since I was getting ready to come to your aid single-handed." A farfetched argument is one which is based on something too remote, as the maid of Medea who said, "Oh, God, would that the timber from which the ships were made never had been cut." Inappropriate arguments are of three kinds. There is one which mentions properties which are common with something else; for if you were to ask me the properties of a rebellious man, and I say that a rebellious man is one who is wicked and trouble-some among men, it is clear that these properties belong no more to a rebellious man than to a vain or foolish man, or some other wicked man. A second kind establishes properties which are not true but false; for if you asked the properties of wisdom, and I said that wisdom is nothing but earning money, I would be establishing untrue properties. The third kind establishes some properties but not all; for if you ask the properties of folly, and I said that folly is the desire for fame, certainly, even though this is folly in one sense, I have not mentioned all the properties of folly. An exchangeable argument is one which through doubtful reasons seeks to prove a doubtful case, in this way: "Great princes of the earth, you should not fight against one another, since the gods who govern the movements of heaven do not fight with each other." A self-evident argument occurs when the speaker con-cludes with that argument which his adversary approves, and omits that which he should prove. Just as the adversary of Orestes did; when he was to show that Orestes had murdered his mother, he indicated that he had killed her; and this was unnecessary, since Orestes did not deny it, but he said instead that he had killed her rightly. An unconfirmed argument occurs when the speaker talks at length and offers much proof upon one point which his adversary completely denies. For example, Ulysses was accused of having killed Ajax, but he said that he had not; nevertheless, his adversary made a great uproar, saying it was a very foul deed that a base man should have killed such a noble knight. A disgraceful argument is one that is indecent because of the place, that is to say, indecent words before the altar; or by reason of him who says them, that is, if a bishop speaks of women or luxury; or by reason of the time, that is, if on Easter Sunday one says that Christ was not resurrected; or by reason of the audience, that is, if in the presence of nuns and monks one speaks of vanity and worldly pleasures; or by reason of the subject, that is, that whoever speaks of the Holy Cross should not say that it is a fork. An offensive argument is one that annoys the wish of the auditors; for if in front of money lenders I were to praise the law which condemns usury, my argument certainly would be vexatious to my auditors. A contradictory argument occurs when the speaker speaks against an action which the auditors have done. For example I go before Alexander to accuse some strong man who had conquered a city by means of arms, and say that there is nothing so cruel in the world as conquering cities and laying them waste; it is apparent that the argument is contradictory, because the auditor, Alexander, had destroyed several cities and towns. An inconsistent argument occurs when the speaker on a point says two different things which are contradictory to one another, as when a person says, "Whoever has virtue has no need for anything else for a good life," and afterward the same man says that no one can live a good life without good health. In another instance, after one has said that he assisted his friend out of affection, he says that he expected much service from him. An adverse argument is one that does more against the speaker than for him; if I wished to encourage a knight in battle, and said that our enemies are big, strong, well-off, it is certain that this would be more against than for me.

It is necessary now to mention the other kind of fallacious argument, the one which does not pertain to what the speaker proposes. This can exist in many forms; if the speaker promises that he will establish several points and then speaks only of one; or when he should mention all parts, he mentions no more than one, that is, if the speaker wishes to show that all women are avaricious and he shows only that one or two are; or if he does not defend himself against that which he is accused, like Pacuvius, when he wished to defend music which was attacked by others, he did not defend music, but praised wisdom greatly. The same was done by him who was accused of vainglory because he did not defend himself against it, but said that he was very bold and hardy at arms; or if something is blamed because of the fault of men, as it is with those who speak evil of the Holy Church because of the wickedness of the prelates; or if I wished to praise a man, I would say that he was very rich and well-off, but I do not mention that he possesses any virtues; or if I make a comparison between two men or two things in such a way that one does not believe that I can praise the one without blaming the other. Or the speaker praises the one and does not mention the other, as if we were to take counsel to establish which is better, peace or war, and I would not make an end of praising peace, but make no mention of war; or if I asked about a specific thing and you responded about a general thing, as if I asked you whether a bear runs and you told me that men and animals run. Or if the reason which a speaker gives is false, because if he says that money is good, since it gives more happiness to life than anything in the world, it is certain the reason is false, because money gives to men the greatest labor and trouble, according to God and mankind. Or if the speaker gives feeble reasons for his account, as Plautus did: "It is not good," he said, "for one to castigate his friend for his misdeeds (for the misdeeds he has done)."[2] Or if the speaker gives such reasons in his account that it is only a restatement of his case, because if he says that avarice

2. The example from Plautus seems broad enough here in its meaning to support Latini's idea. It seems, however, that Latini has taken liberty to change the meaning of the example as Cicero uses it in *De inventione* and as Plautus uses it in *The Trinummus*. Plautus says in the first lines of Act I:

> To chide a friend for any fault which merits blame
> Is thankless task, yet useful in this life of ours
> And profitable. So today this friend of mine
> I'll soundly chide for fault which richly merits blame.

Titus Maccius Plautus, *The Trinummus*, trans. William Ritchie (London: Simpkin Marshall and Co., 1921), p.5.

is a very bad thing because greed for money has already done much great damage to many people, it is certain that avarice and greed are the same thing. Or if the speaker gives an unimportant reason where he should give an important one, because if he says friendship is a good thing because one derives much pleasure from it, it is certain he could give better reasons, and say that there is in it much to be gained, and decency, and virtue.

LXV. The Fourth Type of Refutation Which Establishes Reasons as Strong as or Stronger than the Adversary's[3]

The fourth type of refutation occurs when, after your adversary has established his argument, you reply with one against it as strong or stronger; and such arguments belong more to controversies over making decisions than to other matters. You should know that this refutation can be accomplished in two ways. The first occurs when your adversary mentions something to which you agree and is thus confirmed, but you immediately reply contrariwise with a stronger reason which is confirmed by logical arguments. When Caesar said: "We should pardon the conspirators since they are our citizens," Cato replied, "It is true that they are our citizens, but if they are not sentenced Rome perforce will be destroyed by them." The second kind is used when your adversary says of a thing that it is profitable, and you say that it is true, but you show at once that what you say is honorable, for without a doubt honor is a more solid thing than profit, or just as much so. At this point the present writer leaves the discussion of the fifth part of the discourse, refutation, on which he has said what he knew about it; and he will now speak of the sixth part, which is conclusion.

---

3. Gaiter's title is "The Fourth Type of Refutation." [Ed. note: Gaiter is the editor of the most recent Italian edition of the *Tresor.*]

32. GILES OF ROME

On the Difference between Rhetoric, Ethics, and Politics, Part 1[1]

Translated by Joseph M. Miller

Shortly after the appearance in 1280 of the Latin translation of Aristotle's recently rediscovered *Rhetoric* by William of Moerbeke, the Augustinian doctor, Giles of Rome (Aegidius Romanus, 1243–1316), a disciple of Thomas Aquinas, composed the first scholastic commentary on the work.[2] The commentary did not make any significant contribution to the technical understanding of the rhetorical art; on the contrary, it illustrates almost to the point of stereotype the scholastic approach to many classical texts.[3] Giles constructed a Procrustean bed of scholastic principles and resolutely shaped the Stagyrite's treatise to fit.

Basically the same quality of scholastic structure characterizes Giles' subsequent tract, *On the Difference between Rhetoric, Ethics, and Politics.* As the later Scholastics found a major challenge in the attempt to identify the relative importance of intellect and will in man's actions, so Giles found it necessary to determine whether the art of rhetoric was an intellectual activity (one of the *artes sermocinales*) or a science designed to affect human behavior (one of the *artes morales*). In the first part of the work Giles eliminates rhetoric from consideration as a behavioral study, before proceeding to a lengthy discussion of the difference between ethics and politics. Since the latter question is not of immediate interest to the rhetorical theoretician, only the first part of the document is offered here.

---

1. Trans. from Gerardo Bruni, "The *De differentia rhetoricae, ethicae et politicae* of Aegidius Romanus," *New Scholasticism* (1932), 1–18.
2. Giles of Rome, *Commentaria in rhetoricam Aristotelis,* ed. Alexander Achillinus (Venice, 1515; reprinted, Frankfurt, 1968).
3. S. Robert, "Rhetoric and Dialectic: According to the First Latin Commentary on the *Rhetoric* of Aristotle," *New Scholasticism* 31 (1957), 484–498.

*A Letter from Brother Giles of Rome, of the Order of
Hermit Friars of St. Augustine, to Oliver,
of the Order of Preachers, a Student at Anjou.*

Brother Giles of Rome, of the Order of Hermit Friars, sends
greetings and a genuine expression of love to his dear brother in
Christ, Oliver of the Order of Preachers, a student at Anjou.

You have asked me, God bless you, to explain for you a little
something about the difference between Rhetoric, Ethics, and
Politics. Surely, if you have studied carefully what I have written
about the *Rhetoric,* you cannot fail to distinguish between
Rhetoric and the other two. Granted that Tully seems to classify
Rhetoric under Politics; if that were so, there would indeed be
some difficulty in differentiating them. But if Rhetoric is indeed
the handmaiden of Dialectic,[4] and is therefore more Dialectic
than Politics, then it is easy to establish the difference between
them.

First, Ethics and Politics are specific sciences and are of a
clearly defined kind; they deal with human actions as the subject
matter with which they are concerned. Not so, however, with
Rhetoric; as we read in Book I of the *Rhetoric,* "Rhetoric is the
handmaiden of Dialectic." Both deal with the kinds of things that
somehow fall into the province of general knowledge and not
under the purview of any specific science. But if we say this, as I
believe we are quite justified in saying, then there seems to arise
a certain area of doubt: Rhetoric thus appears as a sort of middle
area, somewhere between the behavioral sciences and the intellectual,[5] and it seems to derive from two areas of study, namely
Dialectic and Politics. But Book I of the *Rhetoric* tells us that it is

4. The translation of the opening sentence of the *Rhetoric,* "Rhetoric is
the handmaiden of Dialectic," and the subsequent conclusions from that
translation depend upon the Latin word *assecutiva,* which William of Moerbeke and Giles both use in place of the Greek *antistrophos. Assecutiva* implies much more inferiority or dependency than the Greek term.

5. This illustrates the scholastic conviction that all knowledge must be
viewed in light of whether it is primarily an intellectual exercise or a system
of acting. I have translated the Latin *moralis* as "behavioral," since that
modern psychological term reflects its import more accurately than the
traditional translation, "moral."

the lot of Rhetoric by its very nature to serve as a kind of part of Dialectic and to deal with the subject matter of Dialectic as if it relates to behavior. But if Rhetoric embraces these elements, then it is more Dialectic than Politics, and we must agree with the Philosopher who joins it to Dialectic rather than with Tully, who seems to subordinate it to Politics.

We must note that a science is identified according to the subject matter with which it deals. Now since Rhetoric deals with the knowledge of those things which are common to several sciences, and since it does not directly concern itself with the knowledge of moral issues, we are therefore justified in saying that it is of an indeterminate subject matter and thus of the same nature as Dialectic; therefore it is not proper to look upon it as of the same nature as Politics. The art of questioning applies certain common principles to individual areas of study, and thus it examines specialized sciences. For example, it examines Geometry in terms of these common elements, with the result that Geometry seems to be composed of two areas of study, Dialectic and Geometry. In reality, however, the art of questioning in this manner does not deal directly with the subject matter of Geometry or of any other specialized science; similarly, the questioner who is not trained in a specific field, but who knows only the elements which are common to all knowledge, is not examining the field at all, but is applying Dialectic to it, as the *Sophistical Refutations* makes clear.[6]

In the same way, Rhetoric considers points which are common to all questions of behavior; nevertheless it does deal directly with the issues of specific questions of behavior by means of these common points. Rhetoric is not proper, therefore, to Politics because it is not concerned with the foundations of behavior; instead it is proper to Dialectic because it treats of elements common to all knowledge, as the *Rhetoric* indicates.

Moreover, since the art of questioning indicates by its very nature a knowledge of common elements rather than of a specific science, when it focuses those generalities upon a specific science

6. *De sophisticorum elenchis*, 11 (Didot, I.287).

such as Geometry, it becomes sophistic Geometry in that it does not proceed from those elements which are properly Geometry. So also, the orator whose province it is to know common principles of behavior, but who moves from those common principles to a specific area like Politics, can be called a political sophist,[7] because he does not argue from a real understanding of Politics.

In the remainder of the treatise, Giles drops Rhetoric from consideration; he sets norms for distinguishing Ethics, as the science of individual behavior, from Politics, as the science of public behavior.

---

7. A more accurate rendition of Giles' words, *sophisticus politicus*, might be the twentieth-century colloquialism, "an ivory-tower pundit."

33. DANTE ALIGHIERI

De vulgari eloquentia, VI[1]

Translated by A. G. Ferrers Howell

Despite the great fame of the *Divina Commedia*, Dante's lesser work, *De vulgari eloquentia* was virtually unknown for almost two hundred years after his death in 1321. Although Boccaccio (1313–1375) mentions it in his *Vita di Dante*, and Leonardo Bruni (1369–1444) mentions it in connection with Dante's *De monarchia*, implying that he was not familiar with the manuscript, it was not until 1529 that Gian Giorgio Trissino brought the work to popular attention. Trissino agreed with Dante's insistence that the language and literature of Italy should be called Italian rather than Tuscan. In his letter to Pope Clement VII (1523–1534) and in his published dialogue *Il Castellano* (1529), Trissino thrashed out the issue of "Tuscan vs. Italian," quoting liberally from *De vulgari eloquentia*. During the same year an anonymous Italian translation of *De vulgari eloquentia* appeared; Trissino's contemporaries were certain that he was the translator and editor of the work, since the same publisher who issued the edition also published the *Il Castellano* and the letter to the Pope, the paper and type form were identical with the other two works, and certain new letters were used which Trissino had invented.

The *De vulgari eloquentia* offers no real rhetorical insights. Instead it describes Dante's understanding of the early development of human speech and language traits to the point where it reaches perfection in the ideal vernacular, Italian. Although the work is of minor importance to rhetoricians, all students of oral discourse will appreciate the method by which Dante establishes the identity of man's first vernacular speech.

---

1. Dante Alighieri, *De vulgari eloquentia*, trans. A. G. Ferrers Howell, in *A Translation of the Latin Works of Dante Alighieri* (London, 1940), pp.1–124. Chapter VI appears on pp.15–17.

Chapter VI

Since human affairs are carried on in very many different languages, so that many men are not understood by many with words any better than without words, it is meet for us to make investigation concerning that language which that man who had no mother, who was never suckled, who never saw either childhood or youth, is believed to have spoken. In this as in much else Pietramala is a most populous city,[2] and the native place of the majority of the children of Adam. For whoever is so offensively unreasonable as to suppose that the place of his birth is the most delightful under the sun, also rates his own vernacular (that is, his mother tongue) above all others, and consequently believes that it actually was that of Adam. But we, to whom the world is our native country, just as the sea is to the fish, though we drank of Arno before our teeth appeared, and though we love Florence so dearly that for the love we bore her we are wrongfully suffering exile—we rest the shoulders of our judgment on reason rather than on feeling. And although as regards our own pleasure or sensuous comfort there exists no more agreeable place in the world than Florence, still, when we turn over the volumes both of poets and other writers in which the world is generally and particularly described, and take account within ourselves of the various situations of the places of the world and their arrangement with respect to the two poles and to the equator, our deliberate and firm opinion is that there are many countries and cities both nobler and more delightful than Tuscany and Florence of which we are a native and a citizen, and also that a great many nations and races use a speech both more agreeable and more serviceable than the Italians do. Returning therefore to our subject, we say that a certain form of speech was created by God together with the first soul. And I say "a form" both in respect of words and their construction and of the utterance of this con-

---

2. Pietramala was a village in the Apennines, about twenty miles south of Bologna. Fraticelli quotes a similar ironical saying about another insignificant place: "So and so has travelled a great deal; he has even seen Peretola."

struction;[3] and this form every tongue of speaking men would use, if it had not been dissipated by the fault of man's presumption, as shall be shown further on.

In this form of speech Adam spoke until the building of the Tower of Babel, which is by interpretation the tower of confusion; and this form of speech was inherited by the sons of Heber, who after him were called Hebrews. With them alone did it remain after the confusion, in order that our Redeemer (who was, as to his humanity, to spring from them) might use, not the language of confusion, but of grace. Therefore Hebrew was the language which the lips of the first speaker formed.[4]

3. By "construction" Dante means the grammatical arrangement of words in sentences; by "utterance of the construction" he means the pronunciation.
4. The statement here made as to the permanency of the language spoken by Adam cannot be reconciled with *Paradiso* XXVI.124–126, where we are told that the language of Adam had disappeared long before the building of Babel; and we must accordingly take it that Dante's opinion had undergone a change by the time he was working on the *Paradiso*. Several scholars feel that the passage in *Paradiso* was inserted expressly to correct this one.

34. ROBERT OF BASEVORN

The Form of Preaching[1]

Commentary

Robert of Basevorn was a fourteenth-century writer; almost nothing is known of him. His *Forma praedicandi* (*c.*1322) is a fine example of the medieval *artes praedicandi* dealing with the "thematic sermon"; this genre takes its name from the use it makes of Scriptural texts or themes as a basis for amplification and division by the preacher. The origins of the thematic sermon are obscure; such early handbooks and manuals of preaching as Guibert's *Liber quo ordine,* the *Speculum Ecclesiae* of Honorius of Autun, and Alan of the Isles' *De arte praedicatoria* do not indicate an awareness of the method. On the other hand, there is a strong indication of thematic development in the *Sermones* of Anthony of Padua (1195–1232), and in the University Sermons preached in Paris during 1230–1231. By the middle of the fourteenth century, however, the technique was quite popular, the subject of numerous treatises like Robert's.

The *Forma praedicandi* consists of an explanatory preface and index, followed by fifty chapters. Chapters 1–5 define and limit the field of preaching; 6–12 describe the preaching methods of Jesus Christ and certain saints; 13–48 deal with various types of "embellishment," ranging from "Invention of the Theme" to "Reflecting on the Subject Matter." This is followed by a brief addendum dealing with cadence. The translation by Leopold Krul is worth comparison with such other preaching manuals as those by Humbert of Romans,[2] Henry of Hesse,[3] and Simon Alcock,[4] all available in English translations.

1. Latin text in Th.–M. Charland, *Artes praedicandi: Contribution à l'histoire de la rhetorique au moyen age* (Paris, 1936), pp.233–323; English translation by Leopold Krul, O.S.B., in *Three Medieval Rhetorical Arts,* ed. James J. Murphy, pp.109–215.

2. See above, 29: Humbert of Romans, *Treatise on Preaching,* II.8–9.

3. Harry Caplan, " 'Henry of Hesse' *On the Art of Preaching,*" *PMLA* 48 (1933), 340–361.

4. Mary F. Boynton, "Simon Alcock on Expanding the Sermon," *Harvard Theological Review* 34 (1941), 201–216.

35. THOMAS OF TODI

The Art of
Giving Sermons and of
Preparing Conferences (EXCERPTS)[1]

Translated by Joseph M. Miller

Little is known of Thomas of Todi, who flourished toward the end of the fourteenth century, beyond the fact that he was a master of theology in the Order of St. Augustine. His treatise, *Ars sermocinandi ac etiam collationes faciendi,* contains seven sections: Part I discusses the divisions of a topic; Part II, the subdivisions; Part III, proofs; Part IV, expansion or embellishment; Part V, arrangement; Part VI, the introduction of a theme; and Part VII, the construction of parallel clauses. Thus it resembles in many ways the *Forma praedicandi* of Robert of Basevorn.[2] The following excerpts are drawn from the opening of the treatise and the last section. The translation is based on the critical text compiled by June Babcock in 1941.

The art[3] of giving sermons as well as of preparing conferences is basically divided into seven considerations. The first of these hinges on the division of the theme; the second on the subdivisions of the primary division; the third on the proofs for the separate items; the fourth on the development and embellishment of them; the fifth on the structural organization of the sermon; the sixth on the introduction of the theme; the seventh on the construction of rhythmic parallels.

---

1. June Babcock, "*Ars Sermocinandi ac etiam Collationes Faciendi* of Thomas of Todi, Ms. Paris, Bibl. Nat. 14965," M. A. thesis, Cornell University, 1941.
2. See previous selection, 34: Robert of Basevorn, *The Form of Preaching.*
3. Babcock, "*Ars Sermocinandi,*" pp.1–8.

In dealing with the first point, the division of the theme, we must preface the division of the theme by considering it in five ways; the first of these is to view it as undivided, so that what is determined about the theme can be expressed in some kind of a series of parallels. In this step, the theme is not broken down into parts, as in the example (Matt. 6:21): "Where your treasure is, there also is your heart." In these words, two seem to have particular importance: "treasure" and "heart." As to the first, there are four kinds of treasure: the treasure is nobler and so should be desired; the treasure is baser and so should be despised; the treasure is inward and so should be guarded; the treasure is outward and so should be cast out. Likewise in the theme given, the remaining part of the undivided text can be explained so that what applies to the noun "heart" can be applied particularly to the "heart of man." It can be located in a place of delight, that is, in external things; it can be located in the seat of life, that is, in interior things; it can be located in what it desires, that is, in nobler things.

The second way it can be considered as a theme is by studying certain characteristics, of which one is perfect latinity. Now perfect latinity is that style which depends upon a properly placed verb and its predicate, implicit or explicit. It can indeed be implicit to the extent that this phrase, "Peter runs,"[4] seems to be imperfect by reason of lacking one of the parts (it does not have a predicate); but if in the example given the verb given as "runs" is changed, it can be changed into "is," with the participle of the verb, "runs"; in this case it will be perfect latinity and will have all its parts fitting together, as "Peter is running." A theme, then, in which this process immediately becomes evident can be this: "And when you fast do not be gloomy like the hypocrites, for they disfigure their faces" (Matt. 6:16). This can be conveniently treated in two parts, each of which demonstrates perfect latinity. The first will be, "When you fast, do not be gloomy like the hypocrites"; the second will be, "they disfigure their faces." In the words of this text, two points come up for consideration, specifi-

---

4. *Petrus currit;* Thomas later compares this to *Petrus est currens.*

cally: the mortification of those who are struggling, which ought to be encouraged, and the deceit of the evil ones, which ought to be destroyed. First, then, "When you fast, do not be gloomy like the hypocrites"; secondly, "for they disfigure their faces."

Thirdly, the theme can be studied as divided into parts of which one is perfect latinity, the other not, as in this example: "And I saw another angel ascending, as from the rising of the sun" (Rev. 7:2). In the words of this text, then, two things are taken together as one, namely the beautiful countenance glorious in many ways and the admirable ascent, luminous in many ways.

Fourthly, the theme can be studied as made up of parts, none of which is perfect latinity. For example, one part of the theme is supplied in such a way that by itself it might be one of the parts of a perfect composition, yet nothing is added to it so as to embrace all the parts of a perfect latin expression, as in this example: "And I saw another angel." This text contains three parts: the first is the word "I saw," the second is "another," and the third is "angel." It is perfectly clear that none of these parts can be taken by itself as perfect latinity, though each might be part of a perfect expression. In the words of this text, then, three things should be quickly treated: the clear vision of what is seen, the holy companionship of being joined to another, and the noble sublimity of perfection. The first of these is "I saw," the second is "another," and the third is "angel."

Fifth and last, the theme can be considered as rhetoricians would consider it, by making a principle division of one word. From this standpoint, a phrase or word can be divided into the letters which make it up, insofar as parallels can be formed according to the will of the preacher, as I make such a division in the text, "I saw another angel." In this case, I take or adapt from the text the word *angelus* (angel), to demonstrate what the letters represent which compose the word *angelus*. There are seven letters altogether, A N G E L U S, according to which parallels can be formed which relate to the angels, as in this way: Through A is signified the *adherence* to God of the angels; through N is signified the *nunciation* of secrets which angels perform truthfully; through G is signified the *gaudium* (or joy) which angels always experience; through E is signified the fact that angels *elevate* the worthy soul; through L is signified that angels *laud* the divine essence; through V is signified that angels look upon *veritas* (truth), through S is signified that the angels love *sanctity*. There you have the word *angelus* divided into letters, so that appropriate parallels can be formed, each fitting together with the others.

Thomas gives two more examples of this method of dividing a single word into its component letters; he uses the text, "Peter and John went up to the temple" (Acts 3:1), and deals with each name in the same way. He points out that in the name PETRUS, P represents punishment for sin, E represents equality of treatment for all who beg, T represents tranquility exhibited by the needy, R represents rigorousness for those who are negligent, U represents (h)umility by those who do good works, and S represents softness of speech. Similarly, in the name JOHANNES, J represents the just man; O, the (h)onest man; A, the amiable man; N, the man nourished in virtue; N, the fact that John was named by his parents in a miraculous way; E, that John was one of the elect; S, that he was submissive. He then explains that the letter H is omitted because it is not truly a letter, but only a sign of breathing. Then, having completed his discussion of how to analyze the text before dividing it, he proceeds to the rules for "Division of a Theme."

There follows[5] the seventh and last section, which deals with the construction of rhythmic parallels.[6] The first rule for this section is: a rhythm must be constructed so that its melody and charm will enchant the ears of the listeners. The second rule is: all the components of a rhythmic parallel must be balanced in phrasing, both as to the number of syllables and as to the accents. Thus, if the first phrase is composed of three words, so should be the second, the third, and if there are more the fourth. And if the first word of the first member is bisyllabic, the first word of the second member should also be bisyllabic; likewise the first word

5. Babcock, *"Ars Sermocinandi,"* pp.68–75.
6. Thomas uses the word *rhythmus* in many different senses. I have therefore translated it variously, according to context, as "rhythm," "rhythmic parallel," "member (or part) of a parallel," "clause," "phrase," etc.

of the third member should be bisyllabic, and so on with the others if there are more members in the series. Again, if the second word of the first member is a trisyllable, the second word of the second member should also be a trisyllable, and so on with the third and fourth, if there are so many. Likewise, if the third word of the first member has four syllables, the third word of the second member ought to have four syllables, and so on with the others; all this appears in the following example:

Salus hominis proponitur;	The salvation of man is assured;
Sensus daemonis confunditur;	The intent of the devil is thwarted;
Cursus sideris dirigitur.	The paths of the stars are laid out.

The third rule is that a syllable sometimes has one letter, sometimes two, sometimes three, sometimes even four. An example of the first and second is *amo* (I love), a single bisyllabic word, the first syllable of which is the one letter, *a*, the second the two letters, *m* and *o*. An example of the third occurs in the word *sensus*, which is made up of two syllables, each containing three letters. An example of the fourth occurs in the word *scrutabar* (I searched), which has three syllables, the first containing four letters, the second two, and the third three. Thus it seems quite clear that although one syllable may contain more letters than another, the accent of the word does not necessarily change; this is clear from the words *amabor* and *scrutabor* (I will love and I will search): the first syllable of *amabor* is one letter, the first syllable of *scrutabor* contains four letters.

The fourth rule is that the sermon-giver ought to try his best to arrange that the words around which the parallelism is built contain identical vowels; this rule must be understood as referring to the penultimate and ultimate sounds. If it cannot always be observed in both the penultimate and ultimate syllables, it must be observed always without deviation in the ultimate. For this reason, words like *deficientes* (lacking) and *contaminatas* (befouled) are never appropriate partners, neither in the beginning of a parallel clause, nor in the middle, nor at the end, since the final vowel of the first word is *e*, and the final vowel of the second is *a*. But the words *deficiens* (lacking) and *subveniens* (assisting)

will sound well at the beginning or at the middle or at the end,
since the penultimate and ultimate vowels of the words are
identical.

The fifth rule is that one rhythmic construction may contain
two words in place of one, in the case where one of the phrases
contains a word of three syllables and the other replaces it with
two words, one a monosyllable and the other a bisyllable, as in
this example:

> *Justus quilibet summo opere coronari tenetur*
> *Animum dirigere, nam hoc est utilitatis;*
> *Ad Deum recurrere, nam hoc est necessitatis;*
> *Mundumque despicere, nam hoc est salubritatis.*

> (Every just man is certain to be rewarded at the end of his life
> For governing his will, which is a useful act;
> For returning to God, which is a necessary act;
> For despising the world, which is a sensible act.)

It is obvious that at the beginning of the first member there
appears the three-syllable word, *animum;* the parallel at the
beginning of the second member is a two-word phrase, *ad Deum,*
the first a monosyllable, the second a bisyllable, as is evident; and
at the beginning of the third member appears a word compounded of two words, *mundum* and *-que.* The same technique
can apply when a four-syllable word occurs in one member: in
the other members there can be two words of two syllables each
or one of one syllable and a second of three, as in this set of
members:

Apostoli in hoc mundum viderunt
Verbum Patris revelatum humanata deitate;
Signum legis mundo datum prophetata veritate.

(The Apostles saw coming into this world
The Word of the Father revealed in humanized godhood;
The sign of the law given to the world in truth clothed with prophecy.)

Here you will note that the word *revelatum,* a quadrisyllable,
occurs in the first member, and that two words correspond to it in
the second member, the words *mundo* and *datum,* both bisyl-
lables. Or we might say:

Apostoli in hoc mundum viderunt
Verbum Patris revelatum humana deitate;
Signum legis jam firmatum veritate prophetica.

(The Apostles saw coming into this world
The Word of the Father revealed in humanized godhood;
The sign of the law, now confirmed by the truth of prophecy.)

Here you will note that the word *revelatum*, a quadrisyllable, occurs in the first member, but that the words *jam* and *firmatum* are a monosyllable and a trisyllable. Finally it should be noted that in rhythmic units and their construction there cannot be any absolute rules propounded, since the composition of phrases can be varied in ways beyond number.

Thomas concludes his work by suggesting twelve basic rhythmic forms, ranging from parallel phrases of two words each to phrases of ten words each, and including three types which depend upon climactic structure in each part.

36. POGGIO BRACCIOLINI

Two Letters[1]

Translated by Joseph M. Miller

In the fall of 1416 there occurred one of the most important events in the transition from Medieval to Renaissance culture, the rediscovery of Quintilian's *Institutio Oratoriae*. Briefly the background for this momentous development was as follows: in an effort to end the Great Schism which had divided the Christian world since 1378, one of the claimants to the Papal tiara had summoned a Council to meet at Constanz, a city in southwest Germany, and the other major claimant agreed to accept its solution.[2] Thus in the spring of 1416, the Council had deposed its convener, John XXIII,[3] and accepted the resignation of his rival, Gregory XII. It then took over two and one-half years for the prelates to find a candidate acceptable to all parties; during that time the officials of the Papal Court were unable to function normally. One of the Apostolic Secretaries, Poggio Bracciolini, a brilliant humanist, took advantage of the leisure thus afforded him to embark on pilgrimages to monasteries throughout southern Germany and France, in search of the ancient manuscripts which report insisted lay buried and neglected in various monastic cellars and towers. The success of his search is attested in the two letters here translated.

The author of the first letter was Leonardo Bruni (1369–1444), also

---

1. Translated from *Latin Writings of the Italian Humanists,* ed. Florence Alden Gregg (New York: Charles Scribner's Sons, 1927), pp.93–94 and 138–139. The omissions, indicated by asterisks, are carried over from this version.
2. For a history of the schism, an important example of the kind of political-ecclesiastical maneuvering that characterized the later Middle Ages and the early Renaissance, see John Holland Smith, *The Great Schism,* in the *Turning Points of History* Series, Sir Denis Brogan, gen. ed. (New York: Weybright and Taley, 1970).
3. John XXIII (also numbered XXII) was later denominated anti-Pope. He occupied his portion of the Papal throne from 1410 till 1415. Because of an earlier confusion in Papal enumeration, there is doubt as to his number; this was finally rectified in 1958 when Angelo Giuseppe Roncalli took the name of John and insisted on repeating the enumerative identification.

known as Leonardo Aretino, because of his birthplace, Arrezo. He had been Apostolic Secretary to John XXIII from 1410 until 1415, and was a close friend of Poggio. A brilliant scholar, Leonardo was famous for his Latin style as well as for his mastery of Greek.[4] The second letter is from Poggio himself to another friend, Guarinus of Verona.[5]

Leonardo to Poggio: Greetings

I hope you are well; I am getting along nicely. I have read your letter to our friend Nicholas,[6] in which you have written of your recent journey and your discovery of certain manuscripts. I feel great cause for delight, not only because of this, but because of the great hope I can tell you entertain of discovering others. It will certainly provide a crown for your glory that you are restoring to our age through your own perseverance and skill all the writings of outstanding figures long lost or neglected. And it is not only a cause for rejoicing among us, but it will be one also for our posterity (I mean to our successors in scholarship). For now these works will no longer be overlooked or ignored; instead, your memory will remind us that these writings, so long neglected and so openly wept for, were recovered by your labors and were restored to us. So, as Camillus[7] is called the second Romulus because he restored what had been destroyed in the city which Romulus gave birth to, so you will quite properly be known as the second author of all those works which your talent and determination have restored to us from their oblivion.

For this reason, I want to beg and implore you that you will not

4. This brief biography of Leonardo is summarized from the Introduction to *LWH*, pp.xi–xii.

5. The only biography of Poggio in English is that by the Reverend William Shepherd, *The Life of Poggio Bracciolini* (Liverpool: Harris Brothers, 1837).

6. Probably Niccolo Niccolai, a Florentine citizen at whose funeral Poggio delivered an effusive eulogy, attributing to the deceased the "support, inspiration, encouragement, and even prodding" for his own work. *Oratio · in funere Nicolai Nicoli civis Florentini*, in *LWH*, pp.117–122.

7. Marcus Furius Camillus (*d. c.*365 B.C.), the Roman general who conquered the city of Veii and who was given credit for driving the Gauls from Rome after the invasion of 390 B.C.

rest content with this glorious achievement; rather, bestir yourself and take heart. And to insure that a lack of financial assistance will not be a handicap to you, I myself will guarantee proper
provision. For you may be sure that in this discovery of yours
you have earned a greater reward than you seem to realize. For
Quintilian, formerly mutilated and maimed, will, through you,
regain the use of his limbs.[8] I have now examined the outlines of
the books; the work is complete now, where before we had only
a part, and that part badly deformed. Oh, how great a gift! How
unexpected this joy! Do I really behold you at last, Marcus Fabius
[Quintilian], whole and unblemished? And how precious you will
be to me now, when I loved and treasured you for your beauty
before, despite the wounds cruelly inflicted on your face and on
both your hands, despite the ravages of time which had mutilated
your ears and disfigured your nose with vicious cuts!

I beg you Poggio, send me a copy of your work as soon as
possible; if human considerations move you at all, let me see it
before I pass from this life.[9] For although both Asconius[10] and
Flaccus[11] are pleasant enough, I do not consider either of them
worth any effort, since if neither had ever lived, the study of
Latin would be none the worse off. But Quintilian, as the father
of rhetoric and the master of oratory, is so special that when you
now set him free from the cruel prison of barbarism after so long
a period of time all the scholars in Italy ought to assemble to
welcome him. Thus I am shocked that you and those who were
with you did not immediately put your hands eagerly to this task
of transcribing; instead you turned to such lesser works, ignoring
this manuscript which I do not hesitate to call the most valuable
of all in the eyes of Latin scholars, except for Cicero's *De Re-
publica,* and the one most despaired of.

8. George Kennedy points out that after the ninth century only a mutilated text of the *Institutio Oratoriae* was generally available, missing parts
of Books I, V, VIII, IX, X, XI, and XII, and all of Books VI and VII, in
Quintilian (New York: Twayne Publishers, 1969), pp.139–140.
  9. Since Leonardo was only 47 at the time, his anxiety seems somewhat
unnecessary.
  10. A commentator on Cicero, whose *Commentaries* Poggio discovered
at the same time.
  11. Q. Valerius Flaccus, whose *Argonauticon* Poggio unearthed at St. Gall.

It remains only for me to warn you then not to waste your time on the works we already have; no, search out instead what we do not have, especially the works of Varro and Cicero. Farewell, then, and keep me in your love; remember me to the authorities in Milan and in Arezzo. Again, farewell. Given at Florence, on the Ides of September, 1416.

Poggio the Florentine, Apostolic Secretary, Sends Warm Greetings to his Friend Guarinus, the Veronese

Although I cannot ignore the fact that in your generosity to all, and especially in your kindness to me, you have always been quite enthusiastic over this work, yet now I beg you to give very particular attention to a consideration of what I have to tell you.*** Oral discourse is the unique tool which we men use to express the power of intellect which distinguishes us from other living creatures.*** As you know, many authors of the Latin language treated of how to embellish and enhance this faculty, of whom the chief and most distinguished was Marcus Fabius Quintilianus. He discussed so brilliantly and so completely, with the most exquisite attention to detail, all the elements which help in the training of the very finest orator that it seems (at least in my judgment) that nothing is lacking in his work, either as to the most wonderful content or as to the singular beauty of his presentation. In that work alone, even if Cicero, the father of Roman eloquence, had never lived, we might discover the science of speaking correctly. But until now that work has been so badly truncated in the versions available to us (the Italians, I mean) and so mutilated, as the result, I believe of passing time, that none of the form, none of the pattern of the man could be discerned in it.*** For by Hercules, if we had not come to his aid, we would have had to bury him within a very short time. There is no doubt that this splendid man, urbane, sophisticated, full of moderation, witty, could not have survived much longer the foul confinement, the squalid prison, the vicious warders. He was so oppressed, like those men condemned to death for a crime, defiled, his beard unkempt, his hair thick with grime, that it would appear from his face and garb that he had been summoned to an unjust sentence. He seemed to be holding out his hands, to be begging the trust of his fellow citizens, to be urging that they defend him against so unfair a condemnation, to be showing humbly that he who had once used his own power and his own eloquence to ensure the safety of many could now find no patron at all to take pity on his state, no one to consider his well-being or to prevent the execution of the unjust sentence.

"But how often some things happen in a way which we dared not hope for," as our Terence puts it. For it was certainly his good fortune, and even more it was my own, that while relaxing at Constanz, I was assailed by a great longing to see the place where he was being held, a solitary prisoner. The monastery of St. Gall is near the city, about twenty miles distant. I betook myself there for the purpose of refreshing my spirit and at the same time in hopes of examining some of the books, of which it was said they had a great many. There, amid a rich treasure-house of volumes which had not been looked at for a very long time, I came across Quintilian, still safe and unharmed, though covered with mold and filthy with dust. For the volumes were not in the library as their importance warranted, but in an unbelievably dark foul cell at the base of a tower, where not even men convicted of a capital crime would be kept. In fact, I think it is beyond question that if any men had to endure the same kind of treatment in such a barbaric pesthole as that to which these volumes were relegated, they would have exposed and made public in the manner of the ancients the many tortures which I now complain of. In addition, I found the first three books and half of the fourth of the *Argonauticon* by C. Valerius Flaccus, and the commentaries of Q. Asconius Pedianus, a most eloquent man, a sort of essay on eight orations of Cicero; concerning these latter, Quintilian himself made mention. I copied them out with my own hand immediately, and sent them to Leonardo Aretino and Nicholas the Florentine, who, when they learned from me of the discovery of this treasure, begged me profusely in their letters to send the Quintilian to them as soon as possible.

So you now have, my dearest Guarinus, all that can be offered at present by a man completely dedicated to you. I wish also that

I could have sent you the book, but it has been placed at the disposal of my friend Leonardo. However you know where to find it if you want it (and I believe you do want it as soon as possible), so that you can easily lay your hands on it. Farewell, then, and keep me in your love when you respond in turn. Constanz, on the eighteenth day before the Kalends of January, of the year of Christ, 1417.

BIBLIOGRAPHY

Abelson, Paul. *The Seven Liberal Arts* (New York, 1906).

Aristotle. *The Rhetoric of Aristotle,* trans. Lane Cooper (New York, 1932).

——. *Topica* and *De sophisticis elenchis,* trans. W. A. Pickard–Cambridge in Vol. I of *The Works of Aristotle,* ed. W. D. Ross (Oxford, 1949–1956).

Atkins, John W. H. *English Literary Criticism: The Medieval Phase* (Cambridge, 1943).

Auerbach, Erich. *Literary Language and Its Public in Late Latin Antiquity and in the Middle Ages,* trans. Ralph Manheim, Bollingen Series 75 (New York, 1965).

Augustine. *On Christian Doctrine,* trans. D. H. Robertson (New York, 1958).

Baldwin, Charles S. *Ancient Rhetoric and Poetic* (New York, 1924).

——. *Medieval Rhetoric and Poetic* (New York, 1928).

Benson, Thomas W. and Michael H. Prosser, eds. *Readings in Classical Rhetoric* (Boston, 1969).

Blench, John W. *Preaching in England in the Late Fifteenth and Sixteenth Centuries: A Study of English Sermons 1450–c.1600* (Oxford, 1964).

Burke, Kenneth. *A Rhetoric of Motives* (Englewood Cliffs, N. J., 1950).

Caplan, Harry. "Classical Rhetoric and the Medieval Theory of Preaching," *Classical Philology,* 28 (1933), 73–96.

——. *Of Eloquence: Studies in Ancient and Medieval Rhetoric* (Ithaca, 1966).

Carlyle, R. W., and A. J. Carlyle. *A History of Medieval Political Theory in the West,* 6 vols. (London, 1903–1936).

Cassiodorus. *An Introduction to Divine and Human Readings,* trans. Leslie Webber Jones (New York, 1946).

Chaytor, Henry J. *From Script to Print* (Cambridge, 1945).

Cicero, Marcus Tullius. *De inventione, De optimo genere oratorum, Topica,* trans. Harry M. Hubbell (Cambridge, Mass., 1949).

Pseudo-Cicero. *Rhetoric ad Herennium,* ed. and trans. Harry Caplan (Cambridge, Mass., 1954).

Clark, Donald L. *Rhetoric in Greco-Roman Education* (New York, 1957).

Clarke, Martin L. *Rhetoric at Rome: A Historical Survey* (London, 1953).

Curtius, Ernst R. *European Literature and the Latin Middle Ages*, trans. Willard R. Trask, Bollingen Series 36 (New York, 1905).

Dargan, Edwin C. *A History of Preaching*, 2 vols. (New York, 1905).

de Wulf, Maurice. *History of Medieval Philosophy*, trans. E. C. Messenger, 2 vols. (New York, 1935–1938).

Denholm–Young, Noel. "The *Cursus* in England," *Collected Papers on Mediaeval Subjects* (Oxford, 1946), 26–55.

Dieter, Otto A. L. "*Arbor picta:* The Medieval Tree of Preaching," *Quarterly Journal of Speech*, 51 (1965), 123–144.

East, James Robert. "Brunetto Latini's Rhetoric of Letter Writing," *Quarterly Journal of Speech*, 54 (1968), 241–246.

Farrar, Clarissa, P., and Austin P. Evans. *Bibliography of English Translations from Medieval Sources*, Columbia University Records of Civilization 39 (New York, 1946).

Gilson, Etienne. *The Spirit of Medieval Philosophy*, trans. A. H. C. Downes (New York, 1936).

Haskins, Charles H. "The Early *Artes dictandi* in Italy," *Studies in Mediaeval Culture* (Oxford, 1929), 170–192.

Haskins, Charles H. *The Renaissance of the Twelfth Century* (Cambridge, Mass., 1927).

———. *The Rise of the Universities* (New York, 1923).

Horace. *Satires, Epistles, and Ars poetica*, ed. and trans. H. Rushton Fairclough (Cambridge, Mass., 1955).

Howell, Wilbur S. *Logic and Rhetoric in England, 1500–1700* (Princeton, 1956).

———, ed. and trans. *The Rhetoric of Alcuin and Charlemagne* (Princeton, 1941).

Hugh of St. Victor. *The Didascalion of Hugh of St. Victor: A Medieval Guide to the Arts*, trans. Jerome Taylor (New York, 1961).

Hultzen, Lee S. "Aristotle's *Rhetoric* in England to 1600," unpublished Ph.D. thesis, Cornell University, 1932.

Kennedy, George. *The Art of Persuasion in Greece* (Princeton, 1963).

LaRusso, Dominic A. "Rhetoric and the Social Order in Italy 1450–1600," Ph. D. thesis, Northwestern University, 1956.

Leach, Arthur F. *The Schools of Medieval England* (New York, 1915).

Leff, Gordon. *Paris and Oxford Universities in the Thirteenth and Fourteenth Centuries: An Institutional and Intellectual History* (New York, 1968).

Lewis, C. A. *Medieval and Renaissance Literature* (Cambridge, 1966).

Lloyd, Roger B. *The Golden Middle Age* (London and New York, 1939).

McGarry, Daniel D., trans. *The Metalogicon of John Salisbury* (Berkeley and Los Angeles, 1955).

McKeon, Richard. "Rhetoric in the Middle Ages," *Speculum* 17 (1942), 1–32.

McKeon, Richard P., ed. *Selections from Medieval Philosophers*, 2 vols. (New York, 1929).

McNally, Robert E. *The Bible in the Early Middle Ages*, Woodstock Papers 4 (Westminster, Md., 1959).

Moody, Ernest A. "The Medieval Contribution to Logic," *Studium Generale* 19 (1966), 443–452.

Mosher, Joseph A. *The Exemplum in the Early Religious and Didactic Literature of England* (New York, 1911).

Murphy, James J. "Aristotle's Rhetoric in the Middle Ages," *Quarterly Journal of Speech*, 52 (1966), 109–115.

———. "The Arts of Discourse, 1050–1400," *Mediaeval Studies* 23 (1961), 194–205.

———. "Cicero's Rhetoric in the Middle Ages," *Quarterly Journal of Speech*, 53 (1967), 334–341.

———. "The Earliest Teaching of Rhetoric at Oxford," *Speech Monographs*, 27 (1960), 345–347.

———. " 'Modern' Elements in Medieval Rhetoric," *Western Speech*, 28 (1964), 206–211.

———. *Medieval Rhetoric: A Select Bibliography* (Toronto, 1971).

———. "Rhetoric in Fourteenth-Century Oxford," *Medium Aevum*, 34 (1965), 1–20.

———. "St. Augustine and Rabanus Maurus: The Genesis of Medieval Rhetoric," *Western Speech*, 31 (1967), 88–96.

———. "Two Medieval Textbooks in Debate," *Journal of the American Forensic Association*, I (1964), 1–6.

Owst, Gerald R. *Literature and Pulpit in Medieval England*, 2nd ed. (Oxford, 1961).

———. *Preaching in Medieval England: An Introduction to Sermon Manuscripts of the Period*, c.1350–1450 (Cambridge, 1926).

Paetow, Louis J. *The Arts Course at Medieval Universities with Special Reference to Grammar and Rhetoric* (Champaign, Ill., 1910).

Petry, Ray C. *No Uncertain Sound: Sermons that Shaped the Pulpit Tradition* (Philadelphia, 1948).

Poole, Reginald L. *Lectures on the History of the Papal Chancery, down to the Time of Innocent III* (Cambridge, 1915).

Putnam, George H. *Books and Their Makers During the Middle Ages*, 2 Vols. (New York, 1896–1897).

Quintilian. *Institutio oratoria,* trans. H. E. Butler, 4 vols. (Cambridge, Mass., 1953).

————. *On the Early Education of the Citizen-Orator,* trans, the Reverend John Selby Watson and James J. Murphy (Indianapolis, 1965).

Rashdall, Hastings, *The Universities of Europe in the Middle Ages,* ed. F. M. Powicke and A. B. Emden, 3 vols. (Oxford, 1936).

Robins, Robert H. *Ancient & Medieval Grammatical Theory in Europe* (London, 1951).

Ross, Woodburn O., ed. *Middle English Sermons,* Early English Text Society 209 (London, 1940).

Rouse, Richard H. *Serial Bibliographies for Medieval Studies,* Publications of the Center for Medieval and Renaissance Studies 3 (Berkeley and Los Angeles, 1969).

Rubenstein, N. "Political Rhetoric in the Imperial Chancery during the Twelfth and Thirteenth Centuries," *Medium Aevum,* 14 (1945), 21–43.

Sandys, John E. A History of Classical Scholarship, vol. I: *From the Sixth Century to the End of the Middle Ages;* vol. II: *From the Revival of Learning to the End of the Eighteenth Century,* 3d ed. (New York, 1964).

Savage, Ernest A. *Old English Libraries: The Making, Collection, and Use of Books During the Middle Ages* (London, 1911).

Smyth, Charles. *The Art of Preaching: A Practical Survey of Preaching in the Church of England, 747–1939,* Society for Promoting Christian Knowledge (London, 1940).

Taylor, Henry O. *The Medieval Mind,* 2 vols. 4th ed. (Cambridge, Mass., 1949).

Waddell, Helen. *The Wandering Scholars* (London, 1927).

Wallach, Luitpold. *Alcuin and Charlemagne: Studies in Carolingian History and Literature* (Ithaca, 1959).

INDEX